Books by Marcia Seligson

The Eternal Bliss Machine: America's Way of Wedding
Options: A Personal Expedition Through the Sexual Frontier

OPTIONS

OPTIONS

A Personal Expedition Through
the Sexual Frontier

Marcia Seligson

Random House New York

Grateful acknowledgment is given to:
Warner Bros., Inc.: For permission to reprint lyrics from "Desperado" by Don Henley
and Glenn Frey. © 1973 WB Music Corp. and Kicking Bear Music. All rights reserved.
Used by permission.

Library of Congress Cataloging in Publication Data
Seligson, Marcia.
Options.
1. Marriage—United States—Case studies.
2. Sex customs—United States. 3. United States—
Moral conditions. I. Title.
HQ535.S4   301.41'7973   77–90292
ISBN 0-394-42587-1

Manufactured in the United States of America
2 4 6 8 9 7 5 3
First Edition

This is for Dick, with my love

Acknowledgments

I would like to thank all of the women and men who opened their homes, gave their time, surrendered their privacy and allowed me to poke unmercifully into the corners of their lives. In order to protect their trust, most names and locations have been changed. Their stories have not.

I also want to thank—for their wisdom and support—Bob Loomis and Lynn Nesbit.

And above all, my very special gratitude to my mentor and friend, Steve Gelman.

Contents

PART ONE

The music at a wedding procession always reminds me of soldiers going into battle.

—Heinrich Heine

I think that where a marriage is fruitful and both parties to it are reasonable and decent the expectation ought to be that it will be lifelong, but not that it will exclude other sex relations.

—Bertrand Russell,
Marriage and Morals,
1929

I

The Expedition

September is the crest of the summer in Southern California. Most of America has by then packed away its bikinis and camping equipment and leftover suntan oil, as well as the remnants of summertime frivolity. Now one stoically awaits the inevitable long dark winter. A hurricane has just pummeled the Gulf States, some city or other is immobilized by a teachers' strike, four plays have already been born and died on Broadway, the Congress has resumed its relentless annual whirligig.

We blessed California Sun Beings, however, have it made in September. On this particular balmy Sunday, toward the end of the month, some of us recline contentedly on matching sea-blue chaise longues on a friend's redwood deck, basking in our hot golden dreams. The spacious deck connects on the east with a sprawling wood and glass home, and on the west with the glistening sands of Malibu. Twelve of us are present here, on an afternoon typical of leisure hours in this region. We tan ourselves single-mindedly, jog on the beach with our dogs, sip white Napa Valley wine and munch Monterey Jack, read *The New York Times Magazine* section, and congratulate ourselves for being here. We are lucky, my God. I think that thought over and over on this perfect happy Sunday as I calculate our individual and collective blessings. We are healthy folk and attractive, talented, productive, kind, not poor and not crazy. If there is an American Dream remaining these days, a Good Life, we dozen comrades are surely it.

There is something else to notice here. Amongst the twelve of us, there have been nineteen failed marriages.

Marriage and Divorce. The plague of our age. It used to be tuberculosis that did everybody in; now it's matrimonial misery. We can transport men to the moon as efficiently as dispatching the Super Chief to Chicago, yet we cannot seem to find a formula for happiness in the family. Our technology explores unfathomable universes, transforms the hoary Truths of Science, propels us into undreamed-of territories, conquers the limitations of being human. Is it conceivable that death—the ultimate titan—will be vanquished by technology long before we figure out how a man and a woman and their children can live together in harmony?

On the deck at Malibu, everyone bears a Russian novel's worth of marital drama. Fred's first wife ran off to New York to become an actress, leaving him with two tots; he remarried quickly, produced three more kids, is now divorced again, raising the initial two himself, up to his nose in alimony and guilt. Dyanne, divorced three years, is still obsessed with her ex, even though *she* left him and he's ensconced with another; she cries biweekly as every new man flunks the Alex-comparison test. Bitter Jonathan turned to homosexuality after his marriage crashed, admits eight years later he still isn't over it, waits for Carolyn's second marriage to self-destruct so he can go straight again. At forty-four, Enid has been married four times, is currently living with a twenty-three-year-old unemployed actor whom she would marry if her business manager would let her. Peter left his first wife for his second, his second for his third; all three look exactly alike; he is thirty-four. Helen and Dan spout the blisses of their second, "mature" union and patronize the unwed among us; yet it's risky inviting them anywhere, as they frequently use each other for target practice, and when the bullets ricochet innocent bystanders bleed. Claire's gynecologist husband ditched her after discovering her fifteen-year affair with his partner. Marilyn dumped her mate, a premature ejaculator, immediately after taking *est.* There are more stories, but you get the point.

The bronzed faces are but roadmaps of our psychic territory: Marking the eyes and environs are fatigue, wariness, disillusion and . . . oh, yes—hope. Tension, fury, intractability have settled into the jaws. And the mouths—ah, the mouths—bear witness to the generalized ache of things not having turned out quite the way they were promised. But observe this too: All eyes wander appraisingly, expectantly, over the others in our pretty crowd, like a radar scanner looking for *something* of importance. No one here is without optimism, immune to romance. Maybe next time . . .

We are not some tiny bizarre fragment of the national scene, my group of winners on the beach. Not some depraved corner of society, inmates of Bedlam, no resemblance to you and yours. Peyton Place teems with such tales, so does Omaha, and all along the edges of the Pacific and Atlantic. The saga of Marriage and Divorce is nothing less than the encyclopedia of American life in the 1970's.

Consider the statistics. They indicate, indisputably, a divorce rate steadily soaring, highest (contrary to belief) among the poor and blacks, rising most notably in the category of couples married from fifteen to twenty years, for whom the rate has doubled since 1960, and increasingly being instigated by women—in 1969 2 percent of the runaway spouses were wives;

four years later the figure was 50 percent.

In 1972 33 percent of all marriages in America ended in divorce. By 1975 the figure had leaped to 40 percent, and in some West Coast urban communities it was even more staggering—70 percent. Even the evidence from the 1950's of second marriages being significantly more durable than first no longer holds true.

In 1975, for the first time the number of divorces passed the one million mark, up 11 percent from the previous year. If we continue on our current track, before the end of this decade more divorces will occur in America each year than marriages.

The correspondence between marriage and ill health, mental and physical, is well documented. In a 1973 study of psychological stress by the U.S. Public Health Service, never-married citizens report fewer symptoms of nervousness, insomnia, inertia, fainting, headaches, etc., than married people—and single women are the freest of all symptomology. In terms of mental health as reported in several studies by the National Center for Health Statistics, although married men claim greater happiness than single men, unwed women manifest more stability, less anxiety and more joyfulness than their married counterparts.

Things are even more dismal than they appear. The horrendous divorce rate is not an accurate barometer of the dilemma, since, clearly, not every sufferer heads for the lawyer. Recent studies indicate that no more than 25 percent of the bonds that remain tied find their situation satisfying, and more than 80 percent of the currently married population has seriously contemplated divorce at some time.

One further cheery tiding: The entrance of children does not, contrary to our starry images, cement connubial bliss. On the contrary, say the experts. With the arrival of the first baby the quality of the marriage tends to sag, and the more children, the graver the enterprise. The highest divorce rate of all, in fact, appears in couples having a child in the first year of their union.

Where are you now that we need you, Norman Rockwell?

Where are all the glowy, shiny, flawless jubilant families in the Geritol/chewing gum/breakfast food/Pepsi ads, those pimple-free paradigms of what American life is supposed to be? Is it possible that the mythology of the American Family is just that—myth? Could it be, remaining for the moment with the perpetrations of the media, that the swampy chaos of *Mary Hartman, Mary Hartman* is more *cinéma vérité* than the hip friskiness of *Rhoda,* the milky schmaltz of *The Waltons?* Does *True Confessions* indeed render more accuracy about us than *The Ladies' Home Journal?* How did it all go awry?

Where *are* the happy families of yesteryear, whose immutable images are so ingrained on our national consciousness that we identify them by their silhouettes: The family consists of two grownups and two children; Daddy is six inches taller and a bit older than Mommy; Sonny is a little bigger and older than his sister. The picture, the model of How It Is, is so entrenched in us that safety signs at school crossings which illustrate two figures must, *by law,* show the boy taller than the girl—or everybody would assume the sign to be mother and son. We knew once what a proper family looked like. We knew what to aspire to.

Today, at a private school in Manhattan, the application form carries separate lines for the mother's and the father's addresses.

The family has been humankind's most enduring institution. Religions rise and die, as do political, economic, philosophical systems. The family has survived, in whatever forms or permutations, but eternally it has survived. That it is, in truth, in stormier straits than ever before in America is no minor issue. Civilization can bear, probably, the rumored death of God, the decline of capitalism, even the demise of patriarchy. Should the long-predicted apocalyptic vision of a California earthquake come to pass—thrusting the entire West into the mid-Pacific, making Kansas City an ocean port—we will somehow make do with that cataclysm. Will we, though, live through the upheavals which currently beset the American family?

—An advertisement soliciting subscribers for *Psychology Today* appeared in *Ms.* The illustration was of a grinning Mommy, Daddy and three kiddies. The copy read: "This family will self-destruct in five years. Or sooner. Because this man and woman will find it impossible to live with each other—and with the pressures and pretense that marriage, family and society will place upon them."

—From social scientist Ashley Montagu: "The American nuclear family is an institution for the systematic production of mental illness in its members."

—". . . rigid conformity to the middle-class design for marriage and family life is the prime cause of physical and psychological breakdown in our time." (Sidney M. Jourard, former president of the Association of Humanistic Psychology, author of *The Transparent Self.*)

But the "middle-class design" is all we know, all we have ever known or seen. Do we have any options, any alternatives to its bleak and ungratifying picture? Most of us don't believe so. A few do, however, and I have spent much of the last years wandering among them, listening and watching and occasionally living their particular crusade. They are a fistful of citizens who search and grapple and even invent new structures for that central unit of our lives—The Family. These rebels start from the thesis that what we've been doing, how we've set it all up, just doesn't work any more, if it ever did. Norman Rockwell, we must now admit, will not save us. Is there anything that will?

One of the early stops on my expedition into marriage options was the Sandstone Ranch. It was, simply, the farthest reaches of experimentation in alternatives that America could offer to date. And it exists, with some predictability, in California—the cradle of new lifestyle movements, the vanguard of trends in thought and behavior that surge through the nation and eventually become household clichés. I went to Sandstone because I live in California. And because I travel, from time to time, through a realm where sexual monogamy has a heartbeat so faint it is barely discernible. And because I experience around me, every day, two inexorable tidal waves: the sweeping failure of traditional marriage and the valiant gropings for something new. In 1972 when I started this voyage, the Sandstone Ranch in Los Angeles was as far removed from my entrenched beliefs about the world as anything I could imagine. It was a likely place to begin.

> Sandstone is an experiment in social and recreational alternatives and a center to explore those trends in education, religion, philosophy and the physical and behavioral sciences which emphasize the potentialities and values of human existence. Its activities consist of seminars and workshops, residential programs, consulting, research and a private membership club.
>
> —from the Sandstone newsletter

When I walked through the front door of Sandstone, the first thing my eyes caught and held was a naked man and woman sprawled on the floor in front of the fireplace, performing oral sex on each other. Eleven people were with me. We all gaped and gasped, but the oral sexists did not even look up. I wanted nothing more than to flee. Mind you, as far as I know in my own life, I do not think fellatio and its partner to be disgusting. But at that instant I was sure I had never before witnessed any act so fearsome or repellent. How could they? And like that, right out in the open? The punch line of the old joke seemed ludicrously appropriate: Who do I have to fuck to get out of here?

Sandstone. It is somewhat of a legend in these parts. If you begin a dinner-party dialogue with "I went to Sandstone last night," you are guaranteed the floor for at least two hours. You can also assume the following predictable responses: 75 percent of the assemblage will make nervous, hostile jokes, but they will not change the subject; 13 percent of the women will say they want to go, at which revelation their husbands will freak out; 28 percent of the men will assure you they could never get an erection under such circumstances. ("I couldn't get it up with a derrick," I once heard a fellow exclaim.) Everybody will demand a precise accounting of who was doing what to whom. The subject of Sandstone causes more hysteria at Hollywood dinners than a dollop of mescaline in the gazpacho.

It was the lifetime dream of Sandstone's founders, Barbara and John Williamson, to build a utopian experimental community, a dream finally realized in 1969 (and suspended, probably temporarily, in 1977, when Sandstone ran out of money and had to abandon its eight-year location). John, a businessman, inventor and social scientist by hobby, had come to the conclusion (as reported by the February 1975 *Penthouse Forum*) "that many social ills existed because people were alienated from themselves, those they supposedly loved, and from their social environment. He theorized that if people could be openly intimate and remove the life-negative taboos against sexuality, they might improve their state of mind and their regard for others."

That is the nature of the rhetoric employed to describe Sandstone. Robert and Anna Francoeur, authors of the book *Eve's New Rib*, write that Sandstone is an "intentional or engineered environment which facilitates the formation and evolution of various types of communities among its members. Sandstone simply tries to facilitate human relations and intimacies of all types and intensities within an atmosphere that respects human dignity and individualities. It is a search for possibilities of what communities might be." Writer Gay Talese, who discovered Sandstone and put it on the Manhattan media map, labels its purpose "very profound." The founders, original communal family, and succeeding governing forces discuss Sandstone to the accompaniment of harps, view it as an intensely significant tribal experiment, a model for both future community and heterosexual relationships of the 1980's.

Less lofty citizens of the City of the Angels define Sandstone simply as "a fucking ranch."

In the winter of 1972, at the time of my initial visit to Sandstone, I was a newcomer to California living. In my early thirties, I was at a time in my life when the impulse to make grand changes, to explore, had been so gnawing for a while that nothing but titanic uprooting would satisfy. The sexy sixties with its explosion of consciousness was over, and I'd never be the same, of course. I'd found the Women's Movement, become a writer after years of aimless splashing, discovered I was no longer waiting for Mr. Perfect Prince to arrive and stamp me "Valid." But New York City, the whole Eastern seaboard, had been my lifelong nest and was as familiar and cozy as my own Greenwich Village bedroom, as predictable as the route of the Fifth Avenue bus. I was stale and numb; I knew everything and everybody. I had to get out.

I'd been settled in the Los Angeles sunbelt only a few months, but long enough to realize that very few parallels existed between my Manhattan existence and that which was rapidly encircling me here. The California folk I was meeting considered the cornerstone of life to be something called Personal Growth. Nothing else, no other goal, was as meaningful here—not success, power, money, relationships, contribution to society, being on the cover of *Newsweek*, winning the Pulitzer Prize.

The divorce rate was twice as high here as anywhere else in America, due largely to the ethos of Personal Growth: If it is not growthful to stay married to one's current spouse, one is obliged as a Californian in good standing to split, regardless of all other considerations and mitigations. Personal Growth accounts for our particular brand of sunny narcissism, for our perpetual restlessness that causes the average Californian to change residence every two years. Fads and booga-boogas and nut-things circulate like the intestinal flu if they promise a touch of Personal Growth. Why do you suppose we're all immersed in rolled oats and kelp pills and growing our own alfalfa sprouts and sensual massage and cucumber-juice facials and jogging at five in the morning across Mulholland Drive and playing tennis maniacally like every weekend was The Last Tournament, and having our charts read and our *I Ching* tossed and our tarot cards dealt? Why are we hoarding mantras like nuclear war is imminent? Or devouring Gurdjieff like it was *The Story of O?* Personal Growth. Maybe we believe that with enough of it stored up in the ledger, we'll cancel out our debit to death. Maybe we will.

Let me tell you something about heterosexual relationships in California. This is not off the point; it is so you will have a minuscule edge in understanding Sandstone, more of an edge than I had on that first bizarre trip, before I understood relationships here. The truth is that they are not like relationships anywhere else in the country. Oh, on the surface, I suppose, things appear the same. We still date, fall in love, fall out of love, break up, struggle, live together, get married, break up, find new people, struggle. So far it's like Peoria. What's different here is that our baseline concern, our compelling impetus, is not relationship. It's Personal Growth. If that's not there above all else, our feelings wither; if it's not there enough we turn our eyes outward in its search. We don't really know what it looks like, this microbe that courses through our veins, we just know that it's central and that we cannot seem to get as much as we need. Ever. So the eternal quest tends to become feverish, and its manifestations confound us. Sandstone is one of its boldest manifestations.

The first man I involved myself with when I moved to California was a superstar in the Personal Growth scene. He runs a popular Topanga Canyon nudist club and growth center, which he defines as "an experiential, recreational and clothing-optional educational facility." (You see what I mean; in the East it would be simply labeled a "nudist camp." This one, in addition to permitting you to romp around the grass unclothed, offers workshops in "Pathways to Sensuality" and "Biofeedback and You.") He was a man in his mid-fifties, heroically handsome and unswervingly committed to growth. Having been married five times, he no longer believed in monogamy or any such form that ostensibly stultified growth, so that for the three months I was with him, he was concurrently sleeping with four other women that I knew of. There would be times, after my having nestled in with him for some days at the club, that I would be leaving the grounds, only to pass my replacement on the way in. I knew he cared for me a lot —he called me his "cosmic joy companion," after all—and I couldn't understand why he was not even thinking about, as I was, abandoning all others and burrowing in together for a long stay. How on earth could he go from one to the other, while the satin-sheeted waterbed was still warm from me? He must be sick, I satisfied myself with.

However, my friend Tom, one of America's very few natives of Beverly Hills, explained the truth to me over and over, patiently. I was from New York and he knew I would not comprehend easily. He said: "It's called California Casual. It doesn't mean he doesn't love you. It just means that there are all those other terrific ladies out there to love, too. And that you alone can't fill *all* his needs. When he's not with you, he probably doesn't think about you too much, and he doesn't need to be with *you* all the time. But, then, when he's with you, he's with you."

Afraid of commitment. Can't love. Terrified of women. I was sure my self-serving analysis was correct. How could anybody make love to five different women in a week? Repressed homosexual, Don Juan complex. Of course. That's it.

Tom said no. I was still an Easterner. The answer was merely "California Relationships."

I didn't fathom any of it that first Western winter that I traveled to Sandstone. By the time I did, I had partially turned into a California Casual myself.

The Williamsons spent their life savings on the Sandstone property, a fifteen-acre estate in wild, remote Topanga Canyon, twenty-five miles north of downtown L.A. It is a magnificent spot at the crest of a secluded canyon in the Santa Monica Mountains, with a remarkable vista of the Pacific, Malibu and on a crisp day, Catalina. Over the years, the facilities enlarged and changed; by 1977 Sandstone had a spacious two-story ranch house, center of the club activities; two houses for seminar programs and workshops; a huge, indoor heated swimming pool, sauna, outdoor Jacuzzi, rolling green lawn, and a variety of living quarters for the communal family, which originally numbered ten and by 1977 stood at twenty. Sandstone was traditionally supported by members, who at the time of my first visit in 1972 paid $280 per couple a year for the privilege of using the facilities and participating in activities that they could not find, in quite the same way, anywhere else.

Los Angeles abounds in swing clubs—establishments (generally private homes) where, for $10 or so, you get your clam dip with crinkled potato chips, your quick conversation about last week's Rams game, and your orgy. It's all quite anonymous and unspontaneous and doesn't rate real high on the Personal Growth scale or in the Yellow Pages of serious alternatives to regular marriage. Swinging is essentially a hula hoop, a phenomenon of impersonal sex largely passé, preposterous and thoroughly irrelevant. Therefore, by means of elaborate screening of potential members, swingers were discouraged from playing at Sandstone. Not that they would have relished the scene. People who feature swinging are not famous for their willingness to create relationships with those they screw ("It's all right to ball my wife, just don't you dare take her to the movies"), and Sandstone has always had this doctrine, this THING about relationships. We don't want you if you're only here for sex; you have to *care*. Fortunately, caring, according to the way it works up here, can happen mighty quickly. Like, for instance, the woman I met who'd been here every weekend for a year with her husband but she'd never gotten it on with anybody. Then, one night, standing on line for the buffet, she got to talking with this fine nude young man in front of her, and six minutes later they had stepped out of line and were caring for each other right there on the floor. They finished speedily and returned to the line—somebody had generously saved their places—just in time to reach the bean salad. But I digress.

> The setting offers a welcome relief from city tensions to the relaxing serenity of natural privacy, fresh air and a variety of activities. At Sandstone you may float in a skin-temperature swimming pool, play volleyball, take a hike or unwind in the hot Jacuzzi. Lounge and dine in the luxurious lodge or on the terraced lawn. Bask in the high-altitude sun with or without clothing and feel free to express your enjoyment of sensual pleasure.
>
> —from the Sandstone brochure

Twelve of us had decided to journey to Sandstone that wintry Wednesday night in 1972. One of our group was a well-known therapist in town; she begged an invitation from the Williamsons, then collected this frightened but curious gaggle of friends. None of us had been there before, although we were all either members of or frequent visitors to Elysium, the aforementioned nudist retreat only a few miles from Sandstone. Six men and six women comprised our solemn-spirited party, the even ratio being a steadfast rule of Sandstone—one of the devices to prevent its becoming, or at least resembling, a hunt-and-prowl singles' bar, or a whorehouse in Dodge City. They do not care whom you bring, or what your relationship, they only demand it be a member of the opposite gender. As it happens, about half the troops are married and bring their mates.

Why was I so panic-stricken? Why, in fact, did the winding, uphill, desolate road to the ranch seem the grimmest odyssey of my life? What was the peril? Group nudity was easy and comfortable for me, and I had not the smallest intention of leaping into open sex. I was going only to observe an arcane phenomenon, and I've spent a major chunk of my workaday life in that delectable pursuit. I was with friends and should have felt sheltered. Why did I think I was about to land on Iwo Jima?

At first, I reasoned it off to mere unfamiliarity. I had never witnessed people making love and assumed I was about to. Furthermore, I didn't know the social etiquette, the rituals of behavior, how I should BE. If I were going to a cocktail party, I would know precisely who I was and what were the codes. At Sandstone, if a man offered me a drink, or spent an hour chatting with me—well, what? What were the expectations? Would he be furious if he'd put in that time, then stood up crooning, Okay-let's-go-downstairs (one of the few things I knew ahead of time was that the major sex spots were "downstairs") and I said, Sorry-I'm-not-that-kind-of-girl? Would I permanently be branded as what we used to call in high school a "cock tease"—a crime second only to showing up in class with fingermarks on the chest of your white cashmere sweater? Would I be dismissed as a turkey, and would the word about me spread through the city so that, after only a few months of my glorious new California life, I would be a pariah?

But mere fear of the unknown couldn't really explain these thunderbolts of negativity. The truth was I carried as much disgust as dread, equal portions of fright and self-righteousness. My unswerving convictions about relationships read like a personal version of the Ten Commandments: Sexual freedom was good so long as you were single, discriminating, and didn't do it too much. For couples, I believed unalterably in monogamy and sexual fidelity, and I looked with contempt upon anyone who practiced otherwise. If you had a good marriage, I knew (although I wasn't at all sure what a "good marriage" looked like), you did not fool around outside it. Either secretly or openly. You probably didn't even have the impulse, except for rare drunken moments or when in Cincinnati at a convention. I had known scores of married men (and a handful of women) who chronically indulged in furtive affairs, and it was perfectly clear to me—no matter what they said—that their marriages were listless, loveless, angry businesses whose only connective tissue was the terror of aloneness.

The Sandstone main house is quite beautiful, like a wealthy family's mansion, but unquestionably designed for comfort and sex. The forty-foot living room is thickly carpeted, with a stone fireplace and a few soft sofas but not much else in the way of furniture or clutter. The lighting is very, very low, as is the rock music emanating from somewhere and floating through the house. Outside the living room is a wide redwood deck, reaching out to the most spectacular mountain view I've seen in these parts. I was surprised at the whole ambiance: I thought it would be smarmy; instead it was elegant.

Ah, but downstairs reveals all. A tiny room for dressing and undressing leads into the "Playroom," about 60 feet long, 20 feet wide. King-sized heated waterbeds, mattresses and pillows rim the walls, an aisle down the middle. One wall is floor-to-ceiling mirrors, a massage table at the near end. It is very dark. Over the entrance, at the bottom of the stairs, a sign reads: "Beyond here, no food or smoking, nor words not soft and loving. Trespassers will be eaten." Oh, ugh.

At the far end of the playroom there is a little bathroom, just a toilet and sink—with no doors. It is the only passageway to the "Ballroom." Now, the ballroom has the look of the really heavy-duty hot stuff, a smell of steamy flesh and iniquitous doings. It is only maybe 15 by 20 feet, and entirely mattressed. All the mattresses are covered in gaily patterned Yves St. Laurent sheets.

Perhaps the most unnerving realization for me on that night at Sandstone, a night utterly out of reach of my own reality, was that in order to go to the bathroom downstairs you had to endure a parade of players strolling back and forth between rooms while you sat in front of them. Of the whole array of affronts to my sensibilities, *that* was the most difficult, the gravest violation.

Wednesday night was potluck supper at Sandstone. The sixty or so members and guests paid $5 and brought a dish to share. We drank jug wine from plastic glasses, ate sitting on the living room rug. Most people were naked—the house kept at a temperature of about 80 degrees for that purpose. I neither took off my clothes nor went to the bathroom all night. In retrospect, I found it amazing that my body would even accommodate the presence of food.

My discomfort did not disappear as time went on; it escalated. On the surface, the early-evening scene was benign enough: People "getting to know each other," "relating," "sharing"—all those worthy California credos. Except for the initial Deep Throat tableau, nobody in my range was even *talking* about sex, and the closest thing I saw to actual carnality was a guy sucking on some girl's ponytail. The members were a soufflé of ages and types, so much so that I cannot make any generalizations, except that there didn't seem to be, surprisingly, any movie bizniks. A scattering of teeth-clenched greaseballs with darting eyes, some quite overweight women and many beefy Rotarians. There was virtually nobody of either sex who looked interesting to me.

I was thrown directly back to junior high school that night, to being trapped at the weekly kissing parties at Mickey Kulick's house. With all the attendant confusion and inadequacy that I then carried—pain that one assumes to be only a hand-maiden of adolescence. Quickly it became evident that those bruises had not vanished at all. I felt ugly and awkward and inept. I yearned to be popular. I yearned to be left alone. I felt smugly superior and utterly without charm. I was terrified that someone would ask me to "kiss," equally afraid that no one would. I knew everybody was watching and judging me, and simultaneously that no one was paying me the slightest bit of attention. I said and did all the wrong things. I didn't know where to talk or sit or look. I loathed myself. I longed to escape. And I smiled and lied and pretended not to care about any of it. And—here's the big one—I knew that everybody was hav-ing a wonderful time but me.

You'll be glad to know, I hope, that somebody *did* ask. As I crouched in the corner of the dining room, joylessly eating my zucchini and eggplant casserole, a young man asked if he could join me. He was naked except for a huge and fake May Company squash-blossom necklace. He worked in aerospace, was terribly earnest and married. (Where was his wife? What was she doing, and to whom? Was she watching us?) He belonged to Sandstone, he said, because here he "could be real with people." Monumentally humorless he was, and I know I must have been rude and surly, not to mention fixated on *not* staring at his extremely large penis which kept edging too close to my salad plate.

We talked pointlessly for no longer than twenty minutes, during which he told me that he always liked smart women and that I had lovely breasts and then the dreaded words: "Why don't we go downstairs?" I cannot remember exactly how I declined, but I pray to God it wasn't "What-kind-of-a-girl," etc., etc. After that, our chatter seemed to run down rapidly and he excused himself to get more wine. He did not come back.

I was secretly very pleased that at least somebody had asked.

After my token triumph I spent the rest of the evening huddled with my gang. One or two had gone off to have sex; the rest of us just watched. At a given time, around 10 P.M., as if by signal, nearly everybody in the living room ambled downstairs, cohort in tow. In the real world, at a party, one can generally tell who is married to or paired with whom. A couple-chauvinism pervades, subtly if not overtly, and one just somehow knows. Perhaps it is that we keep a semiwatchful eye on our mates, always, and if danger lurks in the presence of too-engrossing a conversation, or too close an eye-contact, or too flirtatious an exchange, we rush over to stake claim on our possession. "He's mine, keep away" asserts itself at some point. At Sandstone, it was impossible to tell who "belonged" to whom, and that of course is the way it's supposed to be. Partners separate upon entering, and often do not connect again until heading for the parking lot.

So that, as we meandered through the playroom and ballroom watching people fornicate, I had no idea what the alliances were, and that was one of the strangest aspects of all. On one waterbed two separate couples undulated, each oblivious to the other. I found myself wondering if perhaps one man was the husband of the other woman, especially when he reached over, midstroke, to touch her arm. Does anybody here have sex with the person they brung?

There is no privacy at Sandstone, that is a key feature of the ideology. You cannot go off into a room or space to be solitary with your lover, nor can you ask observers—who may be perched on the corner of your mattress peering at every parry and thrust—not to observe. In the past, you could find a hidden niche on the front lawn, but outdoor gambols were barred after a police helicopter cruising overhead nearly crashed into the main house. Dr. Alex Comfort, a staunch Sandstone supporter, writes of their tenet of public sex in *More Joy of Sex:*

"It's not obvious why having sex in company should have so

big a beneficial effect on some people, a question which is bound to be asked by a culture brought up on privacy. That in fact may well be the reason—privacy means that we experience others as hostile to our sexuality. Either they would disapprove and punish it, or they're Peeping Toms, or they would try to take our partner away. To drop privacy, stop checking if there's a crack in the shades, and experience others outside our sexual relation as approving, enjoying, encouraging, even applauding, and only joining in to reinforce, not threaten, our primary relationship can well be encountered by some people as a total reversal of attitudes they've learned to their hurt. Most of us have learned such attitudes, even if we rationalize them by saying that love is a secret and private thing which would be devalued if other people saw it—which is another way of saying that it would be threatened or disapproved of."

It seems to be true for many Sandstone members that a sizable chunk of the turn-on is in the exhibitionism and voyeurism. One man told me he can recognize his wife's unique sounds of orgasm, and when he hears them from across the room he gets further aroused in his own frolic. That night I found the public aspect dumfounding. I could easily feature the occasional appeal of anonymity, of making love to a stranger, the "zipless fuck," the momentary explosion that occurs apart from time and space and the complexity of ongoing relationship. But to endure the absence of privacy, reaching orgasm while the audience cheered or jeered or even peeked, was not just unerotic to me, but unthinkable. And perhaps Comfort is accurate about the reasons. But then, as somebody said (Norman Mailer, I think), if you take the dirty little secret out of sex, it wouldn't be fun to do any more. Certainly there are two schools of thought on this one. A woman told me that after belonging to Sandstone for six months, she no longer enjoyed sex quite as much if nobody else was around . . .

Witnessing people make love was odd and powerful for me.

At first, I could not relate it to anything I had ever done myself. And my fear related to my own divine covenants of fidelity and secrecy being broken before my eyes. In some dark place I believed *this* was a form of Original Sin.

From every outside vantage point the act looked impersonal and utterly animal. No different from two dogs humping, no different at all. I could not visually perceive caring or connectedness, and that rather scared as well as embarrassed me. And so I found myself leaving the playroom frequently—to get a glass of water or call my answering service or deliver a witty commentary to some of our group. But something always drew me back to watch.

And eventually I started to like it. It was never sexy to me, but I began appreciating the sight on several planes. One, the clinical: Oh, she does it *that* way, too; what do you know? Rather like scrutinizing Chris Evert's serve to pick up pointers. Then, I was captivated in the same way that I am at the ballet, by the motion and choreography of beautiful bodies pulsing together. I rambled through the rooms, becoming aware that some partners did it well, looked good, others looked grotesque. I felt like Pauline Kael at the Cannes Film Festival.

Although some were practicing group grope, the main body of activity was in couples, entirely heterosexual. (Gay couples cannot come to Sandstone because of the equal male/female strictures. Unless, of course, they bring another gay twosome of the opposite sex.) And I saw nothing unorthodox—no chains, Victorian corsets, or funny gadgets.

I was quite relieved to see that nobody was doing anything that *I'd* never done, or executing any wondrous and Olympian feats.

Once I passed the aerospace engineer spread-eagled on his back, his hands clasped behind his head as if he were sunbathing, while a mane of chestnut hair crouched above his loins, moving rhythmically to and fro. He winked at me, smiling, and made a motion to suggest that I join the jolly screw. I declined wordlessly, feeling a swell of revulsion. Humanistic social experiment, my ass, I thought.

I abandoned the playroom permanently. Upstairs, a handful of people talked in the living room. These were clearly the bench sitters, as at this hour everybody that was into fucking was already into fucking. Two things happened that remain etched in my mind: I got to talking with a woman named Judy, whom I had noticed when she arrived earlier with her husband, as they both were attractive and looked more interesting than anybody else. While I had not glimpsed him again, I watched her park at the far end of the couch and hardly move all night. She was dressed in black sweater and slacks, no jewelry or make-up; her message was surely "Don't notice me." I asked her what she was doing here, since she obviously hated it, or at the very least was as ill-fitting as I. "My husband said it was either Sandstone or a divorce," she answered, with a wry smile and more than a little sourness. "We've been married for seventeen years and we're bored to death with each other in bed. Neither of us could tolerate an open marriage, it just seems so frightening, but this place is safer. You know, he's just downstairs, surrounded by other people, and somehow I figure 'What could happen?' So we come up here every Wednesday and Saturday nights and he disappears and just screws his brains out all night. Then he's happy for a couple of days, and *we're* more turned on to each other now than we have been for five years."

—What about you?

"Well, I haven't been able to get into it yet. I'm just not ready. Or maybe I just haven't met anybody I want to get it on with up to now. But I think I'm open to it. It'll happen one day."

—Can you watch your husband making love to somebody else?

"Are you kidding? No way. Never. I can't even think about him doing it."

So twice a week she plays watchdog of the living room and custodian of the marriage, while downstairs hubby swings.

The second thing happened to my friend Jeremy, part of our entourage of onlookers. We were clustered by the fireplace, eight of us, comparing our responses to this peculiar planet. Jeremy was nude. A lovely woman of about thirty, named Emily, naked and evenly brown all over, moved into the midst of our circle. Pleasant, easy and natural, she listened and bantered as if she knew us all well, although we'd not seen her before. She lived at Sandstone with her husband, was part of the original family, and refreshingly spouted no oratory. She was just here because she liked it.

About ten minutes after she arrived, Emily suddenly leaned over to Jeremy and said, in a manner reminiscent of Dorothy in *The Wizard of Oz:* "I just love your cock, Jeremy. It's so beautiful. Would you mind if I take you in my mouth?" We were flabbergasted, Jeremy more than anybody. But in fact—and you'll have to take my word for this—the girl was truly unself-conscious in her forthrightness, and that episode, more than anything else I saw all night, gave a thimble of credibility to the Sandstone philosophy. As they disappeared downstairs, I thought that if there *is* a growing shift in American mores and if Sandstone represents—as they claim—the vanguard of a new model for relationships, then Emily was perhaps the flagbearer, and her approach The Future.

God knows we could use a better model than the one we now cleave to. Our "middle-class design," the nuclear family of the mid-twentieth-century, carries a Sears, Roebuck catalog of faults and ills. It is rigid, patriarchal, child-centered, lonely and monotonous. It deadens and dehumanizes, undermining rather than nurturing love and intimacy. The Family—ideally the fortress of comfort and support—has become the locus of the harshest disappointments and bitterest isolation that we ever experience. There must be a better way, one is compelled to insist. But . . . Sandstone?

Folks say that if you view Sandstone through old tired eyes you will see hustling, competition, promiscuity, nonrelatedness, obsessive screwing. If we can cast off those filters, they say, we will see the true Sandstone environment, the experiment in fresh patterns of thought, new ways of human interaction. And thence follows the litany of words like "intimacy," "freedom," "sharing," "fulfillment." I had trouble that night and long into the future whenever I remembered Sandstone. I tried to be open, nonjudgmental and objective, whatever that means. But what I saw was what I saw.

And what I saw was mostly unsavory and absurd, a cartoon of the lengths to which people will go to juice up our lives. Don't blame me for distortions or misrepresentations, friends. Blame these tired old eyes.

I vowed, as we drove down the mountain into safe and sane country, that I would never go back to Sandstone. But I did, recently. I returned a few years after my first visit, at the tail end of an expedition that was to take me across America, into the heart of an unfamiliar, infant frontier, and deep into the webbing of my own flustered life.

By the time I returned to Sandstone, one or both of us had changed mightily.

II

Genesis

I grew up in the 1940's and 50's, in a middle-class suburb of New York City, and I never knew anybody who was divorced. No one. We had a black maid for a while—although of course we did not refer to her as "black" then. She was from Georgia, had two children a few years younger than me, whom she sometimes brought with her when she came to our house. I got the idea from my mother that Savannah (yes, that was her name) didn't have a husband and maybe never had had one. But that was different, if you know what I mean. Savannah was exotic, not divorced.

There was Rose Lipton, who lived down the block, was a friend of my mother's and had two daughters a bit older than myself. I never knew her husband and was forbidden to speak of him. A scoundrel—according to neighborhood folklore—he had vanished one day, abandoning Rose and their little daughters, stealing her diamond engagement ring on the way out. He was never heard from again, and the detectives hired could find no trace. Later, when I was a junior in college, Rose Lipton went crazy and was locked up for a while to have shock treatments. My mother, with the unfaltering Talmudic certainty that characterized all her opinions, declared Rose's condition attributable to "that-good-for-nothing-bastard" who had deserted her twenty years earlier. But that wasn't divorce either.

The only thing I knew about divorce was that movie stars did it regularly, as did the very rich. Neither category of person, however, was particularly real to me.

Over the years, before I left home to go to college, I had a couple of friends whose fathers died, unanimously of heart attacks. Some of the widows remarried, and even that ostensibly respectable act was disfavored, somehow tainted. One didn't quite trust them so much any more, not like the brave women who elected to remain alone, loyal to the memory . . . In my world the portrait of The Family was untamperable, granite. Nothing could be allowed to chip away at its permanence.

My own parents, like most others I saw, were not happy together, that was clear to me from the beginning of time. Locked into the unaltering cycle of their forty-two-year bond, they would squabble incessantly for some weeks, then lapse into a long stretch of arid silence. Regularly my father, who was a traveling salesman, would disappear for some months and the house would be, at least, peaceful. My brother and I often wondered whatever drew them together in the first place, they were so different and so uncomplementary, and seemed hardly fond of each other. For as long as I can remember, they were angry and disappointed, the anger hardening into turgid knots over the years.

My mother had her romantic dreams when she started out. An exceedingly beautiful woman who, above all, loved to dance, she wanted marriage to be gay, her husband to be a courtier. She told me many times that when my father proposed, he vowed to her that for the rest of their lives together they would dine frequently in formal clothes. She believed his promise and never forgave him its betrayal. I always thought this silly, poignant story was her moonstruck fantasy—my father was a simple and inelegant man—but it dominated her feelings about him and thus about her life.

I think that my father did not confuse happiness with marriage. Marriage was something you did, just as work was something you did. Happiness, or pleasure, or satisfaction—I don't know what words were in use then—was a function of performing that which was expected of you, taking pride in your children, being a moral man, having a fine reputation in the community. He was not the romantic fancier his wife was, had few expectations and small hopes, consequently he was less dispirited. Or at least he felt obliged to keep his sorrows well-hidden.

As children are, my brother and I were often the receptacles of their bitterness and their complaints against each other. During these moments, Mother tugging at me from one side, Father from the other, I imagined "divorce." With extreme self-pity and no compassion for their plight, I saw myself as an unfortunate victim, a prisoner of their war, and felt that nothing short of their severance would be my tunnel of escape. I suspect now that despite their anguish they probably never discussed divorce, and perhaps did not—even in the protected realm of private thoughts—contemplate it. My mother told me, often enough so I can remember her self-sacrificing tone: "I made my bed, now I have to lie in it." The slogan, one could say, of my parents' era. The shame of divorce was more unbearable to them than a dismal lifetime marriage.

Just as divorce wasn't a relevant concept then, neither was "working at the marriage." If such a professional category as Marriage Counselor existed, my parents were not among its patrons. They surely would have thought "Personal Growth" had something to do with eating enough. Each was convinced the other was uniquely at fault, neither had the tools for exploration of self, nor the techniques, consciousness or vocabulary to "increase open communication." So they walked along separate avenues, fulfilled their duties as parents and citizens, provided home and hearth and regularity. And they abided.

Several weeks ago, I was driving a teenager and her girlfriend to the movies. I eavesdropped on their animated conversation about plans for Christmas vacation. Laura, fifteen, who lives with her mother and her mother's boyfriend, wanted to go to Aspen, where her father and his current wife and their new infant live. "But now it's all screwed up," she whined, "because Dad's wife's two sons, who are in prep school back East, decided at the last minute they want to come out and ski, so there's probably no room for me to stay with them." Mary Lee, the other lass, told a similar tale of holiday complexity and displacement, about not wanting to be with her father, with whom she and her brother live, because she hates his girlfriend, and she was invited by her stepmother (Daddy's second ex-wife) for Christmas but her father doesn't want her to go. I stopped trying to follow the plotline. Instead I just absorbed the extraordinary tangled circuitry of these childrens' existences.

"Do all of your friends come from broken homes?" I asked at a lull in the chatter.

They thought for less than a minute. "Yeah," Laura nodded. "Everybody but Todd. He's the only one I know with two regular parents who he lives with."

Something very big has happened in the last twenty years.

The problem may be, simply, that marriage was never intended to bear the weights we lately have shackled to its limbs. One burden marriage was never meant to pull was that of lifelong sexual fidelity. Another was that of love. And still another was happiness. At no time in history has matrimony ever embodied so much to so many.

In Western culture, the momentous jolt of the Industrial Revolution in the nineteenth century transformed the quality of human life and all its institutions. Marriage, as we now think of it, began to blossom. All the knotted, atomized roads of history then led, in America, to the nuclear family—the middle-class, urban, industrialized, close-knit unit. Here are the seeds: People became mobile and moved away from the broad extended family; the status of women saw a minor escalation (if not equal partners, at least they advanced beyond sheer enslavement); contraception was hurled into popular use; there was a new and burgeoning acceptance of sex in marriage for its emotional and pleasureful, as well as procreative, facets.

In the past, different needs—friendship, carnality, expedience, *grande passion*, household help, protection—were often satisfied by different companions. Suddenly, we required having everything, all gratifications, incorporated in one mate, forever. That state of affairs, those colossal demands upon marriage, were unprecedented on this planet.

Let us look to history. Arguments have raged for centuries over the origin of the family unit, over whether its roots are buried in economics or physical survival or convenience or sexual attraction. The sturdiest voices of anthropological opinion—Edward Westermarck, for example—insist that the institutions of marriage and the family were architected with one purpose in mind: children. To produce children, to protect their legitimacy, to create a stable system in which they could be nurtured and flourish. For many primitive peoples a marriage could not even begin until either a child was born or signs of pregnancy appeared; today it is still common for an unwed pregnancy to lead, without argument, to marriage.

In a brutal world, one in which all persons were polarized into literal friends or enemies, children spelled survival. "A man without offspring," wrote Westermarck, "is an unfortunate being under savage conditions of life, where safety and welfare depend upon family ties and the old have to be supported by the young."

And children signified a bridge to immortality. Among ancient Aryans, says Westermarck, a man's tranquility "in the next world depended upon his having a continuous line of male descendants, whose duty it would be to make the periodical offerings for the repose of his soul."

As contraception did not exist, people reproduced like ivy, thus limits had to be created to avoid intramural anarchy. Those "limits" could also be labeled "family." Women had to bear ten children in order to produce two or three survivors, so marriage took place early in life. And as children offered the surest guarantee for maintenance of the union, the marriage was solemnly contracted, for a lifetime. "Lifetime," remember, was a differently shaded idea then, since everybody died at twenty-six.

Dissolution, however, was usually built into the framework —from ancient times until the widespread sweep of Catholicism. Some divorces could occur with the slightest of pretexts —because one's mate was, say, a rotten cook or an inept chopper of wood. Some were initiated by either the man or the woman, some only with mutual consent. The most recognized grounds for divorce: the wife's barrenness or her adultery. The Law of Moses portentously reads: "When a man hath taken a wife and married her, and it come to pass that she find no favor in his eyes, because he hath found some uncleanness in her, then let him write her a bill of divorcement, and give it in her hand, and send her out of his house."

Interestingly, there are no known instances of societies or groups of individuals living in a continuous state of promiscuity. For one thing, in patriarchal systems men seek to control the source and knowledge of paternity, and thus to contain and subordinate women. For another, it is evidently instinctive for people to form relationships, bonds, sexual attachments that persist and, whether monogamous or polygamous, exclude most other humans from their boundaries.

Until the nineteenth century marriage was invariably an arrangement of the most pragmatic sort, a transaction so serious that its control would never be left in the foolish hands of youth. Free selection of mate had no place in the process, particularly for the bride, whose status was that of trophy to be awarded or commodity to be traded. Marriage by Purchase, the most common and perseverant form, still practiced today around the globe, involved a payment of money or goods from the suitor's family to the girl's father. The girl, depending on her intrinsic worth as child-bearer and general servant, was sold off either as one's ripest heifer or as a bag of fertilizer.

Sentiment, emotion, "love"? No association with the state of marriage. Indeed there was no word for "love" in many primitive languages (there still isn't in New Guinea) and marriage for love was considered a crime in Korea until this century. One of the few exceptions was seen among the early Hebrews, who believed a man's love for his wife and his concubines had to be equal with his love for God.

The mainstay of our modern American vision of marriage is the doctrine of monogamy: one man/one woman, sexually exclusive. Until the divorce explosion of these current times made the " 'til death us do part" canon vulnerable to suspicion, we also believed monogamy to include "forever." Both the dictionary and the historical meaning of the word monogamy is quite different—*Marriage with one person at a time.* No stipulations for sexual fidelity or length of stay are built in to the definition—a distinction that is vital to keep in mind.

While it is true that monogamy has been culture's most sanctioned form, polygamy has, to this day, always been an option throughout the world. King Solomon boasted 700 wives, Charlemagne had two plus several concubines, and the all-time record was held by King Mtessa of Uganda, with a total of 7000 wives. (One cannot help but wonder how many unfortunate males were forced to abstinence in order to support the king's habit.)

There are two distinct categories of polygamy: one man with several wives (polygyny) and one woman with many husbands (polyandry). Polyandry has been rare, as it requires both a surplus of men, which is historically uncommon, and a stature bestowed on women which is historically nonexistent. Polygyny was practical when scores of men were killed in war, so that one male was required to impregnate many women. But the dominating motive for polygyny has always been, simply, man's age-old yearning for more than one female. There would be no means, obviously, to have charted woman's drives and hungers throughout a long history in which she was not even considered worthy of research. "The sexual instinct is dulled by long familiarity and stimulated by novelty," historian Westermarck comments on a human condition no less powerful today than in primitive times.

The relationship between monogamy and sexual fidelity is a shadowy one to diagram. Monogamous societies, such as ours, have usually included something the historians ponderously label "informal polygamy," i.e. adultery. Sometimes, as in ancient Greece or Rome, where monogamy was the only legitimate kind of marriage, adulterous alliances—frequently homosexual—were openly condoned. In other societies, like contemporary America, adultery is rampant but essentially deplored and secret.

The only generalization one can make, sheepishly at that, is that in cultures where marriage is an unsentimental businesslike arrangement, infidelity has been accepted. Passion and profane sexual pleasure therein are features of the man-and-mistress game, not the bridal bed. Where marriage has been acceptable only for motives of love, divorce becomes tolerated, while adultery is not abided.

Strict lifelong fidelity has been rare for all people in any given society. Professors Clellan Ford and Frank Beach of Yale, in a well-known study of fidelity in primitive cultures, concluded that our American glorification of sexual exclusivity is a historical peculiarity. Of the 185 societies studied, over 80 percent allowed some form of polygamy; most interesting is the fact that 72 of the societies approved specific sorts of extramarital activities.

Women have naturally been more chained than men, but even so, Kinsey found that 40 percent of all the world's groupings permit adultery for women under special circumstances—your Eskimo wife-swapping, say, or the European *droit du seigneur,* in which brides were deflowered by the feudal lord instead of their grooms. Ford and Beach also point out that in unrestrictive cultures with no patriarchal double-standard, the "women avail themselves as eagerly of their opportunity as do the men." So much for the mythology of women's lesser appetites or more exalted natures.

The chronicled evidence is overwhelming: sexual monogamy is an idiosyncratic state, not a normal one. "The panorama of humanity's other choices," writes Morton Hunt in *Sexual Behavior in the 1970's,* "is proof positive that no one pattern of sexual behavior and mating is instinctive and natural, and that lifelong sexually-exclusive monogamy is perhaps the unlikeliest choice of all." Yet we have glorified monogamy, argued for its "naturalness," simply because it has evolved as our righteous —although most unpracticed—way of life.

The Sixth Commandment notwithstanding, Catholicism's decree of adultery as a mortal sin and the laws of 33 American states making adultery grounds for divorce notwithstanding, infidelity has flourished, unimpeded, since the beginning of time. It is one of life's ageless and universal themes; indeed, literature would be paltry without it.

Now in America, when love is the single motivation for marriage and no other reason seems morally upright, it is jostling to realize that conjugal love hardly existed before the last century. Love, you see, has been the victim of the schizophrenic views of sexuality that have muddled and confounded Western thinking since the dawn of Christianity. For 2000 years love has been seen as an expression of erotic desire, and erotic desire seen as damnable. Necessary—men being animals at heart—but the business of the devil nonetheless. Women, in various eras, have been feared as evil temptresses, pedestalized as goddesses, debased as objects of scorn, or simply dismissed. Thus, remarkable schisms of thought have sprung from such contradictions. Love is a distraction, a *folie;* love is pagan; love is spiritual. One should not have carnal feelings toward one's wife; one shouldn't have them for anybody *but* her; passion and/or idealization of women should be nonsexual but extramarital; one must not love women at all.

Even in medieval Europe, where women were worshiped, died for, married couples abided the grossest expression of married "love": *la chemise cagoule*—milady's coarse-hewn nightshirt with a small hole cut out of the crotch for quick reproductive errands while avoiding any other fleshly or tender contact between husband and wife.

Male chauvinism is the underpinning. Whether women were revered or reviled, they were not looked upon as fully human. So a relationship between man and woman embodying all the dimensions of emotion was inconceivable. Love, therein, was simply not a possibility. Consider an illustration that happened to have taken place recently. It could have occurred 700 years earlier.

I was traveling in East Africa in the summer of 1975. One night at a dinner party in Nairobi, I was told by the hostess that her chief servant, Justin—an imperious black man in his mid-fifties but looking fifteen years younger—was the owner of five wives and seventeen children. Around the periphery, she further explained, lurked several mistresses and a parcel of illegitimate offspring. Justin's entire "family" lived in the same remote hamlet in the mountains a few hundred miles from Nairobi, part of a tribe where polygamy rules. Every few months a different wife journeyed to the city to stay with Justin, working as a maid to the household. Three times a year he trekked to the village to see his brood of children.

Fascinated, I returned the next day and engaged Justin in an hour of light-hearted conversation, via my friend's Swahili interpreting. I told him about Women's Liberation (of which he had never heard) and he bellowed in good-natured disbelief. I teased him that I thought his treatment of his wives and mistresses—the apex of domination—unfair and inhuman. He responded with great gusts of laughter that I was the craziest woman he'd ever met, and what I surely needed was a real man to tame me.

I asked him if he loved his wives. Instead of answering with the hilarity that greeted my other questions, he looked at me with utter noncomprehension, as if I had just asked directions to Neptune. "What do you mean?" he begged. "Well," I tried again, "do you *love* them, any of them? Love. You know what I mean." I thought he was taunting me, but he looked genuinely blank. After a moment's puzzled pause, he grinned broadly and said, "Do I love my cows? Why don't you ask me *that?* How can you love a wife any differently than you do a cow? They're the same thing."

I have a friend who is an Orthodox Jew (a converted libertine, in truth). I asked him if he thought marriages among his crowd looked any better than among mine. "Of course," he said, smiling rabbinically. "Why?" said I. "It's simple. When an Orthodox man and woman marry, each knows exactly what his or her role is—what are their duties and what they can and can't anticipate. They have a literal contract, and if it's broken because he doesn't earn the money, say, like he's supposed to, or she keeps the house filthy, they know precisely who's at fault and what to do to fix it up. Marriage is very clear-cut for us."

Clearly defined roles certainly keep marriage chartable and less vulnerable to attacks of mammoth confusion. But one could rightly argue that the highest crime of the nuclear family has been to thrust men and women into the prison of mechanical, fixed roles, roles which govern our lives. Women, then, are cut off from the world's pulse, busying themselves with unchallenging and unappreciated tasks; men, serving sentences as breadwinners and macho champs, are forbidden the luxury of vulnerability or defeat. As with my African friend, male chauvinism always underlies such rigid role play, but the results are equally unhappy for both sexes, husbands and wives living separated, alienated, strangulated lives, in which the unique humanness of each is somewhere lost.

I would like to tell you something of my grandparents. They were part of the Jewish frontier—Russian immigrants who found their way here, to the Bronx, in the last decade of the nineteenth century, with three young children, no English or money, but armed with a cargo of resolute, dauntless convictions about life. Life, they knew, was essentially brutal. Hardship and suffering were unquestioned, happiness not a word in overuse in their vocabularies, and they would probably have said that the purpose of their lives was to endure, to get through, and to make things somewhat better for their children. Romance and poetry did not suffuse my grandparents' souls nor their days.

Grandpa died of tuberculosis when I was two, and I had only a distant acquaintanceship with my grandmother, so my information about them comes from my Uncle Sidney, the oldest son among their five children, my late father's brother. He was not certain, my uncle once told me, but he thought my grandparents' marriage was arranged; if not, they knew each other for a matter of weeks before they wed. They did not, evidently, marry for love, but for the kind of fundamental survival that inspired primitive pairings. Things were arduous in their Russian village, one needed a mate, and the choice did not shoulder the critical impact of today—despite the fact that permanency was virtually preordained. A sense of responsibility steered them and love was just not an issue.

As it happens, they were not the slightest bit compatible, but that was not an issue either. The replacement then for delight, congruent interests, goosebumps—whatever criteria operate for me in mate selection—was mutual respect, an age-old Jewish value. If their marriage was not perfect, then it was not the vast catalog of emptiness, of missing connections and the absence of love that damaged it. It was the lack of mutual respect, and only that.

Grandma was durable, intrepid and fiercely ambitious. Her own family, the Feinbergs, came to America earlier and by 1910 her three brothers had become highly successful manufacturers of ladies' dresses. Grandpa was expected to do the same but couldn't measure up. He went to work, instead, as a cutter in his brother-in-law's factory, living under the sword of his wife's disappointment, subject to repeatedly voiced comparisons and grievances. He was not as good as her dynamic brothers, he was not doing his duty to her and his five children, he was not a *mensch.* The reason Grandma never grew to love her husband was that he did not make enough money.

Yet my grandparents did not, all in all, have a bad marriage. They made a little money, saw my father and Uncle Sid go into business together, saw another son through an Ivy League law school. In their old age they were taken care of royally by their doting children—each of whom had amounted to something in their terms. All things considered, most particularly their expectations, their marriage was a moderate success.

They did not bear much affection for each other, but according to Uncle Sid, a man never burdened with a lack of assurance about his judgments: "Divorce never would have occurred to them. There were no psychiatrists then, and 90 percent of today's divorces are caused by psychiatrists." It would have been futile to do combat with my uncle and, then again, I'm not so sure he was wrong.

The axis of their lives was work, as with all pioneers, and work meant sixteen hours a day, six days a week, in the sweatshop and the home. They considered themselves middle-class, and the ethic was Getting Ahead, Making It in America. Leisure did not play a role in their days, nor did frivolity. And, simple-minded though it sounds, they had neither time nor energy nor the sort of mentality to fret about their marriage, about whether they were "fulfilled." According to my uncle: "You didn't worry then whether or not your wife was good in bed. You were mostly too tired at night to have sex anyway." Were they faithful? I asked. "Of course. There were no opportunities to fool around. Everything centered around the home and the shop, and everybody knew each other. There was no way to keep a secret. But you have to understand. My parents wouldn't have permitted themselves the luxury of contemplating affairs. They were practical and down-to-earth. They didn't think about being happy or being miserable. They just never asked themselves, 'Am I happy?' "

When you come right down to it, I hardly think about anything else. And that is probably the farthest distance I have traveled from my ancestors, and it is very, very far indeed.

Today it is very likely no easier nor more difficult living with another human being, loving, raising children, facing intimacy —the million ingredients that coalesce into marriage—than it was for my grandparents, or for my parents, or than it has ever been. Today we simply tolerate less and demand more. Or, as the experts in these matters declare: You can best understand the calamity of marriage in terms of factors that have nothing to do with marriage itself. It is not the institution but the climate in which we live that has rendered our traditional ideas of matrimony impossible.

A friend of mine, a wise student of the human condition, said to me a few years ago: "There's only one thing that causes misery in life. Unfulfilled expectations. Nothing else. You can't find an example of unhappiness that stems from any cause other than expectations that aren't being met." I thought, at the time, his words shallow and unconvincing—my own privately held visions of psychic life were infinitely more convoluted and ambiguous. Now I believe he is right. And that that principle is about as complex and all-embracing as American life itself.

The American Dream, after all, feeds on nothing so much

as on expectations. Out there is something—lots of things, in fact, infinite things—better than whatever we now have. With toil, ingenuity, God, luck, capitalism, we can get all of it. And it will surely make us happy.

Happiness—once sheer survival is taken care of—is the true purpose of the dream, the only remaining American ethic. Yearnings, dissatisfactions, strivings toward that elusive state of happiness, form the very heart of our system. To be sure, this is not just American but universal: My grandmother fled Russia with presumptions of a richer life, but unmet expectations resulted in her frustration in marriage. What she did *not* expect—that dream which is a landmark of the time and place we now inhabit—was *everything*.

I'm a consequence of the fifties, with its spread of leisure, higher education and moral apathy. My upbringing had assured me repeatedly that I was capable of and entitled to everything, to towering triumphs on all fronts. (Hadn't Daddy told us, over and over, that all he wanted from life was to provide for our comfort?) Triumphs, by the way, without skirmish or setback, easy victories. Didn't I assume that almost every child on earth received a red Pontiac convertible for her seventeenth birthday? We grew up a flabby and lazy-hearted generation, greedy, self-absorbed, drowning in myths. Our Olympian expectations were perfect setups for crashing defeat.

We are, please remember, the first generation to contract large-scale divorce fever. It was we who started the epidemic.

"Everyone was led to expect a marriage that was a great personal achievement, like the celebrated love affairs of history," writes journalist Caroline Bird of my era. "Everyone was required to improve his sexual performance by virtuoso standards. Married couples expected their marriage to grow, and a marriage that served as a means to any other end was snubbed as mean-spirited if not actually immoral. Rising divorce rates and disillusion with domesticity were the inevitable result, and thoughtful sociologists were beginning to lay the blame not on the frailities of human beings, but on impossible standards for marriage."

One married then because it was time, because we should, because he had good prospects or she was a likely candidate or we wanted to get laid regularly without effort. But we called it Love and expected lasting rapture. We bought all the mythology: The Simultaneous Apocalyptic Orgasm Myth, the Mixed Doubles Myth (he will be my perfect recreation companion), the Family That Prays Together Myth. And the natural, unquestioned concomitant of those comforting blankets of Nirvana was the myth of Sexual Fidelity.

All of us know some golden couple—the couple who plainly has everything, the couple we envy and compare our own blemished relationships to, the couple whose obvious bliss is a thorn in our heads, a rankling reminder that *we* don't have it all. The couple who one day electrifies us by announcing their divorce. Usually their friends take longer to recuperate than they; then, too, having found one willing host, the divorce bug circulates wildly through the neighborhood. I asked Melinda, formerly of golden Melinda and Don, why. "I don't really know why," she said ruefully. "It's not that I didn't have a good marriage. Don was a marvelous husband, a dear man to be around. But for the last two years I woke up every morning sobbing, just wanting to die. I suppose I just couldn't believe that this was *it*, this was my life, and there wasn't ever going to be more."

We ask ourselves, about everything in which we engage: "Is this all there is?" Our work, our trip to the Far East, our last orgasm, our current growth experience. Most assuredly we ask it of our marriage, sometimes daily. When the response rises from our bowels, as it occasionally must, "No! Please God, no!" we do what is decreed by our era: We go crazy, we have an affair, or we get divorced.

Psychologist Abraham Maslow, the founding father of the Human Potential Movement, explained this pocket of the psyche more accurately than anyone. Human needs are not, as Maslow saw them, organized in a random bundle, but rather as a ladder, a hierarchy. What he calls "lower-order needs"— the fundamental drives for food, shelter, safety from external harm—must be filled first; when they are, we automatically move up to satisfying needs for love, belongingness, respect from others, dignity—the "higher-order needs." At the summit of the ladder are our highest aspirations, those of growth, the quest for identity and autonomy, the yearning for excellence. In Maslow's words, "Self-Actualization."

The point is that we never do reach the top of the ladder of needs. As 1970's Americans of the middle class, having polished off our primary requirements, we're as absorbed in the quest to stuff our bellies with self-actualization as citizens before us have struggled after meat. "Apparently," says Maslow, "we function best when we are striving for something that we lack, when we wish for something that we do not have . . ." We live for the peak experience, the ecstatic moment, the great "zap" by which we define and measure our lives. We could probably best be characterized as The Disgruntled Generation, in that we are relentlessly on the prowl for something more, different or beyond what we now possess. But at least the caveman knew when he had meat and when he didn't. How do we know for certain whether or not we've acquired "identity" or "growth" or "excellence"? How much will do it? When, dear God, are we to be satisfied?

I recently asked Dick, my mate of the last three years, if he thought we have common goals in our relationship (I'd been reading somewhere that it only works if a man and woman have common goals). He answered that he has no goals for us, except to "feel good together." Reluctantly, I had to agree. We will stay connected so long as it feels happy, or zappy. If the meter stops registering for a few moments or slips backward, we'll move on. In the absence of those antiquated, lower-order goals which bound my ancestors, "feeling good" may be the only existential purpose that makes any sense today. These are the times; we lack, it seems, some cosmic perspective.

Everything in the culture implants marriage-maiming expectations like electrodes under the skin, nagging us with their constant presence. Psychotherapy and the head-trip revolution lead us down "primrose paths of life's myriad possibilities," as their focus shifts from curing hangups to expanding experience. "You don't have to be sick to get better," the human potential motto chides us, at once affirming our spirit but also tormenting us with the Everest that can never be scaled. The media bombard us with fantasy fulfillment, *Playboy* lures of freedom, airbrushed romantic perfections. And affluence and leisure spark the "there-must-be-more-than-this" pulsing itch that can't be reached. We live with the accessibility of options so numerous and varied that our brains are in a constant state of bewildered overstimulation—overprogrammed computers run amuck.

Rapid change is the tempo of our daily symphony, consumer mania the tune. Planned Obsolescence. Everything wears out quickly, we replace it and do not suffer its loss, as there is always an improved model waiting in the wings. Naturally, our human relationships bear the same temporary, fragmented, avaricious quality; as Alvin Toffler points out in *Future Shock*, we come into contact with more people in a week than our feudal forebears did in a lifetime.

Can anything as fundamentally unsturdy as marriage survive such a cultural conspiracy? Even without the burden of all these tremors rumbling through the country's crust, the marriage institution carries a plethora of its own inherent stresses. Like limestone cliffs on a sandy beach, a long marriage is subject to the natural erosions of time. Domesticity, routine, security, familiarity—all those homey virtues that once beckoned us—over years create the very boredom that entraps and kills. The presence of children can weave the fabric into a rich quilt or irreparably shred it. The imperfect communication that all we humans have with each other can, in wedlock, become an insurmountable barrier of accumulated and unexpressed angers and needs.

The "togetherness" propaganda of the 1950's robbed us of independence, separate space, the power to move freely as entities within the family setup. And so led invariably to stultifying, clinging dependencies. Dependency used to be Good, a signpost of caring and intimacy, two limbs of the same tree and all that. Now having a case of dependency is rather like coming down with hemorrhoids or crabs—humiliating, overly revealing, something you don't want bandied about in the office. Dependency means I cannot survive without you, and that concept has become anathema.

Dr. Richard Farson, behavioral scientist and former president of Esalen, is one of those who condemns the nuclear family. "It is unnatural," he states. "It implies ownership, autocracy, particularly of the man over the woman. It is a lonely and insecure unit and the greatest indictment you can make of it is that it can't stand anything good to happen to it. It can't tolerate any growth, personal fulfillment, success or change; when any of those things occur to any member, it weakens the whole family structure. Consciousness-raising, for instance, has put terrific strains on marriage." In a climate that demands growth, self-realization, the spiraling of consciousness, how does traditional marriage have a prayer?

And what, above all else, of monogamy, the bastion of American matrimony? How can this our most hallowed family myth interface with the expectations and fantasies that drive us like fevered kiddies through a toy store?

In its historical usage, as I've said, monogamy only meant "marriage with one person at a time." But it has been contorted to mean complete sexual exclusivity. At the same time that monogamy's definition was so narrowed, our lifespans were increasing. So that over time the monogamous ideal has become a state that is probably humanly, instinctively preposterous—making love to only one person for fifty or more years. No wonder the respected family counselor Virginia Satir has labeled monogamy "grim, lifeless, boring, depressing, disillusioning." In its current sense monogamy has never worked and undoubtedly never will. Today every surge in the culture, every built-in feature of the marriage framework itself, every aspect of our own psychic make-ups conspire against lasting sexual fidelity.

The real truth, as we know, is that most Americans are not now, nor have we ever been, overwhelmingly faithful to our spouses. Myth is one thing, practice frequently something different. We venerate faithfulness, take vows of "forsaking all others," condemn public figures for their unsacred private dealings, and we screw around. The updated version of the original Kinsey Report states the number of extramarital players in this country to be 60 percent of men, 40 percent of females. Many experts consider these statistics grossly understated. The book *The Wandering Husband* estimates that in certain urban communities 90 percent of the husbands are unfaithful. Alvin Toffler calls widespread adultery "the best kept family secret of our Age of Transience."

Moreover, only one-third of all Americans live in nuclear families (the rest are single, divorced, widowed or residing in other structures). So that in truth only 15 to 20 percent of the population *actually* lives monogamously. Yet it is still the sacrosanct form.

"To try and stay faithful to your wife today is like trying to lose thirty pounds while working at Howard Johnson's. It's impossible." Harvey, my friend the earnest struggler, bemoans his fate, the torturous predicament of maintaining monogamy after eight marriage years, the temptations that trip and stall him on every corner. Our environment is so overtly eroticized, America is like a steambath that never gets turned off. Look at all the symbols of popular culture: laxatives advertised as if they were aphrodisiacs, toothpaste tubes portrayed like Victorian kinky devices. What passes for a "family" movie wouldn't have made it past the raincoat circuit not too many years ago; today it's likely to be the Easter Show at Radio City.

Look at the opportunities for philandering—natural outcomes of prosperity, mobility, liberation of women. The women of my mother's generation stayed at home, encased in suburban stucco, their daily male companionship restricted to various unsuitable handymen. (Anyway, it's only in recent years that the affair-with-the-Sears-man has become trendy.) The men in my father's circle had more freedom, but were Jewish-guilty and chronically exhausted. My grandparents' chances for liaison were even more limited.

Now there seems to be no way to confine our mania for novelty and variety to one bed partner for a lifetime. Not when we're expected to be sexual gluttons before or between marriages but to "settle down" once the ring is passed onto the finger, like a noose to the neck.

Certainly not when we are barraged daily with the message that sex is the key to happiness, to physical and mental well-being. Sex has traveled beyond feeling and relationship, light years beyond the lowly function of "getting off." Having soared in significance, elevated to one of Life's Major Purposes, sex has gotten as lunatic for us as money. We're nothing but inverted Puritans, righteous and sanctimonious. We have giant guilts if we don't make love enough, or in a sufficient repertoire of positions, or with Olympian prowess. We harbor visions of what the "Big O" should feel like, and we're damned if we'll settle for anything less. In my childhood, the cliché goes, you would acquire horrible afflictions if you masturbated. Now we're sure we'll get them if we don't.

In a women's consciousness-raising group, one newly married member insistently begged of her sisters, each session, "How many times did you do it this week?" "How many times did you come?" Her litany of questions was always the same, always urgent. As if her friends' answers would tell her whether *she* was gratified, reassure her that her own coupling was okay. What's enough? And how are we to measure?

We are a crushingly lonely people. The alienation of the stereotypical housewife is well documented, but hers is only more easily visible than that of her family. It is the ever-plaguing sense of emptiness, of *something* missing, which often becomes translated to *someone* is missing. Whereupon follows a frenetic marathon of sexual activity—most often outside the marriage—the creation of thunder and distraction in order to anesthetize us, temporarily, from the insupportable loneliness hiding at the core of our family life.

I once knew a brilliant sculptor, reasonably well married, his career on the rise. He fooled around compulsively, laughably, obviously relishing the prowl more than the deed, and I asked him why. It all seemed beneath him, silly. "I get so bloody lonely in my studio all day," he wailed. "It overpowers me, makes me face myself and my work and my relationship with my family and I just want to escape it all. So I fuck."

Especially effective here is the "hit" of brand-new sex, without history, minus complications and collected bruises. New sex can give transitory reality to what someone called "the fusion delusion"—the misguided idea that we can actually become one with another human being, actually overcome our existential fate of true aloneness.

We're a problem-solving breed; every dilemma should yield to American technology, a solution. Preferably a quick and easily defined solution. Sex meets those requirements. Quandaries that may be, but probably are not, sexual at bottom, are treated by sexual prescriptions.

In the void of other overweening values we are obsessed with love. With being loved, being loving, being liked and well liked, competing for love, killing for love. We've come, in our psychiatric age, to view everything that is neurotic or quirky or awry with our heads as the result of an early failure in love. We didn't get enough or we got the wrong kind, or it was too smothering or it was conditional or it wasn't believable or it came too late. So our appetite for love is insatiable, we won't succumb to living without it. We manifest the addiction by the age-old score-keeping method of body count. The more bodies we accumulate and "love," the more alive we feel, the more worthwhile we are.

An elemental fact of the universe: Nothing endures. We become habituated to almost everything that lasts, we notice it less, our energy for it dissipates. Emotions particularly are subject to habituation. Grief doesn't persist, rage runs its course, joy dwindles. Sexual passion certainly does not endure. It depends for its very heartbeat on unfamiliarity, tension, novelty. The fictional lovers in Erich Segal's *Love Story* and in the film *Dark Victory* sustain extraordinary intense fervor for each other, although married. The women however are dying in each case, which helps immeasurably. A man interviewed for this book reported that the long-dormant passion for his wife had a brief rekindling after she had a nose job and came home from the hospital looking like a different and new person. I once had a love affair with a married man, full of stolen moments and illicit raptures. When he left his wife after a few years and we could make love any time, not just on steamy lunch hours, we found to our astonishment that somehow we were no longer quite so turned on. This is not an uncommon tale.

And it's universal. An experiment with mice, conducted by the Worcester Foundation for Experimental Biology, showed that the blood level of a male mouse's testosterone, the hormone controlling sperm output, is equally low when he is living alone or penned up with the same female for a week. When a new female mouse enters the scene, his hormone skyrockets.

We've always known that sexual heat succumbs to the dampenings of time and domesticity; that is neither a new idea nor a consequence of our unique age. What is new, again, is the insistence that it should not be that way. We won't settle for it.

The discovery of a human being, sexually, is one of life's most awakening, transporting experiences. An experience of aliveness, of sensation, massive involvement of bodies and fantasies, peak moments galore. I've never jumped out of a plane in a parachute or climbed Mt. Everest or been elected President. For most of us mortals, the ecstasy of the first electric stages of sexual union are the ultimate available zaps. And given the sorry truth that zaps don't endure, we need to continually rediscover or invent them anew.

In the best of long-lasting marriages other more abiding and richer qualities replace that brand of intoxication. Continuity, trust, shared experience, deep friendship provide a worthy trade-off and, in some cases, a passion of another kind. But most marriages are not built upon such sure bedrock, and when the sexual fire wanes, great gaps are often what remain. Most of the men and women I've talked with, married for many years, are not especially thrilled, erotically, by their mates. They may love and respect them, see themselves walking in their dotage arm in arm into life's sunset. Their sex lives may even be perfectly adequate, no clinical disturbances, nothing concrete on which to pin uneasiness. The fact is that most are no longer very intensely electrified. And therein, from our national preoccupation with sex, a profound restlessness begins to take root.

Margaret Mead and Simone de Beauvoir have written similarly of this state and its outcome. "Eroticism is a movement toward the *Other*, this is its essential character," says De Beauvoir, "but in the deep intimacy of the couple, husband and wife become for one another the *Same;* no exchange is any longer possible between them, no giving and no conquering." Mead writes of couples who "have become so much like a single person that, like most individuals in America, they feel the need of others to complete themselves, to reassure them that they are good, to rid them of the self-searching that comes from being left alone."

A neighbor of mine, a bachelor until age thirty-seven, has

now been married for fifteen years. It is a good connection, one that will persist and has many rewards. He told me: "The hardest part of being monogamous is that I've lost my feelings of attractiveness. It's probably pure vanity, but all the years I was single and with lots of different women, I had a confidence in my sexuality that I just haven't had for years. When you're with the same person and only her for so long, you seem to flatten out or lose touch with those parts of yourself. It's comfortable, you know her body and she knows yours. But it's deadening to the ego, at least to mine." He then admitted to me, reluctantly, that he has sporadic and "meaningless" liaisons with women, just to know that he's still desirable to a stranger, just to feel what he doesn't feel with his wife any more. His way has its costs for him in guilt and rancid aftertastes, but it's obviously worth it. He's been at it for eight years.

He is in middle-age crisis and surely that's a factor. But men and women twenty years younger have reported similar mind-states to me, and I have experienced them myself.

There's a terrible catch in all of this. Our expectation for marriage is that it contain an ocean of sexual fulfillment never dreamed of by my grandparents. We've studied *The Joy of Sex* and memorized two thousand positions instead of two; women have come to feel entitled to and demanding of equal billing in bed. We require our love-making to encompass Herculean feats, magic transfiguring fireworks. And passion—relentless, unflagging. The catch: Said passion won't hang around in a setting of monogamy. What do we do about that sorry state?

Throughout the course of recent Western history, particularly since the advent of the nuclear family, what we've done is what my neighbor is doing—conduct clandestine adulterous affairs. Or divorce and begin anew and divorce and begin anew. Or bury our cravings in corners of the heart so remote that they will never surface to haunt us.

Until just a short time ago, those have been our only options.

But: Today there are approximately two million Americans practicing alternate lifestyles that include sexual freedom. The forms span a range from basic twosomes to triads, to group marriages of two to five couples living together, to urban or rural communes. They encompass "sex clubs" like Sandstone and spread onto Elm Street in Suburbia. Two million citizens are not a giant majority, but that is not the point. There is something mighty in the air, a wind of change that promises to capture us all, and our children, in its vortex. A new world view, a *Weltanschauung* dizzying in its bigness.

Those who make their livings by predicting the future take this business of alternatives very seriously, read its implications with portent. Nearly ten years ago Dr. Richard Farson delivered a paper before the State of California Committee on Public Education which prophetically capsulized the two million outlaws. He wrote:

"In the future even more than today, change will not be an episode in our life, but life itself. Life will be seen, not as being, but as becoming, as process. And only those who can live in process and enjoy change for its own sake will be happy. Change, then, is the one thing of which we can be certain. . . . We will have to become flexible enough to enjoy the transitory quality of life. We will derive pleasure and meaning from temporary relationships and fleeting encounters. Our personal adjustments to life have been anchored in familiarity, stability, the reliable sameness of things, the permanence of values, places, relationships. In the future our adjustment to life will be based on our ability to cope with the process of change."

I don't remember exactly when it was that I noticed that something large had happened to family life since I was a kid. That marriages were obviously rotten, everybody was getting divorced, fidelity was a lie, expectations were nutty, and mostly everyone I knew was yanked apart by black bitterness at one end and purple romanticism at the other. All the belief systems seemed to be eroding and collapsing, and nobody had a remedy.

In 1974, in the painful aftermath of a relationship that by all the rules should have worked brilliantly and forever, but didn't, I set out to investigate open sexual relationships. My lover and I had tried to have an open relationship. It suited, in theory, our needs; it felt—well—appropriate. We had high hopes for its triumph. It became so open it disappeared. But nothing else, no other form, looked any brighter.

So I longed to find an intelligent system, a way to build my future loves wisely, viably. I sought a means to dodge the beartraps, predict the earthquakes, know where the rainbows are hiding. I wanted answers, too, for my bewildered friends and—in grandiose moments—for the world. And as the loyal daughter of technology, I assumed they were readily accessible. If Woodward and Bernstein could bring down a government through journalistic excavation, I could do something as simple as solve the puzzle of my own basic life.

Some arbitrary decisions had to be made. Because it's surely as easy to find a bloody open relationship as a disastrous conventional one, I would seek out and focus on alternate-lifestyle rebels for whom it seemed to work—at least in their terms, if not in mine. Because I could understand and fit them into a personal context, I would only looked at experiments that were essentially heterosexual. And more than all else, I would only invest time with people who seemed to be making serious attempts at new ways of living and loving.

As far back as 1970 I had discovered that there are individuals either stupid enough or desperate enough or courageous enough to travel these unpaved roads. In 1970, in fact, I had had a bizarre adventure with two such people, two outlandish renegades. And then, sometime later, I moved to California, journeyed to Sandstone. And began this expedition.

I have worked the way reporters work—wandering around

the country, poking into homes, peering into others' spirits, delving my own soul. One thread, one consistent theme flows through all the citizens I've chosen to talk about: the desire for personal freedom combined with their longing for a deep sustained commitment in a relationship. Some of them have fallen on their faces, but some have made it.

PART TWO

Anybody who thinks that monogamy is the only way hasn't had any interesting offers lately.

—Pat Meyer

Freedom, oh freedom,
Well, that's just some people talkin'.
—song lyric ("Desperado" by Don Henley and Glenn
Frey)

III

Pat and Steve Meyer

Miami was scorching and wet that June of 1970. Wet from the unmoving blanket of humidity that pressed down on the city and wet from the daily drizzles that only made one feel slimy instead of cool. I was there for ten days, doing research on the wedding industry for a book I was then writing. And I was staying in my mother's yellow and orange condominium on the beach—a complex where the inhabitants' median age was seventy-eight and the sole subjects of conversation were food and disappointment. My days were spent interviewing banquet managers of hotels and princesses about to be launched. And I passed my nights eating compulsively, as I tend to do in the company of my family, and impressing my mothers' neighbors with exaggerated stories of my glamorous journalist's life. I loathe Miami Beach, that gaudy repository of my heritage, and each day my energy lagged bit by bit.

In addition, I had left behind in New York an ailing love affair with a dear man who made me laugh but with whom sex was painfully unsatisfying, with as much unpredictability as my Fiat's journey through the car wash. Before Miami I had worked at convincing myself that good love-making was not really important over the long haul as compared with tenderness and laughing. But after three days away from him the lie of that became inescapable, and so I was depressed about that, too.

Such was the state of my spirit the night I met Steve Meyer.

I had a close friend living in Miami, a woman eight years my senior, who had divorced her husband of nineteen years and instantly become engulfed in the Human Potential Movement. She worked as the manager of Search, a new and flourishing growth center in Coconut Grove, and it was from Libby that I first learned the words "Rolfing" and "macrobiotics" and heard the stupefying news that people attending therapy groups were now getting naked before strangers. Libby was always "into" something—like, "I'm *into* bioenergetics"—and the somethings changed frequently and with similar fervor each time. After a while, though, I started to take her activities seriously because one weekend, at a nude marathon primal-scream gestalt massage group, she met a terrific guy named Mac. They began living together right away, dashing off to naked groups every few weekends.

Libby would write me long, rhapsodic letters about Steve and Billy, her two favorite group leaders, who were already something of a legend in Miami for their unorthodox behavior: They would take a dozen or so enthusiasts off into the country for a five-day workshop and in between "getting in touch with their feelings" and "dealing with unresolved material from the past" and "becoming in harmony with the energy flow of the universe," everybody would fuck each other.

Libby believed in Steve and Billy. They were, she said, the new breed of psychotherapist—human, not remote, not separating their professional personae from their personal lives. She was pretty sure, too, that they were having sex with each other, although both had wives and children and girlfriends. "Minstrels of the New Age" was the way she once described them to me, in a letter in which the capitals are hers.

One steamy night there was a party at Billy's house and Libby took me. Since I always assumed the population of Miami to be composed entirely of retired Jews from New York, I was rather surprised to find a houseful of people my age, very like my own friends, with fur on their faces, jeans and lots of circulating marijuana. Libby knew everybody. They all hugged long, serious hugs and made prolonged eye contact and said "far out" a lot. I was very uncomfortable and wanted to escape, although—or perhaps because—people were extremely friendly and embraced me instantly upon meeting. I was introduced to the famous Billy, who told me I had "high vibes," clearly a compliment of the highest order. I liked his mane of gray frizzy hair and his tubby body. He looked like he should have been a professor of art history at Bennington.

Then I spotted an extraordinary-looking man at the other end of the living room and couldn't take my eyes away. He was about 6 feet 4, with a huge chest, ramrod-straight back, masses of hair that resembled black grapes and the most exquisitely intense, soulful brown eyes I'd ever seen. He was enveloped by a gaggle of adoring girls peering up at him as if they were tourists at the foot of Mt. Rushmore. And I was quite overcome by his towering physical presence. I had certainly felt volcanic rushes before in my life, but this was bigger and more sudden; it frightened and exhilarated me.

I got a little stoned, enough to be more at ease, and eventually trailed him to a corner. We had one of those conversations which pretends to be serious but is actually total seduction. How you recognize it is that the subject never moves away from sex for more than twenty seconds. Through my mind raced the words, "I've *got* to go to bed with him," a thought which startled me in its utter ferocity, and which sometime later he would label "obsessional." Among other tales, he told me about being in bed recently with his wife and another woman. He said, "It was the first time in that situation where I didn't feel left out and could really get behind watching the two women relate to each other." I gulped. He had to be making that up. Nobody really did that; for damn sure, nobody talked about it if they did. Steve's delivery was very professorial; every word he spoke emerged as if it were etched in stone. Like: "I consider it insane to hate one's body, no matter what it looks like. After all, my body is the temple in which I live." Clunk.

I knew, given the immediate intimacy of our conversation, that he must be feeling as much heat for me as I was for him. Later, I discovered that he talks in that fashion to everybody, all the time, and his entire impression of me that night was that I was "cute."

I, on the distinct other hand, felt some blind, adolescent worship of him. He possessed what was to me at the time the most irresistibly attractive feature in a man: he was deeply agonized. Furthermore, he liked to talk about it, which had the singular effect of convincing you that it was *your* unique qualities that allowed him to reveal his agonies thus.

Libby and I went out to dinner after the party, and I was too ashamed to convey to her the urgency brewing inside me. Instead, I asked prudent questions about Steve, found out that he was thirty-three, had been married for about seven years, had two kids, one a newborn girl. Pat was, according to Libby, a "super lady" and they had an arrangement that a few years hence would become known as an "open marriage." In 1970 there was still no such label and Libby didn't understand or accept the notion any better than I. Steve and Pat fucked each other's friends, she said. In fact, they fucked everybody in this tight little growth-center island, members of both genders interchangeably, and they all talked about it and nobody seemed to freak out. It had to be aboveboard, that was the one requirement. Libby was the only monogamous person in the community, and while nobody gave her any flack, she certainly did feel a significant separation from them. I had never known anybody over the age of twenty-two who lived this way. I was at once appalled, thrilled and thoroughly disbelieving. This was, please note, two and a half years before California, before Sandstone.

The next morning I awoke on my mother's couch at 7 A.M. and phoned Libby. I told her I'd had this terrible nightmare about Steve and blood and plane crashes and snakes, and that I was in a state of gripping anxiety, and what did she think about my going to see Steve for a therapeutic hour.

My story, was, of course, a lie. I just needed to see him. I'd never felt before, in my unsensationally neurotic life, so truly out of control. Libby called and set up an appointment for six that night, offering to drive me—due to my current hysterical manner—to the suburb in which he lived. As the day progressed I indeed developed a stomach-churning panic, which by the time we reached his home was quite severe.

He lived, this titanic pioneer of radical departures, in a dismal gray garden-apartment development in a working-class neighborhood. His own apartment was cramped, an abyssmal mess, furnished in cheap Danish modern, broken toys and spilled raisins. Had I not been so crazed, I would have been utterly repelled.

Steve's wife, whom I had not as yet glimpsed, was in bed with a toothache and never emerged, much to my relief. He greeted me bare-chested and -footed, in cut-off jeans, and I could see that he hardly remembered me from the previous night. His office was standard shrink: a brown foam-rubber couch, one fake leather chair, a Kleenex box and a philodendron. I blurted out all that was swirling through my head about him: my sense of mystical connection, my driving sexual heat, stirrings of love and longing mingled with fear. And my sweeping loss of control. We embraced and cried together, although I hadn't the slightest idea why *he* was weeping so.

Indeed, he was a different kind of therapist; he revealed as much about himself as we spoke of me, but I kept wishing he wouldn't talk quite so much. At the end of two and a half hours he took me in his arms, looked into my eyes for what seemed like twenty minutes and said, "I'd like to spend about five hours in bed with you." I wrote a check for $30 to cover the session, and we made a date for the next night. A substantial part of me found all this ridiculous—including Steve's therapeutic approach—but that was quite beside the point.

The following day I rented a room in one of Miami Beach's newer hotels—midway, in tone, between the opulent Fontainebleau types and those where the old folks sit huddled on the porch demolishing all passers-by. We met there at ten that night, after the encounter group he had been leading. We spoke very little but were surprisingly relaxed, as if we had been connected for a long time. Our love-making was fiery and utterly without inhibition or the awkwardness of unfamiliarity, punctuated by a loud range of unrestrained sounds. Yelping, moaning, roaring, slurping, sobbing. We did not laugh or talk and weren't tender with each other. We kept our eyes open the whole time, which was weird and exciting, particularly in the absence of any words. If I thought this ferocious sex would calm my obsession with Steve, I was wrong. I wanted to go on endlessly, mindlessly, to bury myself in him forever.

Our hunger did not end for three hours. When we stopped, finally, and just lay there fatigued and sweating, his first words to me were "God, I'd really like Pat to meet you. Do you want to come for dinner tomorrow night?"

I could neither comprehend nor bear it. Yes, he explained, Pat knew he was with me, it was fine with her. When he got home in the morning he might tell her everything about me, about our fierce coming together, or he might not. It didn't matter in either case. His marriage, he said, was sure and solid. Best of all, he and Pat liked to bring new soulmates home to share. "We're both bisexual," he said, "and more often than not when one of us arrives home with a friend we'll all wind up in bed together. The only thing that throws noise into our system is when one of us is turned on to somebody that the other can't stand. Then it gets hairy."

I passed on the dinner invitation. There was not one single element in my idle fancies of an evening with the Meyers that I could tolerate. It was as simple as that. Not only was I not bisexual, but my mind's conjurings of being in bed with a woman were fearsome to me. When the woman in question also happened to be the wife of a man I adored, my brain was incapable of stretching to accommodate even the notion of saying hello to her. In fact, I hated the idea that she knew anything about me.

Besides, as I've mentioned, I believed unquestioningly in sexual fidelity, its inextricable link to marital morals and success. Before Steve, I had had one adulterous liaison, a two-month fling with a well-known movie producer, as well-known for his dalliances as his films. He claimed that his twenty-three-year marriage was alive and well; indeed, while I accompanied him to California for five days of conferences on a script he was producing, he phoned his wife every night and bought her an amazingly vulgar baby-blue negligée for $200 in the shop at the Beverly Hills Hotel. Nonetheless, he made ravenous love to me whenever we had eleven free minutes, and in somebody's bubbling Jacuzzi during a dinner party; every day we explored each other with lusty surprise. So, despite the negligée and his claims, I knew his marriage was lousy. He would not be with me, in this way, if it weren't.

Two years later he divorced said wife and the same day married her best friend, whom it turned out he'd been seeing for six years.

Thus, trying to understand Steve's pronouncements about the glories of a sexually free marriage was, for me, like listening to a Southerner extol the Ku Klux Klan. They challenged my entire concrete code of belief. Although, in 1970, my own search was still for the one man who would both excite me and make me feel sheltered forever, I was somewhat prepared to forego the "forever" part. I had just come through the sixties, after all, a tumultuous time of myth-upheavals on all fronts.

Most of my married friends had either severed by now or were stewing in blood; I had had some crushing failures myself; the divorce statistics were zooming. Freedom was a new moral imperative.

But the Meyers' arrangement was, to me, inconceivable and terrifying. There must be, I assured myself with righteous conviction, a fat lie going on. It can't work.

Then too, I didn't want it to be working because I longed for him to leave her and marry me.

My feelings for Steve were probably equal parts of adoration and fear. (There was, in addition, a tiny hint of contempt, which I kept neatly buried). He seemed bigger than life, herculean. To be with him, I thought then, was to stretch the limitations of my beliefs and experience, to confront myself and to grow. His own life was immersed in growth to the exclusion of everything else. He didn't give a damn about what was happening in the world or about books or movies, and he had zero sense of humor. His vision only went inward, which I grant sounds numbingly boring, but as most of the men I knew and had loved were precisely the opposite—they had marched in every available demonstration since the early sixties but were paralyzed from any self-revelation—I bathed in Steve's incessant, intensive navel-gazing. One thing he never offered me, for a moment, was comfort, and I couldn't see what I offered him beyond the chance to play Professor Higgins.

For the next year and a half Steve and I were in touch and saw each other sporadically, always in Miami. Often I invented trips in order to be with him for a few days. Each time he pressed my coming for dinner; each time I declined. Once I flew down over a Labor Day weekend to participate in an encounter group he was leading with Billy. It was a disaster. He turned on to another woman and wound up taking her home to spend the night with Pat and him. If only I were hipper, I scolded myself. He punished me with similar sentiments. When I became furious and hurt he reminded me kindly that he owed me nothing, had promised me nothing, was certainly entitled to fuck whomever he pleased, and I couldn't impose my expectations of fidelity on him. Naturally he was right: If he didn't have obligations to be faithful to his wife, well, he surely didn't have them to me. But I ached nonetheless with humiliation and self-hatred.

That same weekend, I met Pat for the first time when she came to the center to pick Steve up after the group ended on Monday night. I expected her to be beautiful, sensual, exotic. She was a plain and flat-chested *shiksa* with bad teeth. I felt reassured. Surely he would leave her.

But we drifted. I moved to California in early 1972, became embroiled in a new life and other relationships. We exchanged occasional phone calls or notes, and after a while my only continuing sense of Steve was that we would be in each other's lives, in some fashion, always.

In the spring of 1973, my book on weddings was published. For six weeks I trudged around America doing the author's whirling dervish publicity cha-cha. One day in each city until every city seemed to merge and I didn't know if I was in Seattle today or in Minneapolis. Or care.

One such morning I found myself in Fort Lauderdale, seated at a table in the bridal section of a local department store, surrounded by a mountain of my own books, waiting for customers to buy one and acquire the bonus of my autograph. It was one of my life's lowest hours, not the least reason being that although hundreds of Saturday shoppers passed me, gaped at me, even thumbed through the book indifferently, only three actual sales were made. In desperation, the store manager moved me and my table and my heap of books to a spot directly in front of the escalator, which only deepened the degradation and did not improve sales. For most of the morning I sat rigidly, with a cast-iron smile, and prayed for a flash flood. Then I looked up and saw Steve Meyer.

For a minute I didn't recognize him. He had lost about thirty pounds, which made him appear even taller, and his black, formerly curly hair was now roped into a single braid down his back. We hugged wordlessly for about five solid minutes, during which I was aware of the surly glances of the store personnel, mostly directed at Steve's shoeless feet. He had seen an announcement of my "appearance" in the Miami *Herald,* had driven up and wanted to spend the day with me. I was supposed to go to lunch with the store people after this debacle, and then fly back to New York, but I made a limp excuse. Steve said he would drive me to the airport later that night.

It was as if we had seen each other last week instead of one and a half years ago. He was as intense as always, as self-important, seemed slightly less tortured and still rarely laughed. I had evidently changed a lot in that time, as I no longer perceived him as quite so Christlike nor myself as so humble. The continuing saga of his kinky lifestyle did not stun me to the core that day.

We drove along the expressway to his newly purchased house on the outskirts of Miami. He said something peculiar, something that seemed to arise from nowhere: "You know, I've always been a little afraid of you and in awe of you because you're a successful writer. I'm afraid right now." I whipped my head toward him, unable to say the words resounding inside me: "WHAT? WHO, ME? WHAT ARE YOU TALKING ABOUT? I'M SUPPOSED TO BE AFRAID OF YOU!" The fixed positions we had held with each other for those years irrevocably shifted after that, the role game we had concocted altered forever.

The Meyers had moved from the garden-apartment ghetto to a boxy ranch house on a flat street of identical ranch houses. Why? What *was* that incongruous aspect of my Viking hero? His explanations were solid bourgeois, having to do with school districts and proximity to shopping centers and superhighways.

Pat and Teddy, his ten-year-old son, were up north for a week visiting family and having acupuncture, so we were alone in the house with three-year-old Liza and the baby-sitter.

Changes had occurred on Steve's inexorable growth journeys. He no longer worked with Billy, was down on encounter groups ("Just an excuse to fuck everything that moves," he confessed), was currently big on dance therapy and massage and Rolfing and vegetarianism. He and Pat were in a "very high space" with each other, and had decided several months ago to have separate bedrooms. She kept the original master bedroom with the kingsized bed, and he moved to another section of the house, next to his office, to a closet-sized cell with single bed and one tiny window. "Now we know," he said solemnly, "that when we come together it's because we really want to, not because of duty." And I thought, once again as in the past, "Bullshit."

He fixed me lunch—one of those mushy gray vegetarian soybean/brown rice casserole things whose taste you wished had even the smallest correspondence to its virtue. I flashed on the memory that whenever I spent more than six hours with Steve, I was always pining for a cheeseburger. And feeling guilty about it. I wanted to be the kind of person whose drive toward my Human Potential was so single-minded, pure and staunch as to cancel out my more indulgent and self-destructive appetites. I wanted to be someone who clearly preferred the broccoli path to the hot fudge route. I was not and feared I would never be. Steve was, and perhaps that was a key feature of why I liked him.

We passed the entire afternoon making love on his ex-bed, currently Pat's bed. I didn't relish that part, it seemed sinful. I said nothing about it, kept reminding myself that everything was just fine. Our sex was not as fiery as before, had a new element of leisurely gentleness that I deeply savored. It was true that I was no longer either intimidated by Steve nor worshipful of him and, as a result, I enjoyed him better than

I ever had. At one point Liza barged in, as we lazed on the bed, holding hands and listening to chamber music on the radio. My impulse was to either hide under the sheets or dive for the bathroom. But Steve was relaxed, invited the child to take off her clothes so we could all give each other massages. I recalled his once telling me his belief that in a world of pure free expression of love and sensuality, it would be natural for parents and children to make love. CHRIST, I'LL DIE IF HE STARTS ANYTHING LIKE THAT. Fortunately, Liza was so wary of the stranger in Mommy's bed that she couldn't wait to make her escape.

That evening as Steve dropped me off at the airport, he said, "Why don't you come down next weekend? Pat and Teddy will be home. I'd love you to know each other." I said I'd give it some thought and phone him in a few days.

As it happened, the schedule of my tour gave me the next weekend free and I had to be on the East Coast anyway. And, my God, I was curious. That sizable chunk of my character that adores eavesdropping on others' lives was titillated by the idea. As I was no longer fanatic about Steve, had no hunger to spend my life with him, even found him slightly silly, the one-time potential for injury didn't seem pertinent. Then, too, life itself had changed, at least in the circles in which I traveled, since I had first met Steve. I had had the mind-twisting Sandstone escapade, and I now knew many people who were experimenting with nonmonogamous behavior as a serious option. Thus the notion of engaging in the Meyers' *scène en famille* was not nearly so queer or fearsome to me. I did toss the invitation about for days, queried friends (Two-thirds said "Go;" One-third, "Are you nuts?") Finally, by Wednesday, it all felt like a grand voyage into a new solar system.

By the time my plane landed in Miami at seven-thirty Friday evening, I was acutely nauseated. The unknown nature of the weekend had moved, in my head, from excited curiosity into black terror. Where would I sleep? What if Pat and I despised each other? What if they expected, or demanded, a sex scene? How would the kids treat me? I did not know whether Steve was picking me up or Steve and Pat, and I prayed neither of them would appear, so I could flee onto the next plane for New York.

They were both waiting at the gate. Pat, even plainer than I'd remembered, seemed truly serene and welcoming. Steve was playing Arabian prince. I was frantic. We went to a vegetable restaurant and within twenty minutes of my guzzling the white wine the Meyers had brought, I was drunker than I'd been since college. The last detail I recall about those three hours was being ushered to a booth for four and not knowing where to sit. Awkwardly, I stumbled into the seat across from the married couple.

Much later, back at their house as we sat around the kitchen counter drinking tea, I grew increasingly, drunkenly dismayed about what would come next. I liked Pat considerably, was flattered and touched by the fact that she'd read my book during the week. I was no longer afraid that I'd be corraled into a group sex frolic. On the other hand, I certainly wanted to sleep with Steve and had no idea if that would happen.

Then Pat stood up, yawned, kissed us both lightly on our foreheads, saying, "Well, I'm going to bed. See you guys in the morning" and vanished into her private territory.

I did not close my eyes that endless black night. We were two large people on a narrow bed but, more than that, in my weary, wine-tinged hallucinations, I was waiting for the inevitable—a deranged housewife brandishing a kitchen cleaver to burst through the door and murder me.

Apparently I must have dozed near morning because I awoke to a ten-year-old male, Steve's midget double, standing over my nude body, hands on hips. Steve was gone. "Hi! I'm Teddy. You're supposed to come to the kitchen for breakfast."

Pat was cooking organic pancakes, Steve was reading the

paper, Liza was hurling orange pits, and the tableau resembled every nuclear family in America that Saturday. It was certainly difficult to remain strained and paranoid in such a harmless setting. For the first time I felt languid, happy to be there. Steve had patients (to whom he referred as "customers") that morning, then he and I would go off to play tennis. What will Pat do? I speculated silently, and just then a strange figure floated out from Pat's bedroom—a young girl. We were introduced, and I sensed right away that Arlene hated me.

She was about twenty and quite masculine, although pretty. Tall, bony, narrow-hipped, black frizzy hair cropped close to her head, and huge black-rimmed glasses. She appeared lost and scared, followed Pat around the kitchen like a displaced puppy. She also chatted shyly with Steve—who was once again playing the role of bountiful Harem Chief this morning—and she eyed me suspiciously, barely answering my attempts at cordiality. I calculated the available data: She had obviously been there last night. Was she sleeping in Pat's bed? Was she the baby-sitter? Were they lovers? Was this combination arranged because of my being there with Steve? Where was this Ship of Fools headed?

At breakfast, a dialogue between Steve and Pat revealed to me the subtle shadings of dominance operative in their relationship. Pat announced her plans for the day: "Arlene and I are going to the camping store to buy sleeping bags; we'll be back in time for lunch. Tonight we're going to the movies for the eight-thirty show. I've called the baby-sitter to come at six because you and Marcia probably will want to go out to dinner. See you later!" And she and her friend loped off to the station wagon.

Steve explained to me, later in the day, that he'd had no idea where I was going to sleep the night before until Pat trotted off to bed. Likewise, he had not planned this day's entertainments. I had assumed we would all be spending most of the weekend together; he had, after all, been spouting group togetherness since the night we'd met three years ago. Interesting that it was Pat, not he, who was in fact choreographing this odd, unpredictable ballet in which I was another one of the swans. I was reminded, as I often am, of the complex interlacings in a marriage, the hidden realities which belie surface appearance.

When Steve's first patient arrived I did the breakfast dishes and walked into the backyard to be in the sun. Teddy joined me, we lay side by side in the hammock. One of my keenest curiosities regarding the Meyers' arrangement was the kids. How could they conceivably accommodate to the procession of bodies through Mommy's and Daddy's beds? How could they trust anchors? Or comprehend the disparity between their family and those of their friends? What kind of psychic price is exacted? I wanted to find answers without asking the questions directly, without putting Teddy on the spot, but I didn't know how. As we just talked, it all came out.

Teddy spoke freely about his folks' friends, as if it were a subtheme that wound its way through all the subjects on his agenda. The couple who had lived with them for three months, and sometimes Dad was with Roberta and Mom with Kevin. The camping trip they'd all taken with Billy, Steve's ex-partner, and the families. A roster of names came out, too many for me to keep straight, but Teddy seemed clear about the intricate machinations and the Virginia Reel partner changes. More important than clear, he seemed truly balanced, wise beyond his years.

I sensed that he had no difficulties in welcoming me into his ever-fluctuating extended family. In truth, he was more open to this stranger/intruder than almost any child I'd known with whose divorced daddy I had spent time. I did not observe in him any suspicion that he would be excluded, no fear of abandonment by his father, no cautions against becoming close to a surrogate mother who might at any moment vanish—all those states that I'd seen in today's broken-home offspring. I was not, to him, a threat, I was a potential new playmate. At his suggestion we wrote poems about ourselves and read them aloud. Mine was funny and guarded. His was searching and open.

Midmorning, Pat and Arlene came home carrying new sleeping bags and knapsacks for a trip the Meyer family was taking to Wyoming in the summer. I had not imagined Arlene's animosity to me—for the rest of that morning she was as silent and staring as a statue. It was easy to ignore her presence, as Pat was more interested in getting to know me than in taking care of Arlene. She seemed quite content to let her child-friend recede into whatever solitary background place she chose. We three sat around a picnic table on the porch, drinking bitter fenugreek herb tea.

Pat was Steve's polar opposite: If he was haunted, she was sunny; if he was solemn, she was ironic. Whereas he considered every rumbling of his stomach to be of cosmic import, she was self-mocking. Steve could not, for example, discuss the issues of Watergate on everyone's lips at the time without lapsing into his "gut feelings" ("Nixon presses my buttons about my father's betraying my trust . . ."), while Pat's universe encompassed the political. Intelligent and witty, she could be trusted, I sensed. We established very quickly that special bond that women weave together these days—that sure knowledge of female commonality of essence and experience that is the base of Sisterhood. The synergy happens all the time and shouldn't have been particularly astounding. But, after all, in this instance I was feeling love for a woman whose husband I was making love to under her very roof.

By the middle of the weekend, it was very evident to me that I cared more for Pat than I did Steve.

Everything began to deteriorate during lunch, when the four of us ate huge green salads on the porch, and Pat and I did most of the animated talking. It did not occur to me then that

Steve's steady, stony withdrawal may have been precipitated by his wife's and my lively rapport, in which he was not especially the focal center, or by the quantity of our laughing together, which surely neither of us could ever achieve with him. Perhaps. Perhaps he didn't want me to feel as snuggled in as I did by then; maybe he secretly longed for Pat to loathe me or to be in competitive anguish.

Steve and I drove to a local park to play tennis. Waiting for the court, we lay in the grass and he suddenly turned his back to me. I felt the punishment in his silent gesture and was scared. We had a brief dialogue which would become agonizingly familiar to me over the next twenty-four hours:

"What's the matter?"

"Nothing."

"Something's going on. Tell me what you're thinking."

"I'm just in my own space. Leave me alone."

"This silence is really uncomfortable. I wish you'd tell me where you're at."

"Fuck off."

Playing tennis had as much delight as open-heart surgery. He would only talk monosyllabically and wouldn't admit anything was out of the ordinary. I swung dizzily between longing to escape and what-have-I-done-wrong, between not getting hooked into his melodrama and trying frantically to fix it. Meanwhile, I was thoroughly confused about his abrupt switch, and to the degree that I still viewed him as Supershrink I assumed I'd done or said or WAS something horrendous.

Back home, he withdrew into his tiny cell for a nap. Later, when I heard him in the shower I walked into the bathroom and stepped in with him. I probably thought I could turn him on, a last-ditch stand to make contact, to dispel these terrible hours. Sleep had not, however, brightened him. He recoiled from my presence in the cramped shower stall. I fled, walked around the neighborhood for an hour. By the time I returned, thinking I would ask Pat what to do, and laughing to myself about the irony of *that,* Pat and Arlene were gone and Steve was sprawling on the living room couch, smoking hash, gazing at the ceiling. He didn't acknowledge my presence. I had had it.

"What the fuck is going on with you?" I bellowed. One last time.

"I need space. Go away."

I should have left, should have gone to Libby's or to my mother's yellow couch. Instead, bewildered and immobilized, I just crawled into bed. Steve must have stayed with Pat and Arlene that night, as I didn't see him again until breakfast time, when at my sharp request he drove me across the city to Libby's house. In the car my only words to him were "I don't know what this number of yours is, but you've been rude and tyrannical and I'm furious at you." He just continued to stare straight ahead, nodding over and over as if a puppeteer were yanking a string attached to his head, and finally he mumbled, "I hear that that's your experience."

Libby, her boyfriend Mac and I spent the entire Sunday dissecting the events of the weekend, one by one, with great mean zest. We concluded that Steve was, in his heart, a square bourgeois shrink, and Pat was definitely in command of the show. I now knew for certain that he was a schmuck, I was embarrassed for all the years of my attachment, and I tried to figure out a way to be friends with Pat. A week later I received a warm letter from her, affirming our friendship but not mentioning the denouement of the weekend. I never heard from Steve. I next saw them both eight months later, by which time I had committed myself to writing this book. The meeting took place in Miami, where I flew to interview them.

The Meyers were to be my first subjects, a logical launching pad. For one thing, my experiences with them had left an indelible mark. Though skeptical about them, their ideology and the alleged beauties of their union, I knew there was *something* there, something as yet indefinable. Something, however puzzling and arcane, to note and to reckon with.

I went to Miami still tightly locked into my essential beliefs about relationships and my cynicism about Steve Meyer as a lifestyle pundit. I also assumed, then, that the theme in all of this was just Sexual Freedom. By the time I left Florida, I was not so sure about anything any more.

Steve

There was nothing in his history that would seem to lead him naturally onto his maverick path. A good Jewish boy from Cedarhurst, Long Island, oldest son of Philip and Evelyn Meyer, nice neurotic fretting middle-class parents. He attended Rutgers University, which, in the 1950's, indicated he either wasn't smart enough or studious enough to get into Harvard or Dartmouth. He majored in psychology, which nearly everybody majored in, he slept with 8.4 girls in four years, continued on for a doctorate and at twenty-four moved to Miami to work as an organizational psychologist for Eastern Airlines.

In 1963 he met Pat Tanner at a beach party, and six months later they were married. She was in her third month of pregnancy at the time.

For five years their marriage was conventional, as was the totality of their behavior. They were doing precisely what everybody around them was doing, and what they had always expected they would and should do, performing like all we dancing bears the '40's and '50's had spawned. "On the surface," Steve remembers, "I had a fierce and grim determination to get ahead, be successful, be a good husband and father and live up to all those values I'd been inculcated with. I was a mechanical person, a windup man. Along with that, I was completely faithful to Pat, I didn't even allow myself to fantasize about other women, was essentially frightened to *talk* to other women. What I realize now, and didn't then, is that the main reason I'd been faithful was because I was so dead.

"Ostensibly we'd gotten married because Pat was pregnant. But it was really because we were both desperately lonely, empty and shellshocked from our respective childhoods. During those first five years we had very little sex. What we did have in the way of physical intimacy, when we weren't being cold or mean, was that every weekend we'd pull the covers over our heads and cling to each other. There were a lot of lies between us—we were trying so hard to have a "good" marriage but were really no place with each other—but it wasn't like the horror stories I've heard. There was always a baseline of good will, of touching, which is probably the only reason we survived those years."

Swirling through the culture at that time, picking up momentum, was perhaps the single factor most responsible for the birth of alternate lifestyle trends in the late '60's: the Human Potential Movement. Sensitivity and encounter groups, mass nudity, people telling each other how they really felt instead of being polite, the glorification of selfishness to replace self-sacrifice as a supreme value. And a newly blossoming, vastly contrasting psychological theorem: Life was no longer about adjustment to or solution of one's problems. Life was about increasing energy, heightening awareness, maximizing experience, being free, living in the moment, actualizing Self. Getting, in other words, all the goodies there were to be gotten.

In 1968, five years into his marriage, seven years into his predictable and earnest rise up the professional ladder, the year of America's third heart-wrenching political assassination of the decade, Steve attended his first weekend encounter group, and the carefully cemented framework of his existence began to crumble.

"I'd never been away from home before and I was terrified. In the course of the weekend I was becoming in touch with all the bullshit I was living by, and the gnawing yearnings I'd been denying all my life. Sex was only one of them, but I got into an absolute frenzy about this twenty-four-year-old girl who was the youngest and sexiest woman there and very much into playing seduction games. I realized I was scared shitless of her and mostly of my own sexuality and what it implied about my rigid rules of faithfulness. I saw that I was holding my life together by suppressing every real feeling I had. I didn't go to bed with her for two reasons: It didn't fit into my image of myself and I was in competition with another guy who was older and more experienced. I saw that I was nothing much more than a creepy, turned off, eighty-year-old dead professional psychologist."

Three days after the group was over Steve was still hooked on her. He phoned her, they both took off from work early, met at her apartment and fucked. "Just as I was coming," Steve says, "something swiveled my head to the right, and I believed I saw God coming down to strike me dead. Only an asexual, tight-assed Jewish boy could have had that vision. And at the same time I was feeling some kind of new life in me, and I went from being eighty to seventeen in an hour.

"I decided I was going to tell Pat straight off—I didn't have any truck with this adultery or deceit stuff. So I walked in an hour late for dinner—I'd never been late before—and I said, 'I want to talk about where I've been'—but my mouth never moved, I felt like I didn't have any teeth. Pat said she didn't want to talk about it, and then it took us three months where I could finally admit that I'd fucked somebody else, and where she could finally listen."

Pat's reaction, when the story *did* come out, was relief—a response I have noticed from her in several situations where others would feel piercing jealousy. "Steve and I were so disconnected from each other that anything that would get him away from me, take the pressure off, was just fine with me," she says.

"I think," Steve says in recalling that first straying, "that the initial experience with outside sex can be very liberating for a couple. It can either kill the relationship or challenge it to a new level of honesty, realizing where you are or aren't with each other. My going to bed with that girl precipitated Pat's and my first six-month 'divorce.' Although there was no geographic separation, we definitely had a divorce, a time to bring out on the table all the values and assumptions we had about marriage, to test, to toss them out. I learned, as hurtful as it was, that Pat wasn't going to automatically love me, even though that's the mythology of marriage. It was a time for us to piss the lies out of our system."

According to Pat, however, Steve's monumental screw had no such dramatic ramifications. "His fooling around never had a sense of continuity or seriousness to it. It didn't interfere with our marriage—such as it was—at all." According to Pat, the apocalypse came after *her* first affair.

Be that as it may, it was Steve's discovery of the 1960's encounter movement culture that launched them both on this journey. Through a colleague at work he met Billy, the most pivotal character in the pageant. At forty-five, Billy was the Big Daddy of Search, the growth center where Steve hung out. What Fritz Perls was to Esalen in those years—guru, live-in trendsetter, figure of mystery and dread and awe—Billy was here. His groups were the most popular, his techniques the farthest out, his body the most sought-after. He was the first prophet of true, limitless sexual abandon in the neighborhood—"Whatever turns you on" was his most oft-quoted banality—and he himself, although married to Abby for twenty-odd years, moved lustily between nymphet-young girls and wispy young men. Billy put open bisexuality into the dictionary in Florida. When he met Steve, Billy quickly convinced him to leave his straight job in industry and come to work at Search. Billy also lured Steve into bed.

He was Steve's first and primary male lover. "He was adoring me," Steve says, "putting me on a pedestal, and I was lapping it up. Also, we were having a physical intimacy that was quite authentic, and which I wasn't having with Pat at the time. When I met Billy I was a stupid ladies' man, a militant heterosexual and a rotten, unimaginative lover. I was very turned off at some essential level. I think the first erection I ever had that I didn't will with my mind, that happened purely spontaneously, was with Billy."

Bisexuality, an erotic ethic that one associates with the counterculture, with a generation born ten or even twenty years after Steve and his comrades, was now wending its way through the steadfast middle class. If, in the late '6o's, folks in Dubuque were not yet climbing out on the distant limbs of sex that my friends in Miami were, could one really be so sure that they were not far behind? I have had to keep reminding myself over the years that although I've frequently responded to the Meyers' shenanigans with shock, they are cut from the same bolt of cultural cloth as I. And that I, shock notwithstanding, am surely no less vulnerable to these transformations than they . . .

Pat, between full-time motherhood and sporadic substitute teaching, set off on the encounter-group trail herself. She was very much under Steve's tutelage then; wherever his footprints trod, her own feet were sure to slip in afterward. At one of her very first weekends she met a man named Roger ("When the pressure was on, you found somebody to fuck," she snickers) with whom she began her first and most intensive extramarital affair. It continued for two years.

Roger was married, lived in Atlanta and commuted to Miami on business once a week. He and Pat would stay overnight at a hotel on the beach, walk on the sand at 2 A.M., get stoned, make love until dawn. Then she would drive back to suburbia and her family. She was living, for months at a time, entirely for Roger's visits. "He took on for me all the qualities that I'd always imagined I'd find. He was the most romantic and treated me the nicest and loved me the best. If he'd wanted to divorce his wife and run off with me, I would have been very tempted." Steve and she were galaxies apart, in that lonely estrangement that afflicts married people who are passing their days in pretense and avoidance. "Nothing meant anything to me but Roger. Not my home, Steve, my child, my job. I was not what you'd call a happy, productive person."

"For the most part," says Steve in a rare burst of self-derision, "I wasn't feeling jealous. Jealousy was a major imperfection and of course I didn't have any. I was very 'understanding.' This was something Pat had to do for *her*—part of her growth and development, nothing to do with me personally. I had played Pat's therapist for five years, in addition to the other noble things I'd done for her. And she played patient, so obviously it was part of her therapy to be with this guy. And we never used the word 'condescending' in those days. I just saw myself as a phenomenologist, studying events."

Steve's work was becoming increasingly exciting to him as he moved into a small spotlight as group leader, Billy's cohort, and mini-swami. He was beginning to experience the seductive elation of having power over people's psyches and the exploding new cosmos of "intimacy" and "love." Soul-baring and sharing, mass weeping, smashing each other with foam-rubber bats called batakas to exorcise one's hidden fury. ALL THAT EXQUISITE FEELING. The encounter game seemed a way of contacting others that was more real and substantive than what was going on in the outside world, and so Steve was not lonely or frightened. He was a rock star on the ascendant. Replete with groupies.

After Pat's affair had continued for some time, however, Steve became scared. "She was looking at me as if I didn't exist, and suddenly I couldn't deny how strong her fixation for Roger was. I was living in total disbelief that she didn't care for me, when I loved her so."

Steve's sexual experience and patterns were different from

Pat's and still are. She followed a highly romantic, exclusive, possessive path, looking for the quintessential Great Love. Steve fooled around. Intensely, because that is his nature, but fooling around nonetheless. Whereas he was eager to be friends with Pat's lover, she wouldn't let him in, didn't want him around.

Pat's affair with Roger came to a climactic turning point on a Tuesday evening which the Meyers now title "The Fateful Night." Pat invited Roger home for dinner and to stay over. "It was becoming clear," she says, "that Steve *was* important to me, more than I had thought for many years. The grand design in my mind was for the three of us to be friends, for everybody to love each other, to remove all this soap opera. Roger had never been to our home before, in fact Steve and he had only met once or twice. Early in the evening things went beautifully. We laughed and ate and all went swimming together. But I really wanted to sleep with Roger, and I didn't know how to work that out."

Steve continues: "Pat was giving me double messages all over the place. 'Go away, come here; I love you, I hate you.' What happened to me was that I became a child in relation to the two symbolic parents. I was anxious for their approval. If I hadn't succumbed, I would have gone off into my own space and said, 'Okay, they're into each other.' But instead I hung around, feeling more and more rejected. I felt Roger was a much better friend to me that whole night than Pat; he could see my pain and she didn't want to at all.

"When it was time for bed she said, 'I want to be with you tonight, Steve, and Roger will sleep on the couch.' So I got into bed and waited, expecting she would be there in a minute. After a half-hour she hadn't come in. I walked into the living room and they were lying together on the couch, fully dressed. I went crazy; grabbed her off him and started beating the shit out of him. I had a superhuman strength I never knew I was capable of and I knew at that moment I could break his neck.

I let go, and he and I immediately fell into a hug."

Why did he attack Roger, not Pat? Roger was, in some sense, the innocent, as much the tormented object of Pat's confused manipulations as Steve. Steve agrees that logically his impulse should have been to vent his rage on his wife, not the stranger. But literature and folklore affirm his actions as most common: When wife is in bed with somebody and husband barges in, he shoots the interloper, the challenger, not the deceiver; his instinct, it would seem, is to protect what's his rather than seek revenge against the villain.

Steve continues: "So then the real ice was broken, the three of us talked for a long time and I became friends with Roger. It was natural for the three of us to wind up in bed together. After Pat and I made love, we all dropped off to sleep. All of a sudden I was jarred out of a very deep sleep to see the two of them fucking right next to me, Pat sitting on top of Roger. I was terrified, particularly the way they were grinding away, like animals. I thought, God she's never been that way with me. Right then I was probably minus-two years old. I literally crawled out of bed and to the living room couch, crying like a baby, so sorry for myself. When they finished, they got into the bathtub, giggling like children, not even noticing that I was gone."

It was 4 A.M. Steve called Billy, drove to his home and got into bed with him and Abby; they held him tightly for two hours while he sobbed. At eight he went home to get dressed for work, and the moment he walked in the door was the first time Pat and Roger, still in bed, realized he hadn't been there all these hours. "I felt absolute disgust and contempt for both of them," Steve says. "From my point of view, they were utterly insensitive to me, saying things like 'Oh, is there something wrong?'"

From a clear viewpoint, though, it seems that there was nothing the slightest bit insensitive about these machinations, that the evening was a series of exquisitely honed torture de-

vices, each calculated by the participants—albeit unconsciously—for the precise level of agony it produced. It further
seems that couples in open relationships—merely because they
wave flags of "honesty" and "communication"—would be no
less prone to seething hostility, power plays and the capacity
for inflicting pain than humans in traditional matches, and that
sex can be the most lethal of weapons. Alleged "honesty" does
not, of itself, ensure good will.

Steve says, "I drove to work numb, dazed. At ten Pat phoned
me and said, 'I want you to know how sorry I am that I stood
in the way of you and Roger getting together.' I was shocked
beyond belief that she could think the issue was that. The tears
started streaming down my face. I ran out of the office and the
minute I hit the sunlight I knew I could go home and kill her,
and I was gleeful. I realized I wouldn't go back to the house,
and for the next two days I stayed with a guy from work, didn't
tell anybody where I was. Billy and Pat finally found me after
scouring the city, and I went home."

Their relationship changed starkly after that night; the cre-
scendo of inflicting agony ceased; the fear of all that potential
violence had traumatized and sobered both of them and, at the
same time, they seemed to have realized the depth of their
involvement with each other. Pat saw Roger just two more
times. "It was over after I spent the night with him at a hotel.
At 6 A.M., I was driving home and I just said to myself—for
the first time after I'd been in this same scene hundreds of
times—'What the hell are you doing to yourself?' And it was
just as clear as it could be. I pulled in to my garage, jumped
into bed with Steve and I finally felt, 'I'm home.'"

For Steve, there then followed a two-year period of adolescent fucking around during which, he says, "I was wearing my
prick on my sleeve." It was at the height of that era that he
met me and our relationship developed. But he has never fallen
in love, had an affair whose intensity or longevity was a threat
to his marriage, nor become even a fraction as consumed

romantically as has Pat. Since I met the Meyers, I've observed this exact phenomenon over and over among open marriage-ites, and it seems to bespeak stereotypic roles even within unconventional structures. Men fuck around, women seek True Love.

I once asked Steve why he had avoided long and serious contact with another woman; I did not think it was accidental. He said, "I don't know if that's a conscious choice. Sometimes I can get into a mind-fuck about it, like 'I must be a shallow person.' More to the point, though, is for me to look at how I like to spend my time, and see how much I have left over for other things, like a heavy relationship. For the last couple of years I've really enjoyed being alone. I've been doing carpentry, building a sundeck, and there just isn't enough time to get into another energy-consuming thing besides Pat. I guess I'm just really not interested in it." I felt unsatisfied with his answer, which seemed glib and trite. I suspected the truth to lie in a denser and more concealed place. A corner of guilt, or ambivalence over this outlandish trip, perhaps. I couldn't help but remember his way with me that weekend.

After Steve emerged from his phase of mechanical sex-seeking he moved into what he perceives as a much freer ethic. "What I was doing was the lowest level of sex—compulsion. Slightly above that is the level most of us operate from, contract sex: We do it every Wednesday and Saturday, once a night, and we always go down on each other. The levels beyond that are where sex really starts to get interesting.

"Now I don't go looking for sexual partners. It's natural to my life and it happens or it doesn't. I've gone for six months being celibate. The first time, last year, I really got high from it. The second time, which I'm just coming out of, lasted eight weeks, and I've been feeling sick. My body feels numb and exhausted."

Part of what Steve labels as his journey toward sexual free-dom—defined by him as spontaneous, nonautomatic behavior

—has been his bisexuality. Steve claims no real preference of one gender over the other, but I have never known anybody who was equally turned on to both sexes, who didn't perceive huge differences in quality and texture and identity in the love-making act with each sex, and have some ultimate preference. I don't pretend to understand Steve's sexual bent, or how he arrived at the niche he now occupies. It seems too complex, these days, to reduce the matter to "latent homosexuality," a name tag that once served to explain and dismiss all such spiny puzzles.

My comprehension of Pat's path is clearer. She was, I am certain, deeply stunned by the cataclysms wrought by her relationship with Roger. He was, thus, her last affair with a man.

Pat

She had never experienced that quantity of passion or poetry for Steve. Or for anyone else besides Roger. And she equated the degree of hurt, confusion and loss of control over her life with Roger's being a man. She didn't need it, want it, couldn't abide being so erupted ever again. So for the next few years Pat retreated into the benign fortress of motherhood and wifehood and solid citizenry. Other hungers would remain silently entombed.

Pat had married carrying all the certainties of her generation. Steve would be her one and only, forever. Or, if the gods were uncharitable, until they could no longer stand the presence of each other. But she would definitely be married; there was no other option in her world view. Today, it is slightly more common for fledgling couples to start out together debating the theoretical and pragmatic validities of "open marriage"; in the early '60's we didn't even have the vocabulary, much less the mind.

"We never sat down and discussed it," recalls Pat. "Just as

I never said to myself, 'Oh, I think I'll have an affair.' Those were not acceptable alternatives to people like Steve and me. Not that we didn't *do* them, obviously. We just couldn't face making a choice about doing them. They had to sort of 'happen.' In our case, something really dramatic would have had to happen to put a crack in our nice respectable superstructure. The 'something' was my affair with Roger." Rashomon. Steve has claimed *his* first breach of contract precipitated the jolt; Pat says hers. I believe Pat. She has never been endangered or even very affected by Steve's meanderings, while he has been gutted by hers.

Pat, like her husband, does not seem a likely candidate for the sexual revolution and for such radical departures. She grew up in Cincinnati, with a mother who was earnest Midwestern Bible Belt, and a stepfather (her own father died when she was two) deeply embedded in Catholicism. Bright but not ambitious, unexposed to literature or music or ideas, she was unquestioning about her inevitable female destiny. Majoring in education at the University of Massachusetts, she then moved to Miami to teach grade school and play in the sun. By the time she married Steve Meyer, when she was twenty-two and pregnant, she had had just three boyfriends—only one of whom had been her lover.

Like Steve, she was resolute and unhappy for the first five years of her marriage, disconnected from and disappointed in her husband, powerless to know how to repair things, frightened to leave. She had been sold out by her expectations.

It was easier for me to grasp Steve's leap into the whirlpool of free sex than it was Pat's. She does not give the impression that he does of self-conscious "hip," or of righteous rebellion against background structures. I asked her if she thought the impetus for her affair with Roger was retribution for Steve's initial breaking of the Big Rule. She pondered a moment, but seemed sure it wasn't. "There was just a sense that this was the culture we were moving into, where everybody was sleeping around freely, and when in Rome it becomes much simpler to do what everybody's doing. And we felt *right* doing it. Billy's influence hung heavy on our whole crowd. You just weren't living up to your human potential if you only went to bed with the person you were married to."

In retrospect, Pat sees the relationship with Roger as "my way of breaking out of this terrible downward spiral I was in with Steve, where I always lived in his shadow, where he was playing big-strong-wise-prince-therapist and I was the patient. Even though I always had a job and a life outside the home, I was superconscious of *his* needs all the time, above my own. That's the way I was raised, that's the way my mother was with my stepfather.

"But the affair with Roger shifted my head in a way that lasted even after it was over. It put me in touch with my autonomy. I realized, 'I'm a person, I have a life; the marriage is here, but I also need to do the things I need to do for me.' "

Autonomy. For most, we will see, it is one of the cardinal issues of open relationships. The assertion of independent self. Women, for reasons that are self-evident, make this proclamation more fiercely than do men. It comes up again and again; it is beyond sex. Pat then makes a striking claim: "It was having a really intensive affair with a man that got me in touch with my autonomy, and having affairs with women that got me in touch with my sexuality."

Not only had she no experience with homosexuality, she had few women friends. She was one of those females who prided herself on being a "man's woman," told herself women were petty and competitive and untrustworthy, and men were more intelligent, more fun to be with. One could put forth, I suppose, that Pat's rejection of women was a denial of her own fearful impulses. But many of us until recently held the same view of other women, measured our sisters solely in terms of whether or not their thighs were thinner than ours. And, in truth, I think Pat's enterprise to be more fascinating and subtle than that reductionist view permits.

The spreading encounter-movement mentality was, above

all its other effects, opening up sexuality. Billy, the prophet, had eyes for Steve, which shook Pat deeply. She says, "I'd gone through a relationship in college where the boy I was in love with also had a guy at the same time. That was agonizing to me. So when Steve and Billy got friendly, it was watching that same movie once again, and it scared the hell out of me. But after they became lovers Billy also became a close, dear friend of mine, and all the fears slowly went away. I saw that their relationship didn't jeopardize me or my bond with Steve, and that changed most of my negative feelings about homosexuality. But . . . it never seemed like something I personally wanted to do."

One weekend Pat participated in a group that Billy and Steve were leading. The format was that on Friday night everybody would get their clothes off. Saturday morning was kind of slow, then the group would break for lunch and the afternoon was free time. Pat describes it: "One of several things would happen. You'd either get together with the person you had your eye on and you'd go screw, or by yourself you'd go get drunk or you'd go cry. There was a nice, attractive girl in the group, about twenty-five years old. She came over to me and said, 'I like you, I'd like to spend the afternoon with you.' I had planned to be alone but I said okay. We went to the beach and talked all day. And that was the first time I was aware it was possible to spend a long time with another woman and be totally there, be enjoying it as much as with a man. In my prior experience you only spent time with a woman if you didn't have a guy to be with. She and I got very close that weekend. There was no sexual involvement, but it was in the air between us, and contemplating it was very scary to me."

Locked doors had been pried open a few inches. Afterward, Pat allowed herself her first fantasies about making love with a woman and the more she thought about it the more appealing the idea seemed. Fantasies about men always reawakened in her the trauma of Roger. "The thoughts and wondering didn't worry me. I didn't have any 'homosexual panic,' like 'Oh, my god, I'm a lesbian.' That came much later," she laughs ruefully.

About a year later, the summer that Liza was a year old, Pat, Billy's wife Abby, and another friend, Ellen, a local therapist, piled into Ellen's Volkswagen camper and took off for northern Florida, to a five-day marathon group for women. Ellen, according to Pat, had been sending out some transparent sexual messages to her for many months. They had never confronted the issue directly with each other, but it was clear, in the way that those things are always clear though unspoken. Pat was ready to examine this new province, finally.

She had not been with anyone but Steve for a few years, and sex for her was never a thunderous factor in their union. She had sat by calmly while he raced through those years of interminable Don Juan fucking, and while she was never possessive, was not a keeper of scores, his frolics were a constant reminder of what was missing in her own days. Her dilemma was that she no longer wanted to be with men, and making love to women was forbidden, filled with mystery and dread. She simply had to wait until her internal processes provided a resolution.

The last night of the marathon, after it was all over, the three friends sat around in Abby's motel room getting soused on gin and tonics. The air was heavy, not the least reason being that about two months before Pat and Abby had found themselves in bed together, dead drunk. Whatever had gone on between them had never been spoken of again, and Pat had repressed the whole event. In fact, it was almost as if it had never occurred. She certainly did not classify that episode—whatever happened—as her first homosexual experience.

This night Pat, feeling a boozy bravery, turned to Ellen. "Listen, Ellen, you've been sending out these signals to me for a long time. Let's get it on. I want to sleep with you tonight." They did, and Pat recalls an array of incendiary sensations.

Remembers that she felt virginal, slightly inept, childlike. Remembers that the sex was like none other of her life. Profoundly different, and infinitely better. "For me," she says softly, "there is something incredible in making love with someone who's exactly like you are, physically. I can't explain it without sounding sort of mystical, but the truth is it's like looking into a mirror and really seeing yourself."

Both women were shaken by the night. Ellen sneaked out of Pat's room before dawn, retreating to her camper. And when Pat awoke in the morning, alone, she crawled into a ball under the shelter of the covers and wept for hours. She hitched a ride back to Miami, as she couldn't face Ellen, couldn't deal with the mélange of feelings she was feeling—humiliation, rage, rejection.

Several days later they bumped into each other at a party. Ellen made a sheepish confession, one that astonished Pat: It was her first time with a woman, too.

They began seeing each other regularly. When Steve was away doing groups, Ellen stayed over, and otherwise spent a good deal of time around the Meyer household. The kids liked her, they all picnicked and went to the beach together, and for Pat it was the kind of light, flowing companionship that she wanted—without stress, pain or tempest. Sex was a sizable part of it. As time went on Pat became aware that she relished making love with a woman more than any other sex she'd ever had.

On occasion she and Ellen and Steve would go to bed together—a blending that's occurred with every woman in Pat's repertoire. But the three-part mixture was never satisfying to her. I imagine she enters such a complex drama with unclarity, desiring to include Steve in her jaunts, dreaming of some utopian free, androgynous extended family, yet—at her core—puzzled by her true and deepest impulses, her love for women. The clue came for me from her clipped response when I asked her, "Does this knowledge of being more turned on to women than men put you in conflict?" Her answer, delivered in a tone unusual for her, a tone that communicated I-don't-want-to-discuss-it, was "No. I can't do that. I can't let it put me into conflict." Period. No more dialogue on that point.

Ellen and Pat saw each other for about a year, several times a week. Her marriage to Steve was not being disrupted, she contends, in fact it was improving with the expanding honesty and separateness they were now granting one another. "My relationship with Ellen was something I was doing," she laughs. "Like having a hobby—doing needlepoint or something."

Almost as an afterthought Pat mentions to me that during the entire course of their liaison, Ellen was also married.

As time went on Ellen became clinging, demanding more and more of Pat's dedication and time. Do-you-love-me-best-of-all became the classic refrain, as Pat perceives it, and suddenly she was thrust back into the strait jacket of a possessive connection, something she had been working to free herself from for several years. She didn't want *that* any more than she wanted the *Sturm und Drang* of loving a man. It was finished with Ellen.

But what one believes one wants and what longings in truth drive us are often at odds. Pat thought she was seeking serenity, a tidy life with some frisky diversions. Three months after closing the door on Ellen's demands, however, she fell wildly in love. More in love than she had been with Roger, and with more excesses of emotion. This time it was with a woman.

Diana was a sometime casual bedmate of Steve's and, in many of her facets, a female counterpart of Steve. Yet another charter member of their incestuous growth-center cabal, Diana was also an encounter leader—beautiful, charismatic, commanding, with a capacity to draw worshipers to her fast and intensely. Steve talked of her to Pat incessantly, mostly in terms that soured Pat. "You should try to be like her" was the sort of endearing sentiment he would lay on his wife. "She's the epitome of a woman." He would bring Diana home to stay overnight, and while they were fucking downstairs on Steve's prim cot Pat would be in her own room seething—not with your common low-grade jealousy but with wanting what Diana had, wanting to possess . . . what? Was it Diana she longed to possess or those qualities in Diana that she herself lacked? And, in some way, is that question fundamental to the nature of homosexual love?

Pat recognized the same features in Diana that I had once revered in Steve: the electric, towering dynamism in whose presence we feel infinitely more exciting than we really think ourselves to be. From the first time she met Diana, she needed her approval, and was ever afraid of not receiving it. Steve, for reasons that I cannot fathom even with his heady explanations, actively promoted a merger between the two women. Pat and Diana had casual dinners a few times, a sexual *ménage à trois* with Steve a few times, and very soon Pat was locked into slavish adoration of this fiery woman. They began an affair. Pat then knew the truth: Passion is passion whether the object is male or female. The elements of obsessiveness, loss of power, heights and depths were no breezier for Pat, no simpler to bear, this time around than they had been with Roger. Indeed, they were compounded by Diana's being a woman. Now Pat was plunged into the midst of severe guilt, a true homosexual panic.

"I felt I was losing my mind—literally. I loved and needed her much more than she did me, which is a *bum* position to be in. She was totally unpredictable, I never knew where she was going to be at from one day to the next. And I wanted her desperately all the time. We were never able to talk about what was going on—isn't that weird for two such growth freaks? So I lived waiting for the next ax to fall, having to watch everything I said. The truth is it was no fun at all."

I mentioned to Pat the obvious: It sounded like several torturous love affairs I'd had with men. Exactly. No sisterhood, or special empathy or heightened trust. Just the same old shit. But worse for Pat, because now she began to see herself as a raging, out-of-control lesbian, and for the first time since Roger, she felt the framework of her nuclear-family edifice seriously endangered, some days on the edge of collapse.

She lost interest in having sex with Steve although, she declares, "During this time my relationships with men were really the best they'd ever been. I'd given up all the crappy heterosexual games designed to get some guy enticed, so I could really be good friends with men." And Steve accepted the situation, as both of them have an uncanny ability to do.

The affair was the reverse of Ellen. Now it was Pat who was clinging and pressuring and suffering, and Diana who was feeling smothered. When Diana began to withhold sex, Pat was rapidly driven nuts, and the whole thing exploded. At the time I interviewed her in 1974, Pat was still bitter and troubled about Diana, had not seen her in nearly a year, which indicates —given the minuscule orbit of their lives—that at least one was purposely avoiding the other. Diana, at that moment, was living with a man.

The affair over, Pat—as after Roger—foreswore any more tempest. She settled down once again, turned her attention to the fruitful ordering of her days. There had been some flings with women—Arlene, the student of my weekend with the Meyers being the most recent. But no *grandes passions* to fracture her nest. One has to be willing to allow upheaval when diving into the maelstrom of love. Pat was not.

I was curious about Arlene since my weekend with them. Although I spent two days with Pat and her, I could never get a lucid picture of their relationship. The story is: Steve had led a massage workshop with some college kids, and Arlene was one. As in the typical scenario, he took her to bed on the Saturday afternoon break and several times thereafter. "Then at Christmas a year ago," Pat continues the tale, "we were going to New York for five days and needed a baby-sitter. Steve hired Arlene to stay with the kids. On the plane coming back home he said to me, 'She's never been with a woman before but I know she'd like to.' I wheeled around in my seat and shrieked, not too sedately, 'Are you out of your fucking mind? What are you trying to set up THIS time?'

"Anyway, that night, the three of us wound up in bed together—this is getting into your porny Victorian novel—and Arlene discovered she really liked having sex with another girl, and I discovered it was something I'd missed a lot, but hadn't let myself think about. She's a pleasant little chick and she began coming around a lot. The three of us spent considerable time in bed together; I'd say that's the most enjoyable sex I've ever had in a threesome with Steve, probably because there was so little real involvement for me, it was just play. But she started getting greedy of my time and attention and I started thinking, 'Jesus, you're thirty-three years old, you've got two kids already, what do you need another one for, other than to satisfy your insane lust?' So I eased away from her, except she still baby-sits for us, and occasionally spends a night downstairs with Steve."

The weekend we were all together Arlene was just there on Friday watching the children and hung around after. Pat did not invite her in order to have a "date," or to even the score. She emphasizes—and I believe her—that she has no exclusion problems in such situations, has never felt left out when Steve brings a lover home. "I dig spending time by myself," she says. "I can entertain myself with a book for days and *I love* my room, boy. It's *my place*. I might have felt fairly poisonous if I hadn't liked you that weekend, but I did, so it was all fine with me. I think Steve has a much bigger difficulty with being excluded than I do."

I was baffled by the areas of Pat's concerns and nonconcerns. It's jolly if her husband is fucking somebody she likes, not okay otherwise. Why is that the important issue? "Because if it's some dopey chick who I don't want to have around, I feel as if my space and time have been violated. Especially if there's the implication that I'm supposed to be nice and hostessy."

Pat's apparent lack of jealousy and possessiveness is one of the most fascinating corners, to me, of the Meyer configuration. A dazzling illustration presented itself one evening while I was interviewing and visiting. As we lounged around the kitchen table, several friends dropped by. We all got to reminiscing about teen-age days in the '50's, and Steve told a story. It seems that just the week before, he was having sex with a girl in the back seat of his car, parked on a dark street. It was the first time he'd ever done that act, and throughout love-making he kept being transported back to high school with attendant memories and aches. Everybody in the room, six friends in all, found the story either moderately amusing or hilarious. Except for me. I was terribly uneasy for Pat, projecting how betrayed *I* would feel were I she at that moment. I noticed that she was chuckling as naturally as anyone. Later when I brought it up, she said, "I have no problem with that story. I think it's terribly funny, as I would if anybody told it. I'm not distressed just because the hero is my husband."

It is not as if she's indifferent toward him; it is obviously uncomplicated to feel nonpossessive toward a man one doesn't give a damn for. But she truly loves and likes Steve, treasures her family arrangement and the solid base it provides her. And it does have some of the sturdiest, firmest roots I've seen in an enduring marriage, despite the unconventionality of the plot and the ever-changingness of the supporting players.

Pat, as noted, does not experience a vital sexual connection to Steve, and that is probably the sharpest clue to her absence of jealousy. He is her best friend, her caring and devoted roommate, her partner in child-rearing. That defines their good will and lack of strain, their willingness to let the other soar in whatever direction he or she desires. When they were more like lovers in earlier years, they weren't friends. Then they were vulnerable to each other, capable of causing acute bruisings, and needing to bind their mate in the ropes of false safety. . . .

But now Steve views passion as "excess" and vulnerability as "self-indulgence," and thinks neither has anything to do with love. And he is, I believe, more sexually turned on to Pat than she is to him. At the same time, he persists in denying her true proclivities while he has been responsible for engineering several of her episodes with women. I perceive Steve to be more confused about his own sexuality than is his wife. With other women his relationships are essentially carnal; with Pat everything but.

Sexual passion for Pat, one has noticed, inevitably produces the *Hindenburg* disaster.

I once asked Pat whether she thought best-friend and best-lover to be a possible combination to find in one person, and in the form of the nuclear family. "I just don't know," she mused. "I'd certainly rather be married to my best friend than anybody else. There's a lot of ebb and flow between Steve and me. Last summer we went on a back-packing trip for a week in Georgia, and during those days we had the best-friend/best-lover thing. There was nobody else I'd rather have been fucking or hiking and spending time laughing with. But it's just not possible all the time. We're all looking for the perfect situation where everything's going to be exactly the way we want it every minute. I'm sorry, life doesn't work like that. At least not for me."

I wondered aloud then if she was looking for something now, seeking that elusive "perfect situation." She became wistful at the question, more melancholy than I'd ever seen her. "I think," she said slowly, "at one stage of the game I was out for the next intense affair. Now I'm not. Last summer I was rereading *Look Homeward, Angel*. And there's one part where Eugene has this brief, passionate idyll with a girl. And the tears are rolling down my face, and I'm thinking 'I don't think this is ever going to happen to me again.'"

When she envisions this magic poetic love, is it with a man or a woman?

"It's with a woman," replied Pat softly.

Pat and Steve

The three of us lay on the floor in the Meyers' living room, my tape recorder the center of our huddle. Outside a chilling, gloomy rain had been falling all day. This house was built for the tropics, and we did not feel at all cozily protected. Or perhaps it was the conversation, the probing into regions usually allowed to sleep, that was not permitting comfort. We were all cold, and so we drank beer and peppermint tea continuously over this long afternoon that stretched into evening. The wet coconut palms swayed eerily through the window. It was New Year's Day.

"If you were to stop the tape right now," Steve said, on this, our third day of talking, "you would have one-tenth of the story. All that we've told you so far is just getting the shit out of the way so we can really start making it with each other. And making it in the world as two free spirits, with mutual support to experiment with life."

Pat agreed: "Where I am right now is a product of all the stuff we've gone through in our marriage, all the workings out of independence and commitment. Now I'm ready to be a presence in the world on my own. I'm not clinging to Steve or hiding behind him; I feel both very close to him and quite separate. And that's very much the way I want it."

Commitment and independence, intimacy with selfhood. Is the Meyer's sexual license only a metaphor for bigger meanings?

Some of their verbiage seems disarmingly authentic, some soapbox rhetoric, and much—particularly from Steve—seems closer to what he dreams than what he actually is. But the most penetrating stuff is unearthed by watching how Pat and Steve are together. They are unmistakably fond of each other; kindness always prevails. They listen and laugh and respond. I never notice the poison darts or little murders that permeate so many long-married couples. Nobody clutches on, neither seems fearful of the other, and a great deal of room moves between them. There is a rare absence of sex roles—it is not predictable who will jump up to prepare dinner or who will dominate the conversation. They are not sexy with each other, but then neither are most people under the same roof for thirteen years. And there are no visible lies.

Steve and Pat show remarkable acceptance, a willingness to say "Okay" to the unending variety of phases and stages each moves through. Both their own independent psyches and their marriage—after the first five deadly years—have traveled through more torrents and tumults than a tiny atoll caught in the center of a cyclone, yet the Meyers ride out the storms with an equanimity that is rare. Like jaunty rubber rafts, they bend with the next wave and the one after that, and they survive everything. It was not so in their early years when they were still imbued with our usual preconceptions of the matrimonial state. Then they sank, slowly but ineluctably, into disappointment and despair. Theirs was a case history destined for Reno.

Their priorities, at the moment, coincide. A fortunate harmony. If they clashed, the marriage would not likely remain intact, as the Meyers do not compromise what is crucial to them. Steve recently told me he was establishing a new career, as a bioenergetics therapist, and his time was consumed by study. "It's very clear what's important to me right now. My family is critical to me; they're the underpinning for my sense of independence, my ability to start down a new career road. I'm doing it on my own but it's a shared experience with them. I don't think I could live in the kind of graceful separateness that I feel if it weren't for the sense of belonging that I have with them." The following week Steve was going to New York for two months to study and do workshops. He would be living with a girlfriend.

For Pat too, liberty was the essential priority now. "What I want," she said thoughtfully, "is to be able to feel free to do the things that I want to do, pursue the interests and people that I want. And that has to be the kind of condition that exists between us so it's available for Steve, too. And the things he wants to pursue just might not include me. And that's all right." It is also perfectly all right, she said, for Steve to be leaving for a few months—in fact she was looking forward to it—and certainly "fine" that he was going to be bunking with a lover.

I repeatedly have caught myself wondering why the Meyers stay together. It is difficult and trying to live with another being, to accommodate conflicting rhythms and needs. If the primacy in one's life is for freedom, why not live freely? There is more to this question that readily appears; one could ask it of open relationships across the board. Free sexuality has the disadvantage of eliminating some bonuses of traditional monogamy, like safety and constancy. And open marriage seems to carry the horrors of singlehood—the never-quieting search for new bodies, the strain of frequently shifting ties—without the benefit of true release from responsibility to others.

For Pat, the answer is clear-cut. "I genuinely like Steve very much," she says. "I need to live with other people, be close to them, and explore and grow. I just wouldn't want to live alone." But Pat does not view her marriage as riskier, more open-ended and perilous than monogamy. She feels secure. Or as secure as anybody can realistically feel.

"As far as I'm concerned," Steve says, "the whole business of open relationships is very existential, and not about sex at all. There's a realization that Pat and I are our own persons, that there are very real limits on how much one can share with another. That's a very frightening concept to us, with what the culture has taught us relationships should be. So I really groove on the fact of Pat's and my apartness and that I don't really know her, haven't begun to experience her yet. That's really exciting to me. I have a lot of curiosity about what she's going to be up to in ten years. That's why I stick around, I guess."

He, too, feels sheltered—because, paradoxically, of the flow and movement between them, the very qualities that challenge solidity for most couples. "Pat and I are involved in a process which gives us a better chance of having fresh, open experiences with each other, experiences that aren't preprogrammed. If I were to get divorced and start over with somebody new, I'd have a lot of that preprogrammed stuff to get through. I'm living in a supportive environment which was many years in the making. And as I look around I couldn't possibly see anything that could challenge that. There's such a lot of relief to living this way. Imagine what bullshit it is to live with, foremost in your mind, what expectations you have for yourself and what the other person has for you, and always trying to meet those expectations and constantly thinking your mate is failing you."

Steve is surely a windbag, exhaling streams of '60's platitudes with each ebbing breath. And the Meyers' story is hard for me to identify with in its particulars—three in a bed, bisexuality, jocular nonpossessiveness. Yet there is less probable cause for fracture of this kinship than most. If either were to fall in love with somebody else, the structure provides space—total and accepting space. Many marriages are like a taut string: one unexpected zap of pressure and they break. The Meyers' marriage is so loose it can ostensibly tolerate anything. In 1974, after interviewing them for this book, I left Miami thinking that they were the least fragile couple I had ever known. And *that* was indeed something.

But doubts and dark questions nevertheless enveloped my head. What, for instance, is a woman saying when she claims she wants only to make love to other women and not particularly to the man she lives with and cares for? Is there some vast region of withholding that both Steve and Pat require to keep this thing functioning smoothly? Is the fact that neither of them has yet created another union with endurance, but only short-lived storms, a comment on them, or on open marriage?

Yes, the Meyers were a sturdy pair. But that, for me, was not the only consummation to be wished in a marriage. I had learned from them, yes, stretched my mind some. But there was nothing in their house that sent my spirits flying. Nothing so far that looked brighter than what I had seen around me forever.

Onward . . .

IV

Quartet

One forty-five in the morning. Two men and two women are sprawled throughout a small living room, crumpled over huge, multicolored throw pillows that comprise the only furniture. I hover in the corner, away from the nucleus, wanting to be inconspicuous and inanimate, struggling urgently to stay alert at this low hour. The fire in the fireplace has long since gone to sleep, as has the rest of the world. In here, a quadrophonic dialogue is entering its second hour, with no discernible indication of reaching completion.

Said dialogue is characterized by a tidal quantity of anger, pain, confusion and verbiage. While the majority of America slumbers this quartet in Phoenix, Arizona, is blazing with heat. The topic, ironically, is Who Will Sleep with Whom Tonight.

I will give you the denouement before the details: Since the skirmish will rage until precisely 4:48 A.M., and since there will be no resolution save that of numbing exhaustion, and since one of the males will have to get up at six to go to work, nobody at 4:48 will give much of a damn where anybody is sleeping. All of them will collapse, like overcooked souflés, into the closest soft spot.

Paul and Connie Langden and Jamie and Fred Fox are married to each other, in what is today termed, logically enough, a group marriage. It is a form neither legal nor widespread; indeed there are probably no more than a few thousand arrangements of this nature existing in America. Although much statistical research is being conducted on group marriages (primarily by Ph. D. candidates) one is hard-pressed to find any meaningful data, for two reasons: 1) the shareholders tend to be secretive; and 2) the marriages tend to disintegrate before one can get one's notes typed. It has taken me several months to track down this particular quartet in Phoenix, to convince them to allow my intrusion. They aren't ashamed about their setup, only protective, and I cannot blame them. They make the Meyers look like Betty and Gerald Ford.

A group marriage, to further define, is not a commune, although it may resemble one in numbers. In a group marriage there is no repeated turnover of bodies, folks do not drop in and out; and the commitment is twofold—to the collective and to every individual within. I believe that all such tribes consist of an equal number of men and women, and that each member is considered to be married—that is, connected in a fundamental, intimate way—to each other member. In terms of sex, there has probably never been a group marriage without cross-pollination, but few linkings are homosexual. And hardly any partake of random team sex, but instead favor your usual behind-closed-door duets.

As of this evening, this foursome has been cohabitating for almost three months, along with the Langdens' four children, ages six to seventeen, and the Foxes' two, ages six and eight. They own a rambling "Victorian" mansion built circa 1962, a joint checking acccount under the combination name "LaFox," three dogs, two cats, an iguana called Colonel Sanders, four cars and approximately fifty-five bottles of pills in the medicine cabinets of their five bathrooms.

They also have a great many recurrent problems with sleeping arrangements and thus tonight's dialectics are more fre-

quent than not. Ultimately, nine months and two weeks from
now, there will be a unified chorus of "FUCK IT," an explosive
wrench, a garage sale, some elaborate financial negotiations,
and each couple will recede to its prior ways. Connie Langden
will say to me over lunch, her fragile voice a blend of relief and
disappointment, "Jesus, one year of a group marriage is like five
of a regular marriage. Half our time was spent encountering—
and that gets old pretty fast!" However, like most warriors just
released from the prison of a failed union, with one eye scan-
ning the horizon for the next opportunity, Connie would like
to try it again. Sometime, not right now.

The sleeping arrangements. It is necessary to grasp the sexual arrangements first, and those are that each member of the
group is involved in regular intercourse with each of the opposite sex. No homosexuality and no collective gambols, except
once or twice when they all got very stoned and one thing led
to another, but those didn't really count . . . Straight boy/girl
couplings, just like marriage in Scarsdale, except you have two
bedfellows instead of merely one. It isn't, mind you, some kind
of moral/religious dictum that decrees it rigidly thus. Simply
a matter of personal taste, they say.

When they first got together the alternatives of form were
hotly debated. One possibility was to have the women retain
each bedroom and the men float back and forth; that way the
kids would have the stability of always knowing which was
"Mommy's room." That seemed a fine idea, but how often
should they shift companions? Once a week? Every night?
Perhaps the "real" marrieds should always wake up together
and all other mergings take place before dawn?

What the LaFoxes finally decided upon, unanimously, was
total spontaneity, and that is why they are still awake and
clustered about the living room in the middle of the night. And
why the air is choked with fatigue and brooding. Spontaneity
certainly appeared to be the philosophically correct solution at
the time. They were people, after all, dedicated to experiment-

ing, to breaking away from systems that didn't work, that stifled self-expansion. They dreamed of living by the authentic flow of the moment, not by automaticity or expectations or lies. A noble contemporary notion.

So every day the decision would be made afresh: Whom do I want to sleep with tonight? And what follows is the inevitable outcome, the Armageddon I am witnessing from my safe, uninvolved corner.

Connie begins: "I'd really like to be with Fred tonight. How do you feel about that, Fred?"

"Well, sure. I've been feeling very close to you lately. Very turned on."

Jamie flares: "But you've been with her for the past two nights. That's very threatening to me. I need some time to relate to you, too."

Paul: "Shit, that makes me feel just *great*. Both of you want to screw Fred. Connie, I feel you could be more sensitive to my needs. You're my primary partner, and it seems like you're only wanting to relate to him."

Connie: "You're laying a trip on me, and I'm not going to get sucked into your little-boy game. I won't let you make me feel guilty."

Jamie: "Man, you're so goddamn hard-nosed, Connie. Your desires are causing two people a lot of pain, and you don't give a shit."

Paul: "I'm not laying a trip on you anyway. On a gut level I'm just feeling rejected and lonely, and I'm expressing my feelings. That's what we're supposed to be free to do, isn't it?"

Connie: "Well, I can understand your feelings, but sometimes I need to do what's best for me. And, listen, Jamie, I'm feeling like you're constantly competing with me, and keeping score if you think I'm more 'popular' this week than you, and it's a real pain in the ass."

Jamie: "You may be right, actually. There's something I want to share with you, Paul. One of the reasons I'm feeling distant from you is that whenever we're together I feel like you're only thinking about Connie and feeling anxious about her being with Fred."

Paul: "That's true. Besides, I think I'm still carrying around some anger toward you from last week. When you asked me to stroke your breasts more gently—like Fred does—I really got pissed off."

Fred: "Hey, I thought one of our rules is that we'll never compare. Don't do that again, Jamie."

Jamie: "I know. I'm sorry."

Connie: "Wait a minute, Fred. You don't have to sound so righteous and preachy. Why don't you just tell her what you're feeling?"

The New Communication, a sample of which you have just read, says We Can Only Talk About Our Feelings. No thoughts, ideas, abstractions, *certainly* no judgments. Guts are good, heads are bad. You may never start a sentence with "I think." On the other hand, if you begin with "I feel" you can get away with atrocities. "I feel you're a schmuck . . ." It is like a board-game entertainment: "You said 'I think'; move back ten spaces, pay $50." Purists of this game believe every sentence out of one's mouth, no matter the topic, should begin "I feel." "I feel I would like half a pound of lean pastrami, please . . ."

The *recitativo* continues. It becomes, over the hours, increasingly injured and accusatory. Hidden agendas and withheld gripes spring forth like ancient dust from a newly opened trunk. They struggle earnestly—if humorlessly—these rebels, to be open and honest in their speaking and empathetic in their listening. Although weary and bored, I find myself moved by their valiant efforts at staying afloat in such murky waters. I also think their style of communication preposterous, endlessly circular and mostly ineffectual. I'm filled with the powerful temptation to move into the middle, to settle it easily, quickly, technologically—like some anthropologist watching the Bantus scrapping over how to use the newfangled egg beater. "Listen, you sleep here, you there, hop to it . . ." are the words lurking in the back of my throat. I restrain them.

The LaFoxes cannot go on like this much longer, we all know that. They are not having much fun in their group marriage, not getting much work done, not even getting laid as much as they did before this grand new liberty which is, of course, the largest joke. These late-night contretemps are triggered by the simplest of recurring realities: Two people want to sleep with the same person. It's excruciating for the fourth person, the fourth's spouse, for the two competing for the same bedmate, and even for the desired bedmate forced to select. Surely who's-bedding-with-whom *cannot* be the core concern of their "marriage." And yet it repeatedly seems so. How dreary and trivial, I think. I would not want my days consumed with such logistics.

The quartet finally realizes at about 3 A.M. one night that either they are still too insecure, too fledgling in this new tribe to take sleeping configurations more lightly or the notion of spontaneous selection is simply bullshit.

So, feeling heavily like ideological sellouts and Human Potential flops they inaugurate a brand-new system: They will change bed partners every three nights. Period. Regardless of whom they are feeling more intimate with or estranged from, more or less sexy about, they will follow the schedule. With this decision everyone, especially me, experiences flooding relief. Rigid structure is often more comforting than anarchy, and what does it matter if you're loathing Charlie tonight, just crawl into bed, turn your back and go to sleep. Thank God. It's beginning to look like a real marriage.

In my thoughts, at that moment in 1974, group marriage had sometimes reared its gothic head as The Possible Panacea. (There *was* an Answer out there somewhere, wasn't there?) Some form, I believed, would prove more likely and lovely than the previous ones. It was apparent to me that I was seeking, for myself, a way of fusing with a man while not relinquishing my own liberty and person. Some heady balance that would provide shelter yet air, separateness yet trust. So far, nearly to the middle of my life, I had not found it.

The Sandstone code looked too unsavory, too awful, to be an answer for either me or Mr. and Ms. American Public. Open marriage—well, I didn't know yet. Up until then I had only explored the Meyers, whose trip was as bizarre to me as Sandstone. Communal living, on the other hand, had always carried a fierce attraction: rosy memories of summer camp and sharing weekend ski houses and college dorms and marvelous houseguests. So, before I met the LaFox clan and some other practitioners, I imagined that the architecture of group marriage could possibly be a means to eliminate the scary chaos of such arrangements as the Meyers', while permitting new and fresh experiences, sexual and otherwise.

There are only a handful of experts and gurus in the Alternate Lifestyle kingdom, and it is likely that you would not have heard of them unless having pursued these matters—with the notable exception of Nena and George O'Neill, whose book not only created the expression "open marriage" but in its astonishing sale of three million copies, altered countless marital relationships.

The true swami of this subculture is Robert Rimmer, a businessman-writer of philosophical tracts poorly disguised as novels. His sole theme, repeated now in some nine books, is New Forms of Interpersonal Relating—revolving around sexual variety. His influence has been colossal, a fact difficult to comprehend, as his writing is so truly dreadful and his utopian notions so seemingly ludicrous. But it occurs to me, as I wander through these strange new lands, that Rimmer may well be some sort of cultural prophet, in that his seemingly ludicrous concepts appear to be actually taking place, some years *after* their invention in his books. *The Harrad Experiment,* his most well-known tome, is a novel about an experimental college with coed living facilities, freestyle nudity and multiple sexual liaisons. When it was published in 1966, it was science-fiction; now it is ho-hum reportage.

The same holds true for *Proposition 31,* Rimmer's novel about group marriage. Everybody either doing it or interested in it reads Rimmer as if he were Julia Child. *Proposition 31* is the only "How To" manual around; in fact, when the real-life Langdens and Foxes settled upon three-day sleeping shifts, the model was Rimmer's characters.

It was in relation to this book that I first heard of the group marriage phenomenon and Robert Rimmer. I was working, in 1968, as publicity director for a large publishing house in New York. One day I was presented with the manuscript of a new book and told to devise a plan for promoting it and its author. I read *Proposition 31* in bed that night and I remember my response well: I called one of the editors at home and said, "Why are we publishing this garbage?"

I will spare you my comments about Rimmer's writing style, except to tell you that he cannot seem to create a sex scene (of which there must be hundreds) without using either the word "wondrous" or "joyous" and generally both, and in one place he describes his hero's penis as a "salty limp instrument." More than the style it was the essence of the novel, the ideology, that struck me as so absurd.

In *Proposition 31* two couples, the Herndons and the Sheas, live next door to each other in San Pedro, California. (In 1968 all books and movies about deviant lifestyle were set in Southern California. For credibility.) They each have sturdy marriages but after fifteen years are restless and sexually bored. They peer into each others' bathroom windows with binoculars a lot and have reveries about their neighbors' genitalia even more, and then one Shea and one Herndon get together for an illicit affair. When she gets pregnant and they have to decide whether to terminate their current homes and marry each other, we hurtle into the *real* plot. The other Herndon and Shea consummate their binocular-gazing and find they like it. All four then, with their kids, flee to the woods for a while, agree to form a corporate marriage, and this is where the novel proceeds from merely suburban-sex trash into heavy-duty philosophy.

When I first read the book in 1968, saw the words "group marriage" for the first time, my prevailing response was How Dumb. It is difficult enough to find one person you want to have dinner with, I thought. The premise of lining up three or five to be married to, loving and committed with, sharing of space and money and children and intimacy with, was patently ridiculous. Believing as I did in conventional forms, I could not view any such deviations as meaningful, even for idle contemplation. Nor could I identify my own struggles with such Martians. That the introduction to *Proposition 31* terms group marriage ". . . the only real adventure left in the world for men and women" was not exactly an overpowering argument to me.

Before I flew to Phoenix to see the LaFoxes, I reread this novel—read it in the light of nearly a decade of modulations in the culture, and a metamorphosis in myself. Group marriage now seemed a fascinating possibility.

Proposition 31, however, is still dreadful. Rimmer would have us believe group marriage *is* the ultimate cure-all: Four bouncy folks plunging into this cyclone as though it were a swimming pool on a hot day, never losing their stewardess/surfer effervescence, loving each other's mates with sybaritic glee and spouting ceaseless, problem-free oratory midcoitus. Nobody in Rimmer's dominion becomes jealous or stunned, impotent or destroyed. The previously repressed women are magically transformed into jolly lascivious tarts; the men changed to Olympian studgods. A Cinderella tale for the new age.

That, as we have already begun to notice, is not quite the way it works, after all.

Nancy Herndon says in *Proposition 31*, "As I looked at her blond bush I wondered whether David had kissed her there. Had Horace? Well, they had both kissed me between the legs, so why not Tanya, too? What kind of madness were we all involved in?"

What kind of madness, indeed. What breed of folk enter such odd and intricate bonding, a form for which they have no recipe for victory, no model of behavior save Robert Rimmer's peppy delusions? One's life, it naturally seems, is too jarring and convoluted as it is, one's relationships too difficult and demanding as they are. What is the drive toward being married —with all that that state entails—to three or more other beings?

As we move from a monogamous one-to-one alliance, at one end of the spectrum, to a group marriage at the other—with such interim forms as the adulterous marriage and open relationship—the complexity increases not arithmetically but logarythmically, so that in a group marriage of, say, six adults, in fact thirty relationships exist—including pairings, trios, subgroups of four, and six means of leaving one person out. A staggering jigsaw, a full-time vocation.

In their book *Group Marriage*, Larry and Joan Constantine, the leading researchers in this arena, claim that 58 percent of these unions dissolve within their first year, and only 7 percent are intact after five. My own informal research concurs: I met a quartet in New Hampshire with whom I then corresponded for six months. Their Christmas card said they were doing fine, thinking about having some babies together; four months later not only had the four sundered, but the two original couples had traded mates, remarried, moved to different cities and were living monogamously, in some emotional state resembling catatonia.

What literature exists on the subject claims the motivations to enter group marriage to be in the category of "self-enrichment" and "personality growth potential in interpersonal processes." The Constantines say that "variety of sexual partners" is a considerable impetus, but not the biggest, and improving what they consider to be unsatisfactory marriages, hardly a feature at all.

I don't believe anything in that last sentence, although I cannot prove my point. But I've noticed that sexual variety is *the* compelling surface motivation, the catalyst to making it happen, and that all the marriages are at least somewhat shaky. We are still, at heart, moralists who must fuse sex with love and probably with marriage. Rimmer's prototypical characters are the clearest illustrations. Nobody just wants to ball; they are obliged to fall in love and then forever to gush the litany of "wondrousness" and "joyousness."

Paul and Connie Langden, half of the LaFox conglomerate, are an interesting case to consider. They had been, at the time of their short-lived clan outing, married for nineteen years. From the very beginning they had never practiced sexual fidelity. Twenty years ago, when we didn't even have the language except for perjoratives like "promiscuous," they were pioneers of swinging, communal setups and totally free love. Currently they are open to every possibility but monogamy, but their preference has always been for living with others. The LaFoxes were their first official group wedlock experiment— and probably not the last. Permanence, even longevity, has never ranked high in their value scheme; continuous new experience has.

Most group marriages come together haphazardly, the standard story reading like this: Somebody gets involved with somebody else and instead of rupturing the original pairings, they see if the mates dig each other, and if that works they move in together. A quartet living in Dallas evolved when a couple, vacationing in Sweden, met a nineteen-year-old blond beauty, and arranged for her to move to the States to be their housekeeper. Predictably, like a Swedish movie, the husband and she had an affair, he divorced his wife and married the housekeeper. The ex-wife then married the husband's best friend, and as of this writing the four are merrily cohabiting in west Texas.

Connie and Paul, on the contrary, went out in search of a couple to wed. They haunted the spots and scenes where such a willing pair might appear, asked their friends if they knew anybody to introduce them to, and joined Family Synergy, the organization of alternate lifestyle crusaders at whose outings and programs folks cruise one another. Eventually and appropriately, at a Robert Rimmer lecture, they met Jamie and Fred, also looking. The four explored each other precisely in the same way that singles do their mating dance, and after some months it felt right for them to "marry."

Months later when they broke up, it was not entirely due to the complexity—although Fred Fox had, as a matter of fact, quit his job as an advertising copywriter in order to devote more time to the "relationship." The irreconcilable differences that drove them dramatically apart came out of philosophical frictions. For one thing, their view of child-rearing conflicted, the Foxes being much more authoritarian than the permissive Langdens. Since all the kids were pooled, as it were, such conflicts proved fiercely corrosive and unsolvable. For another thing, the Foxes wanted a closed, sexually exclusive foursome, while the Langdens required liberty to pursue additional new adventures. Connie, when we spoke over lunch, did not see the irony that was becoming evident to me in this unceasing quest for something other than what we have. Two isn't *it*, maybe four; four isn't *it*, perhaps six. Does it ever end? Do these times make it truly impossible to be satisfied, no matter what road we pursue? If so, is there anything more gloomy?

I looked for many months to find a group marriage that had persevered for at least two years, finally finding one in Bethesda, Maryland, ensconced in a two-bedroom tract house in an Archie Bunker neighborhood, not dissimilar to the Meyer territory. An unlikely environment, an even more unlikely quartet. Low- to middle-level government employees dwell here, the paper-pushers, not the decision-makers. Pintos and station wagons dot the driveways, children's swings and bicycles landscape the lawns. In the third stucco house from the left on a flat street live Danny and Marilyn Kamens, Amy and Rick Green. Their neighbors know nothing more than that they are cute young kids, banding together to save money. They certainly *look* average enough. Rick even works for the Department of Agriculture, and if any raising of eyebrows takes place, it's just because sometimes it's hard to keep straight whose spouse is whose when you notice them walking, coupled, on the street or getting into their camper, and the specific coupling seems to shift frequently.

They call themselves "G'Dramak." The "G" is silent. They had that name printed on a bumper sticker for their car, and when asked what it means, depending on the asker, they either tell the truth or say it's a religious order.

I spend three days with them, sleeping in the living room of their one-story, one-bathroom home. The house reminds me of graduate students' dwellings at the University of Wisconsin: slightly messy, very cluttered, a hodgepodge of furniture compiled from garage sales and the Salvation Army. We five trip over each other, it seems, going to and from the small bathroom; whenever one exits, somebody is waiting to get in.

The "G'Dramaks" are all young, twenty-six to twenty-nine. The Greens are Wisconsin Catholics; Kamens, Philadelphia Jews. Otherwise, the similarities in history give rise to speculation on how they found each other and chose this peculiar path. Both pairs were childhood sweethearts, virgins before each other, married before hitting twenty. All four came out of settled families in which there has not been a single divorce. Although they themselves have no children yet, the principle of family is markedly crucial to them, as is stability, permanence and—please believe this—a highly romantic ideal. If you encountered the four separately, you might assign them to the covers of *Redbook.* Together they reside in what could certainly be labeled the most deviant structure in American family life.

As it often happens, the women are more vital, more easily remembered than the men. Months after the visit I confuse Rick with Danny, physically and in temperament; while I'm with them, they remain cautious with me, withholding, cordial but superficial, often not quite honest. My insights into the lives of this strange quartet come from the women and from my own eye. Marilyn and Amy stay distinct in my memory.

Amy is blond, scrubbed like a 4-H girl, not pretty. She still wears braces on her teeth, is too leggy and thin and although she is twenty-seven, you can see precisely her looks at sixteen. Easygoing, a good person, she does needlepoint, wears a yellow terrycloth bathrobe, and doesn't really comprehend the aims of Women's Liberation. She was the girl in your college dorm who majored in Home Ec, was pinned before she got to her sophomore year and never even came close to cracking up. The sort of woman I have never been able to fathom, for her lack of complexity and contradiction. I ask her one morning over coffee whether she feels competitive with Marilyn, who is lovely, dark-haired, exotic. Does she fear Marilyn is sexier? I ask, naturally projecting my sense that Marilyn is sexier. Amy does not show any stress at my tactless probe: "No, not at all," she replies sunnily. "I feel great about myself and all I can give is who I am, so if they like her better than me, that's okay." No, I certainly wouldn't believe a word of this either if I read it. But Amy meant the words. She was not lying. There *are* beings in the world like that.

Marilyn forms a dark Yang balance to Mary's perky simplicity. Moody, introspective, sloppy, she is neurotic enough to be totally familiar and trustworthy to me. She admits easily to being the craziest of the four, the one who has had the most difficulty adjusting, the one on whom the twice-weekly "blow-out" meetings (as in "blow-out-the-shit") tend to focus. How does Amy not feel envious of this raven-haired Rebecca? What certificate of mental health is required to stay clear about one's own subtle virtues in the presence of round Semitic breasts and a mysterious nature? I surely could not do it for five minutes.

The men, as I say, do not shine forth. During my stay I will frequently mistake one for the other and become embarrassed. One or the other, when called by the wrong name, will say calmly, "That's okay. It happens all the time."

During my three days in Bethesda, I feel increasingly claustrophobic in this tiny box that, were I living there alone, would suffocate me. I understand quickly that space and privacy cannot be a priority in such a coalition, when the family is not wealthy. Very soon I come to think that I could never—never—accommodate to all the tiny stuff in the bathroom that belongs to somebody else, or to the differing cleanliness habits of three other people, or to the relentless dealing with the mathematical details of each day.

Dismissal on those scores is simple. If we believe our lives are about who's-not-putting-the-cap-on-the-toothpaste, we can kill *any* connection with another human being who is not exactly like us. What is not quite so easy to negate is the warm appeal of extended family, the richness of living with others—with more than one other. In the days that I am here, I'm swept from one mind to its opposite regularly and swiftly.

They met in Wisconsin three and a half years before my trip. Danny and Marilyn Kamens had gone to the university in Madison and stayed in the city afterward. Amy and Rick had grown up in Milwaukee, never gone to college. Marilyn and Rick worked in the same office, for the state, doing what they term "idiot work." They felt some strong sexual vibrations, which they never acted upon but talked about frequently over lunch —in that if-only-we-could-do-it manner that further titillates.

Although they had never in their lives made love with anybody else, Danny and Marilyn Kamens told themselves they had an open marriage. They approved the concepts and had read Rimmer. Then Danny took his first mescaline trip, where-after, like so many kids of his ilk, his head burst open. He started wearing more flamboyant clothes, eating weird foods, and really looking at other women. "I was just opening up to everything there was," he recalls. "Like, we were best friends with this other couple our senior year and there was a lot of sexual tension between all of us. Chuck and I would sit in the living room watching Marilyn and his wife doing strip teases in front of us. But it never went any further, even though we played this game about six times. Everybody said it was me, my inhibitions, that prevented it. After my mescaline trip, the next time it happened we wound up going off into separate rooms, having sex with each other's mates."

And after that, they felt liberated to go to bed with other of their friends. Because all of the "friends" were a known quantity, jealousy was at a minimum, a refrain I've noticed repeatedly. Similarly, this is one of the reasons the Meyers always like to bring their lovers into the fold.

For the Greens, the infidelity was more conventional. Rick messed around surreptitiously. "For me," he admits, "the need was purely for sexual variety. I wasn't looking for somebody to fall in love with, and I felt my marriage was strong. Sex with Amy was good, you know, but in my mind I kept thinking there was something out there I should be getting or experiencing, so periodically I felt bored or lonely. I'd been with Amy since we were kids, after all."

Something is missing. Another recurring theme of the Alternative Sonata.

One night there was a party at the Greens', and Rick and Danny wound up in the kitchen. They had met once or twice before, but this time the conversation leaped to a new level: Rick stated he wanted to sleep with Danny's wife and wondered if that could be somehow arranged. Danny thought for a few minutes and, as he eyed Amy's slim legs through the open door, allowed as how it was okay with him. Amy, when approached about the entente, wasn't too ecstatic about Danny, but she is an accommodating sort of earth mother and agreed. She had been shoved before by her husband into dating, and had discovered that she too liked the novelty. Besides, the Kamens were leaving in a few months for an indefinite stay in Europe, so this was all light kicks, no commitment, no emotional hassles, just a minisexual jaunt.

—Was group sex the fantasy?

They are, in chorus, startled and dismayed at my wicked suggestion. "Hell, no, we don't go in for that," says Danny. "Just switching," nods Amy sweetly.

So the G's moved in with the K's for a couple of months of connubial blitz, and then the Kamens left for Europe. They corresponded frequently, and as Marilyn puts it, "the letters kept getting stronger and stronger until finally we asked them to join us." With no hesitation the Greens abandoned their jobs, and the four spent the next one and a half years roaming first across Western Europe, then around the United States in a camper, becoming ever-growingly wed to the others. About a year before I met them they settled into the cramped abode in Bethesda to live, in some ways, like every other family on the street, and in other ways like hardly anybody else in America.

One can pinpoint some of the tangible advantages right away. A true breakdown of traditional household roles exists here, arrived at naturally, organically. I hardly know a nuclear family where this is so, where housework isn't a constant political struggle, even when both adults are working full time and are in philosophical accord. We women and men are too automatic in our old roles, too resigned, scared or resistant to change, too lazy to rock the craft. The G'Dramaks somehow have moved quickly from ancient assumptions, so that now they do not view their home as the women's domain and any male contribution as "doing a favor" or "helping out." Thus the house is not a political battlefield, where one chalks up victories or defeats by who wound up doing the dishes that night. Marilyn says, "It's really easy to explain. The men know they can't get away with that crap because there's two of us to come down on them. And Amy and I watch each other to make sure we're not lapsing into playing slave."

I'm always curious about the structuring of households: I think it's indicative of deeper things in relationships. In this case, it is even more fascinating because of the unusual number of participants. When I am there, Amy is not working, so most of the daily chores fall to her. We go together to the supermarket, the laundromat, the hardware store. She is quite willing— it's the least she can do since she's not bringing in any money. Danny is working at home, translating complex electronic contracts from French. He cleans the house and takes care of the lawn. Marilyn is a secretary at a television station in D.C., and Rick, as said, is a clerk at the Department of Agriculture. Each cooks for three nights running, has three off, then does dishes for the next three. The women are distinctly better chefs but Danny is energetic about learning, and if the beef bourguignon dinner he prepares is a smidgen oversalted and underdone, well, we are supportive anyway.

Their joint monthly income is about $1600—which dispels for me the fantasy of get-rich-quick communal pooling. All incomes and savings and gifts are combined, with the exception of $20 a month doled out to each for personal spending without accountability. All else must be decided upon by unanimous vote before it's purchased. Clothes and contributions and presents always come out of the $20.

—What if one of you wants to buy a Linda Ronstadt album?

"We vote. If it's not unanimous, you have to take it out of your own allowance."

—What if I want to see *Star Wars* and nobody else does? Same thing?

"No. We figure movies even themselves out. That comes out of the common pot."

—Does that mean you sneakily watch to see who's drinking more Budweiser than who? Or using the phone more? Can somebody listen to somebody else's Linda Ronstadt album if he didn't pay for it?

I'm starting to feel strangled again. *What do you mean telling me I have to get the group vote for my record?* Who can possibly make this sort of humbling surrender outside a Zen monastery? But this is the least of it, just the most surface. There are infiltrations, self-denials, compromises beyond my own ability to comprehend in such a collective effort, a mass intrusion into one's consciousness on a daily, hourly basis. A kibbutz escalated to the tenth power. Primacies which must, by definition, be squashed, idiosyncracies leveled, privacy aborted. Is not the need for physical and psychic air a primal one?

But even as I become righteous and adamant in my negativity, I veer to the considerable other hand: Four people instead of two come home to each other at night, with more stimulation, fun and less laser focus on a single other human being. The weight does not lie so mercilessly on one frail mate for the total fulfillment of one's needs. Marilyn and Amy have a second man, each other and that new organism created from the amalgam—The Group. It is companionable and peaceable and interesting around the dinner table and later around the fireplace, cheerier than with most twosomes I know. Few of the subtle put-downs, or struggles for verbal dominance, or the dull-witted "couple chauvinism" I see operative in our nuclear lives. Here it is enchantingly alive and, well . . . family. It reminds me again, with stabs of nostalgia, of my sweet college dorm.

Around the fire that night, I reflect on those popular current theories that living in a pack is fundamental and natural, and the compressed family route we've gone in our time is strange, lonely, unviable. Like open relationships, communal living looks like an exciting, nourishing and humane idea. Then why do I start to decline into quiet madness if my own houseguests—even best friends, amiable, never-tiresome or exploitative, loving company—stay two days beyond their allotted limit? Have we lost the talent to share, to relinquish, compromise? Perhaps the toothpaste-tube trivial annoyance governs our choices more than I can bear to face. I can't help but notice that, much as I relished the dorm and have probably distorted its memories, I've never chosen anything resembling that configuration again. Is it so impossible to give up the self-centered habits and rigidities of nuclear or solitary householding? I wonder if I'll ever be clear-eyed and unambiguous about this entire perplexing topic, instead of continually discovering boxes within boxes within boxes, each appearing to contain an answer but only unwrapping another layer of puzzlement . . .

Yes, there are true joys to be witnessed in the G'Dramak house, and there is also the flipside of joy. There is the taunting presence of jealousy.

One rainy afternoon, while Marilyn and Rick are at work, Amy and Danny and I talk in the kitchen, sitting on frayed rattan stools. I have been here a day and a half and, despite the aura of tranquil affection, I haven't seen anyone touch, and that has seemed powerfully odd to me. I remark on this and Pandora's box is wrenched open. When asked previously, all four have stoutly denied any current problems with jealousy. Oh, in the early Bethesda days, Marilyn and Amy had moved through a bad bout of kitchen competition: "My background," says Amy, "was that I had to do everything for my man, and suddenly here was another woman in my kitchen, doing things for him. I didn't have complete control any more, so I wasn't sure I was valuable to Rick. It got to the point where I wouldn't walk into the kitchen if she was there, and we hardly ever talked to each other."

Since the elevating of consciousness and replanning of household roles, this difficulty has vanished. But I imagine the issue was partially a displaced one, anyway. You're-usurping-my-kitchen-power is surely more handleable to the human psyche than one's dread of being replaced by a superior talent in the bed.

Now in the comfort of steaming coffee and kitchen camaraderie, submerged truths spring forth. Where the four have stated they are with one another, where they believe they should be according to Robert Rimmer's gospel, is one thing. We are all married to each other equally, they swear. We do not allow ourselves to compare. (When Danny and Rick play tennis they won't even report the score to the women.) Our original bondings have always been rock-solid and unchallenged, they testify. Where they truly live tends to hover somewhat more to the conservative right. Like Steve Meyer, these revolutionaries spout party dogma, hoping their guts will catch up to the manifesto. The biggest flaw in these matters, I think, is the discrepancy between what is right and what's human.

Need it be said that one member's dilemmas, in a group marriage, echo through the entire union, coloring all the combinations and dynamics of it. You could say the same for a twosome, but collectively it magnifies mercilessly. Danny, soulful and morose, admits he is the source. And the title of his aggravation: Sexual Jealousy.

"I've been the most insecure in this area. You know, the original attraction was between Marilyn and Rick, and I've always worried that he was better in bed than me and she wouldn't want to sleep with me any more. I'd see them hugging and I'd think, 'She hasn't hugged me in four days' or 'She doesn't put that much oomph into *my* affection.' Or I'd be lying in bed with Amy and hear a *thump* next door and I'd think, *'They're fucking, and when she does it with* me *the bed doesn't even creak!'* "

—Doesn't having Amy even the odds a bit, make you feel more sought after?

"Just the opposite," he laments. "I feel guilty about not giving her enough. At first I figured she wasn't even attracted to me, she was just going along with this whole thing for reasons of her own."

Then the spiral winds down: Amy feels unwanted by Danny, who only concentrates on Marilyn; Marilyn and Rick feel guilty or resentful that their parade is being rained on. All compounded by Rick's good-natured personality, which never hooks into jealous emotions, thus making Danny feel like even more of an ass. Soon it all begins to sound, to me, like the Langdens and Foxes at three in the morning, and far more understandable than Steve and Pat Meyer's unflagging cool.

The confrontation with the green-eyed monster is, for them, daily and relentless. Does it ever resolve itself, disappear or diminish? "No," Danny says slowly, frowning. "It just comes and goes."

I see why they don't touch, for God's sake, given the reverberations of a single hug. I mention to Danny that the LaFoxes had a similar difficulty—Paul's self-lacerating fantasies about Fred's bedroom prowess. Their solution, well-planned out at a group meeting, was for the two males to go to bed together *once*, thus being able to forever view the other as a mere imperfect man. Evidently it was a freeing act. But Danny is horrified at the suggestion, as I guessed he would be. I also understand now why they cannot be nude as a quartet, although each has seen the others naked. This tribe is ruled by such quirky boundaries of behavior, codes that seem jarringly paradoxical. Living as they do on a secret island of nonconformity, their own interior regulations are nonetheless so strict, and *so* straight.

Their catechism forbids discussions of sex except between the two partners immediately involved. Two married people presumably talk about their love-making; logically shouldn't four, when they insist they are as one? But how much trickier and more perplexing is this confluence? And how really destructive might such conversations be?

And, in fact, I'm getting the distinct idea even in my short
stay that Danny's perceptions are accurate, that Rick and
Marilyn do form a connection more electric than any of the
remaining three combinations. And isn't inherent in that the
seed of the group's demise? Researchers Larry and Joan Constantine report that although substantial primary relationships
are essential to the working of a group marriage, most members
list their preferred sex partner as *not* their legal mate. I wonder
if the enterprise lasted long enough, would that preference
shift back . . . ?

Perhaps, on second thought, the death knell is my private
illusion. Most of us do not love our partners in perfectly equal
balanced parts at all times. And over time, in unions that
thrive, unevennesses are smoothed or tolerated, or at the very
least ignored.

The really evident imbalance lives in the dynamic between
Rick and Danny, and there one can see a microcosm of the
world. The "boys" are withholding and careful, talk about
sports but not feelings, and never confront pain. The women,
typically, blab and consort and feel as knitted to each other as
to their males. They explore their mutual paralysis about producing children—fears each of them has always carried, but
lately exaggerated by the unique form their lives have taken.
Rick and Danny have never approached the matter while alone
together.

Marilyn says, "I'd rather talk to Amy about my emotional
hassles than to either guy. Like if I'm not too happy because
Rick's spending the night somewhere, she and I will sit down,
sometimes we'll stay up all night bouncing it around. I can't
see either Rick or Danny doing that." Amy adds, "If I have
a problem with one of them that can't be ironed out, I'll go
to Marilyn and say, 'Hey, does he do this with you? What do
you do about it?' See, each of us is more used to our own
husband, so we'll go to the other woman as a resource."

I laugh to myself watching Rick and Danny flinch, scowl and

shudder as Amy admits this horror of which neither man has been aware, but which confirms every male's bleakest nightmares—two women who know him well grinding apart his myriad defects.

—Wait a minute. Back up. What do you mean, "if Rick spends the night somewhere?"

This new information—that the incredibly complex world of the G'Dramaks does not end at their own front door—stuns and utterly exhausts me in the same way as when friends describe their back-packing trips through the High Sierras.

"Yes, we've inaugurated a new policy," says Rick, grinning like a teenager who's just acquired his first convertible. "We switch partners every two nights and then have one night off each week. We're not looking, mind you. We're just open to the fact that if you happen to come across somebody you're interested in, you're free to pursue it."

—And has it happened?

Marilyn answers softly, "Yes, to both Rick and me. And the woman he slept with and the guy I slept with are both good friends of all of us and they met through us and now they're living together. But we still see them regularly."

Musical beds, you may have gathered, is a repeated pastime in these circles, and what amazes me most is where and how they find so many people who turn them on . . . It is wearying for me to contemplate how many of these folks' waking hours are consumed by sexual activity—actual sex or all the busywork surrounding it. And yet, that curious contradiction: Not sexual anarchists, their own credos are as unbending as those of any proper Fundamentalist.

Danny mentions that he is not only in anguish over his wife's and Rick's coalition, but over Marilyn's and Rob's—the new character who has just entered stage-left. Amy cries out, "Well, me too, since we're talking about it. For a while, I was the only one in the house without an outside affair going" (Note: Danny apparently has Tracy, a newly introduced name about whom

I no longer have the stamina to inquire) "and I was goddamn jealous."

"Well," say I, feeling like Dr. Joyce Brothers. "That's not so profound. That's just everybody-has-a-date-for-the-prom-but-me."

Where do they find the time, I ponder again and again, and the vitality? To exist in a group marriage seems to mean the cessation of most of life's activities—merely to remain intact.

The single truest generalization I can make about group marriage denizens regards their uniform lack of passion for anything else. They are not career-oriented, civic-minded, hob-by-freaked. They do not have powerful life goals or a driving interest in tennis, stamps or playing the viola. The Relationship is what juices their motors. Fred LaFox, recall, quit his job to concentrate on his marriage.

"It *is* true that we're not committed to anything except each other," admits Rick, who has changed jobs more times than the IRS can speculate. "For me," Amy says, "everything comes to a complete halt when something is bothering one of us. Even if I'm on my way out to a spectacular job interview, I'll drop it, I just won't go, until things are right with us." The Meyers are the direct antithesis of this foursome. With so many concerns and pulls and tugs outside their union they seem, if anything, to have too much apartness, too little meld-ing. Their relationship is not the nucleus of their lives, the axis upon which all else pivots. Is this, I wonder, the difference in forms or in people?

On the last day of my stay, Amy's father arrives for dinner. A lawyer from Milwaukee, he's in Washington on impromptu business, and his surprise phone call announces he will be at the house within the hour.

Some very frantic and very funny scrambling around ensues. Telltale signs of the odd coupling are cleaned up—Marilyn's bra (Amy does not own one, although one might ask how her daddy would know that) is removed from the dressertop housing Rick's sweaters, a hand-drawn poster reading G'DRAMAKS, FAMILY OF THE FUTURE pulled down from the living room wall. They even go so far as to remove their complete collected works of Robert Rimmer from the bookshelf, while I watch in fascination.

"You don't tell your Catholic parents from Wisconsin about something like this," Amy says a trifle hysterically, while vacuuming the living room in double-time. "All our folks know we live together, but my parents just aren't keyed in to sex, so I don't think it's ever occurred to them to question. I tell them I go to church regularly, which I don't, so that keeps them calm about my life."

Only Marilyn's mother knows the truth, having seen a TV program on group marriage and instantly phoned Marilyn's sister to ask nervously if *that* was what was really going on with her daughter. She's apparently a hip Jewish mother, as mothers go, and has dealt with the information. "She was primarily concerned that Danny and I still have a good and loving marriage," says Marilyn, "and I convinced her that we do." Mama has not, one notes, been down yet from Philadelphia to visit.

Last Christmas, when the quartet drove to see family in Milwaukee, they stayed with Rick's parents and switched partners stealthily every two nights by sneaking in and out of dark bedrooms, so as to conform to their unalterable schedule.

Once Daddy arrives, the scene relaxes, and you would not think a gigantic secret to be in operation. I cannot see any hints that he is searching for slippers under the bed or skeletons in the closets. His kids live in a funky commune, I think he thinks. And I speculate on just how this good Catholic Middle-American sixty-two-year old Republican citizen and father would grasp the real news, whether his consciousness would be capable of stretching to accommodate such overwhelming deviance. I suspect not, but then in the course of my travels, I'm surprised more often than not.

The heaviest irony must, by now, be obvious: Humans drawn to group marriage espouse freedom, cherish variety of experience, downgrade permanence and conformity. They see their way not as merely an alternative but as a more elevated form of living. Yet the few group marriages I've looked in on are more tightly ruled and circumscribed than most of your monotonous monogamies. The G'Dramaks switch beds after two nights and you're not even allowed to sleep on the couch if you're angry or want solitude. You must also, when riding in the car, sit with the person you're currently bedding with. Danny says to me, without a hint of self-derision, "Ideally, if our marriage were working in perfect harmony, every single decision any of us made would be a group decision," and as he finishes the sentence I find myself struggling for air. Thank you, no. That notion, pressing in on me like a steel vise, is infinitely bigger than the pleasantness of the dinner table. If it's *Gemütlichkeit* I'm longing for, thank you, I'll take a cruise.

But the real key to all this lies in Marilyn's offhanded answer to my not-so-offhanded question. "Are you totally satisfied with your 'marriage' now?" I ask. "Got what you want?" "Well, sure," she shrugs. Then she brightens. "Except lately I've been thinking it might be *really* interesting to find another couple to join us. God, that would be exciting."

And I suddenly know that *that* is surely the most central question I have asked in three days.

V

Bud De Leon, Donna De Leon and Marty Simon

Just a few weeks after I saw the G'Dramaks in Maryland, Donna DeLeon, Bud DeLeon and Marty Simon in Los Angeles had their first child, a blue-eyed boy whom they named Nicholas. One knew for certain that Bud and not Marty was the father because the infant had Bud's blinding orange hair. Marty is dark. Besides, the trio had mutually decided that their baby would be sired by Bud.

For one thing, they figured it would be legally simpler for Bud and Donna, a married couple, to co-produce a baby. For another, Marty was more than a trifle uneasy about this weighty responsibility falling to him—an interloper—so he passed the gauntlet to Bud, allowing as how "I thought that it was a natural complement to all the years Bud and Donna have been together."

During the months that Donna was trying to get pregnant she used, theoretically, no contraception with her husband and either a diaphragm or condoms with Marty. But the nature of their trinity is such that she tended to become confused at times, so until the carrot-head made its theatrical entrance, the case wasn't airtight. Bud says he wouldn't have cared: "I thought it would be cute to have a redheaded kid, but paternity is not terribly significant to me. It might have mattered if Marty had an I.Q. of ninety, however." Marty doesn't.

Bud, Donna and Marty had lived together for about a year and a half when Donna became pregnant. They pool their moneys, sleep in the same queen-sized bed with Donna in the middle, and like Steve and Pat Meyer, but unlike the G'Dramaks, they view themselves as close friends and distinctly separate individuals, rather than Siamese triplets joined at the hip.

They registered for Lamaze natural childbirth classes together, the initial amazement of teacher and classmates melting away after a while, to be replaced by welcome and care. "A baby needs all the parenting it can get," spouted the teacher, a sentiment echoing the threesome's own glowing confidence about creating a child in the face of their peculiar family setup.

The hospital was something else. Rules decreed only one "labor coach" in the labor room, but both Bud and Marty sneaked in. After a few minutes a nurse entered, asked them who was the father. "We told her we both were and she got rather upset and left," Marty has written. A hurried conference of agitated nurses and orderlies ensued in the hallway, then the commanding head nurse barreled back to the labor room. "Who is the *husband?*" she demanded this time. "We both are," Bud and Marty responded serenely, in chorus. Turning to Donna, heavily in labor, the nurse begged, "Lady, which one is your *legal* husband?" and Marty was banished to the fathers' waiting room to watch the Dodgers game and pace. During Donna's nine-hour exercise the joint husbands/fathers were permitted, by perplexed nurses, to exchange places several times, and both were there to witness the birth of Nicholas.

"The nurses were very nice about visiting hours for the couple of days that Donna was in the hospital," writes Marty. "We told them the situation, and all of the nurses gathered round. They asked me if I love her, how I feel about the baby, and I told them that we were all 'married' . . . and that Nicholas is a son to each of us. One nurse said, 'I don't know why you're in this thing. Don't you see you're only going to lose in the end?' I left the other nurses arguing with her. I certainly didn't feel that way."

There are more triads—that's what they call themselves, "triads"—than any other bigger-than-two mergings. That they exist at all, that three adults can defy all our paradigms of pairing and live together in close-knit fashion, was an unsettling discovery to me. That triads, by my own observation and the scant available research, seem to be more healthily flourishing than group marriages, than communes in which there is unrestricted sex play, and than many open marriages has continually surprised me. From the beginning I was intrigued, wanted to find out why such an unusual form should be the most victorious of the alternatives.

"Successful" should be defined. I do that, arbitrarily, both in terms of longevity and the degree to which the people involved experience satisfaction. That is, does the relationship suit their purposes? The alternate-lifestyle cheerleaders downgrade longevity as a value, pointing to the centuries of marriages which remained together as if imprisoned for life on Devil's Island. They view constant change as the inevitable thrust of the day and see any wistful yearning for permanence in our current culture as rather like hoping for the return of the bubonic plague. Some truth rests on their side; the fallacy and foolishness of the notion arises when a group marriage is labeled "successful" if it manages to survive the weekend.

How does one judge if a relationship is any good? I often have not the smallest conception of my closest friends' bonds, of what cements or splinters them, of whether those binding elements are "healthy" or "neurotic," growth-producing or murderous. I pace through similar darkness in understanding my own vital ties. Can I really tell you whether the DeLeon corporation is gratifying and noble and happy? Or whether they are all fundamentally full of shit? I often can't answer that one for myself.

I can say that triads tend to stay glued longer than other nonnuclear constructs. They tend to report more pleasure and less strife in their daily doings than, say, those few group marriages I've visited, where wee-hour retchings are the natural order of the day. In all the threesomes I've met—and in each case they were created by a married couple taking in a third individual—the basic two claims its relationship more flexible in a triumverate than before, and the problems more readily solvable. For the newcomer, it depends on how long the three have been a team and—primarily—the quality of relationship with the person of the same sex. If Bud and Marty were not firm buddies, the three would likely be doomed.

I would not have believed such intricate three-part harmony to be possible. The world is run in pairs, we learn early on in life. I dredge up still-sharp memories of grade school, even years before males had invaded my universe. My best girlfriend, inseparable pal, finds another soulmate. I am excluded. Why? Two is the only acceptable number, there is never space for three.

From adolescence, when life becomes sexual, the urgency of pairing is unmistakable. And the inflexible rule of social competition is stamped on us forevermore. He will prefer her to me, I'll be left out. The essential drama of relationship, the plotline from which springs the demonic characters: Possessiveness, Jealousy, Control, Loss.

A cumbersome number, three. Restaurant booths, bucket seats, tennis courts, dance steps, bridge games are designed for partners, or two sets of two. But: Check out the primal and universal sexual fantasies, hidden contents of the psyche. The number three appears again and again. The *ménage à trois* finds timeless, popular expression in *The Arabian Nights, The*

Kamasutra, the sultry pages of *Cosmopolitan.* I research friends of both sexes, delve into my own self, look at the literature. And time after time unearth the same erotic images, varying only in detail. Sexual fantasies of three. For many males the prevailing reverie is concocted of two women, very active, making love to him, utterly passive. Or he is watching two females engaged with each other. One man I know is quite specific: He fantasizes lying inert while two females are simultaneously "doing" him and making love to one another. Men seem to revel in women's imagined homosexuality, probably a reflection of man's common buried fear that women gratify each other better than any male can.

Men rarely place another male in their story; women however often become not only fiercely assertive in our trio conjurings, but actively bisexual.

My own recurring choice fantasy centers about two beautiful and very young men who are not only fiery with me, but free to be loving with each other. (My script doesn't have room for any potential inhibitions or freakouts in that department, during which I would then be forced to play nurse.) They are focusing, these young gods, all their energy, passion and genius on me. One is going down on me while the other is kissing my mouth, my breasts, my neck, gazing into my eyes. Then they change places. The three of us flow together, it is never two and one. Nobody competes or is ignored, and I am bathed in exquisite attention.

Other possibilities come to mind to explain the success of triads. The number three is geometrically far smaller than four —five possible combinations instead of ten—thus exceedingly less complex. In being with the G'Dramaks, I often felt fatigued by the labyrinthine complications. At its best moments their tribe seemed unwieldy; most often, every day was like preparing for an Apollo launching to the moon. Three does not carry that burden.

Three re-creates the original architecture in which we are

born and learn to survive. Although our first family may have added elements like siblings or grandmothers, the Mommy/-Daddy/baby triangle is primordial. Even my threesome sexual fantasy seems infantlike in its self-absorption, its receiving of all the prizes from two worshipers solely devoted to *me*. In one of the triads I visited, to be described later on, that sense of original tight-knit family was so strong that I found myself grappling with feelings that I experienced nowhere else in my travels, feelings of envy, longing and grief—emotions that at the time were surprising and inexplicable to me. Only recently did I begin to associate them with some secret and ancient swellings in myself, a core sense of loss that was stirred by this trinity of adults who love each other and live as intimate family.

Most early triads—early meaning in the late 1960's—were comprised of two women and one man. Traditional sex roles governed that split—polygamy (one man, several women) being historically far more prevalent than the reverse. Women have always been assumed to be natural, instinctive supporters of men, and men more valuable than women; thus it was normal to think of two women nurturing one man, rather than the opposite. The obvious discrepancies in male and female sexual capacity, women being far more capable of prolonged activity and repeated orgasm—which fact should *surely* influence and tilt that logic in the opposite direction—was conveniently ignored.

Lately, according to the experts at Family Synergy who watch for and catalog these matters, the tides are turning. We are seeing more triads which they term "man-heavy," as ingrained sex roles and myths dissolve and men become more able to connect with each other noncompetitively. The "research," though, asserts that the most harmonious of three musketeers are still those which feature two women, and my own observations confirm this. Two women simply get along better, are more willing to be transparent and cooperative with each other, than are two men.

You will probably be surprised to learn, after all our talk of erotic fantasies, that very few triads engage in bisexual or homosexual love. Hardly any indulge in group revelry or even lean so far to the left as to enjoy watching their two mates make love. Those that do are invariably "woman-heavy" triads. Virtually all those that I've encountered confess they would like *someday* to play more unconfinedly, are sure it would add to their intimacy, but say they are not ready. The women admit to periodic homosexual thoughts, the men are unanimously blocked from even that mind-play. The trend-watchers say these strictures are bending a bit, but only after the triad has been aligned for a long term can experimentation even begin to be risked. Just like the group marriages, triads appear to be composed of Daniel Boones plowing through the wilderness riding bikes with training wheels. It is a funny and touching phenomenon to me, this contradiction between thundering on the trails and tiptoeing in the bedroom, and more than anything else speaks to the transition time in which we live.

"In every age there are a few individuals, often academic or professional people, at the growing edge of society, questioning, examining new social issues before most people know they are issues," writes James Ramey in the *Journal of Marriage and the Family*, November 1972. Bud DeLeon considers himself to be one of those individuals, as do the people who surround him. He is a holy roller in Family Synergy, an anthropologist and the Zsa Zsa Gabor of the alternate-lifestyle circuit. Whenever somebody in Los Angeles needs a lecturer, panel-discussant or talk-show guest to rail on about the philosophy and practice of kinky households, Bud is summoned—along with Donna, Marty and now young Nicholas, who made his network television debut when three weeks old.

Bud is scholarly, slow-speaking, pontifical, mostly without humor. And very convincing. He is a man who fervently believes that open sexual relationships are the destined future—

a big step up from dreary old monogamy—and he has set about inventing his life according to his convictions. Unlike anybody else I've interviewed, whose "solutions" have generally been born from surges that were emotional, the DeLeon triumverate is grounded in common cause, rooted in intellectual principle. "I certainly think it is possible," says Bud with the droning and measured delivery that characterizes all his speech, "to make a conscious decision that one can love to the extent and quantity that we allow ourselves, and then proceed to live in that fashion." Sounds more tedious than loving as he expresses it, but concepts applied to matters of the heart generally do.

During the months I had interviewed the Meyers, LaFoxes and G'Dramaks, I had heard Bud expound his views several times, at lectures and Family Synergy seminars. I'd always thought him pompous, which allowed me to offhandedly wipe out his ideas. Then one night I go to his home for dinner, and to meet Donna and Marty. We four talk for six hours, and eventually I find myself dazzled by the logic and reasonableness of their doctrines. I will never be able to tell you what goes on between them, whether this triangle of theirs is as sensational as they avow, as they are public people and committed proselytizers and always control what you see. But I leave their home that night, if not moved in my heart by how they are together, utterly compelled by their arguments, and by the understanding that they are the perfect spokespersons for this new vision of society. They are the theoriests, the dogmatists necessary for all big revolutions. We don't have to like them, we just have to buy their dream.

They live in an old shabby house in Eagle Rock, a smoggy suburb east of Los Angeles. Having known Bud slightly before this evening, I'm quite dumfounded by Donna and Marty. I probably expect replicas of Lenin and Jane Fonda. They are not even close. In truth, all three are so disparate in temperament that the blending doesn't ever compute, even now, some years later. We would never arrange a blind date for any one with the others.

Marty is twenty-five, Semitically handsome, fiery and articulate. His sarcastic verbal style is much like that of the nervously ambitious and defensive urban young men I've known, so I'm rather stunned to find out that Marty's "profession" is being a trouble shooter for the phone company. "A highly skilled job, requiring mass amounts of toleration for boredom" he snarls, both at me for asking his line of work and at himself for doing what he does. Like everybody in this town, he really dreams of making films and always has some project lurking around the corner but never quite coming off. The incipient movie usually centers about the real-life tale of living in a triad—the most interesting thing that's ever happened to Marty.

Donna staggers me. Grossly overweight, hiding beneath a shapeless mud-colored kaftan, she is unkempt and listless. In contrast to the sharp intelligence and verbal flash of her two lovers, she easily fades into the background. Naturally I expected a sex-queen goddess blended with a vibrant radicalizer, the femme fatale of two worshipful courtiers. Why do I resent her not being such a dish?

Donna spends the early part of the evening isolated in the kitchen preparing dinner, a fact which does not for a moment leave my consciousness.

I begin by attack, my skeptical mood framed by the Meyers, the G'Dramaks—humans whose saga I could not purchase for myself. "Don't people open up their marriages because they're in trouble, on the road to divorce and desperately trying *anything?*" Do I still really believe that, or am I partially playing devil's advocate?

"No," Bud says benevolently, "not most. For most it's not because they're loving each other less or their relationship is less valuable to them but because they've gotten to the point where they recognize that their mate isn't meeting all their needs, and that no one person can. You make a choice—either your needs go unmet or you fill them outside the primary relationship.

"All the movies, books and the whole culture is telling you

that your mate is supposed to fill your life totally. So most of us, when that inevitably doesn't happen, are severely disappointed, divorce and go and try to find the *real* person to accomplish that, the *real* knight on the white stallion. But that doesn't work any better, since it ignores the fundamental issue —that no one person can do it all. The alternative is to reevaluate what the limitations of the relationship are, what are the strengths and weaknesses, and be open to finding satisfaction in those areas of weakness from other people."

This is the first of his arguments that invariably seduce me with their seeming incontestability. We are gluttons, we overstimulated and overloaded Americans, and short of retiring to a cavern in Tibet, there may be no exit from that current purgatory. But one also observes that the Elizabeth Taylor syndrome of regularly trading in worn-out models for new doesn't yield much long-range dividend. "So you're saying," I plunge on, "that monogamy is a rotten state, because if it were gratifying, people wouldn't need to expand?"

Bud sits back. He is on sure and effortless ground. "I don't think that's the question. 'Gratifying' isn't an absolute. If you've seen the Grand Canyon, why would you want to go to Europe? If you have three friends, why would you want any more? Why would you want to love somebody else, or experience somebody else sexually, if you already love one person? I believe you only have one life and you want to get as much out of it as you can. I don't want to set rigid limits or cut off possibilities for happiness in my own life. Do you?"

Well, Christ no, what kind of dolt does he think I am? And what a loaded question. Another irrefutable point for the DeLeon team. But, I think as he speaks, even as we yearn for and feel entitled to *everything,* most of us see life as an unavoidable series of bargains. What I will trade off, for example, in order to preserve a stable, quiet and unassailable nest, is a diversity of continuing new frolics with new and exciting people. Traditional marriage—when couched in such perspective —looks unbearably grim and sacrificial.

Bud adds to my shared thought the even grimmer idea that
all our bargains are only lies, at best. There *is* no fullproof
guarantee of untamperable protection, and most traditional
American marriages are not nearly *semper fidelis*. The DeLeons and others of their ilk do not honor the notion of trade-offs,
and that is an element of what so attracts me. They not only
want it all (as does everybody else) but see the feasibility of
building structures that will allow for it all. As I am a human
who longs daily for a secret to thinness that includes lasagna
and fudgicles, I always resent the inevitable choices I must
make, the dues I must pay. My appetites are big and my
acceptance of compromise tiny.

The score so far is two–zero. I have made no hot points for
Monogamy this evening. And the most persuasive argument
for open sexuality—its viability as well as appeal—is yet to
come. It relies on the analogy of friendship. As mentioned,
Bud, Donna and Marty perceive their interraction, their link,
as something much nearer to an intimate friendship than to
the romantic idealization that underpins our conjugal myths.
It is a thought similar to the Meyers' view of their bond, and
in direct lineage from the pre-nineteenth-century ideas of marriage. Within that framework nonmonogamy should work
gracefully. Listen:

"If you have one best friend," Bud says, "that doesn't mean
you don't have any other friends, or that you abandon one
friend for another. You recognize that your best friend is an
individual totally separate from you, with a completely independent life, and that's okay. You don't try to control his or
her behavior, you don't make demands of exclusivity, you don't
try to own him, you don't become crazy if he makes another
close buddy, you don't easily feel threatened or excluded. A
good open marriage has those qualities—much involvement,
yet lots of latitude."

Marty chimes in. "So, if your best friend also happens to be
your lover and you meet another friend who becomes your
lover, why should that be a disaster? In fact, why couldn't the

two become friends? Your lover enjoys your having happiness, right? And if that includes other people, and that's how you work well and dig life, then he'll want that for you."

—Come on, say I. Now you're going off the deep end. (Interesting that the instant he extends the analogy into sex, he loses me.)

Bud grins. "That's totally true of our relationship, and nobody ever believes it. If Donna finds somebody that really turns her on, I'm delighted for her. She gets a kind of glow that I enjoy watching. I just went off on the first leg of a new affair last night, and when I came home this morning and told Donna about it, she was really thrilled. She said, 'Hey, Bud, that's neat.' She likes Barbara and sees that my affair with her will just enlarge our network of friends."

Barbara, you will want to know, lives with Hans and some others in a group marriage, but more of that later.

Within the friendship analogy it makes sense. My good women pals, male buddies and even casual lovers naturally have had many other close ties, not to mention autonomous existences. I do not see myself as locked into "couplehood" with them—with all the carload of demands that that label wields.

Ah, sometimes I *do* feel left out, or fearful that I am not loved as much as I was, if time is consistently taken away from me and devoted to the new friend. The apostles are wrong to claim that one doesn't experience jealous aches with nonlovers. But, for me at least, the occasional sting suffered over a friend has never borne with it the crushing terror or rage that my mate can inflict with a word. A friend's abuses—real or imagined—have never once made me feel, "This I cannot survive."

Bud's theorems are beautifully reasoned. If I could find the key to shuffling my view of my lover from "This is my one and only" to "This is my dear loving roommate," open sexual relationships could flourish, and without the volcanic upheavals they now seem to entail. But I am so conditioned into my certainty that intimacy *must* carry with it the most dangerous cargo that I cannot imagine what sort of reformation of belief and heart would have to occur for me to utter freely, "Hey, darling, that's neat" (or hopefully something more poetic) when confronted with my love's newest flame. Bud, Donna and Marty do not think as I and don't live that way. Earlier on, I would have assured myself they were lying and posturing. Now I am beginning to recognize humans who are just unlike me.

Naturally an open relationship works best if you're intellectually committed to it, as the DeLeons are. If you're a monogamous person trying to save your drowning union, or to be hip or to accommodate your spouse, it's rather like sniffing petunia petals to cure a cold because everything else has failed. It probably won't make it. "You have to sincerely believe," says Marty, "that more is better, that one person isn't enough."

"Aha," say I. "Are two people enough? Three? What's enough?" The G'Dramaks are finding that four isn't quite sufficient.

Marty, moving from flippant to combative, spits at me: "Yes, I've eaten steak, now I don't have to try anything else. Or maybe I'll throw in a potato, surely *that's* enough." It's the old steak-and-potatoes gambit. I'm prepared for that one.

"But," I press on, slightly daunted, "you're living with two people. You want more? When does it stop?" Experience greed, zap greed. My ancestors had no such unreachable horizons in their vision . . .

Marty calms down, condescends to my narrowness of vista. "I live in a whole world of people, so does Bud and so does Donna. And that's as it should be. Don't you?"

Well, of course I do, responding to the loaded question again. But moving beyond, for a moment's pondering, my monogamous conditioning, I can see the only *real* restriction against building carloads of new bonds as that of time and energy. If I chose to spend my awake hours exclusively on the cultivation of friends, the possibilities would definitely be extended about eighty-fold. The capacities for love may or may not be limited; for time and energy they surely are. But I have to keep reminding myself, these individuals *do* see lovers as friends, and seem to be willing to invest the hours, so why not have six going on concurrently? Or eight?

Take Bud. He is married to Donna, living with although not making love with Marty, and has been having an every-Thursday-afternoon affair with Julia. Now, Thursday afternoon is when Julia's husband Brian teaches an art class. Brian, who once had a thing with Donna but it didn't work out, is terribly jealous and thinks that Julia's tie with Bud is platonic. Bud has rationalized the Big Lie which, I point out to him smugly, contradicts his public stance of openness and honesty. He says, "Both of us would feel a lot of loss if we stopped having sex, and it's probably our relationship that keeps theirs good, because Brian wasn't meeting enough of Julia's needs and she was feeling trapped, before me."

"I seem to go in two-year cycles," claims Bud. "I was monogamous with Donna in the beginning for two years and then started branching out. Now I've been with Julia for two years, and I find I'm ready to get into still another significant relationship." And then last night along came Barbara, who of course has two other significant relationships going on at the moment.

I ask Bud if he'll just add Barbara to the roster or if she will replace Julia or Donna, or whoever else fills his dance card. "No, I have no intention of cutting anybody out. The way we look at these things, our lives just expand, not contract. The only way I would leave anyone is if one woman were to give me an ultimatum. Then she would lose."

I still shift to and fro, spastically, like a disjointed seesaw. I'm captivated by the rightness of the concepts. But when they report to me the narrative of their days, with more combatants and machinations than a high-noon traffic jam in Times Square, I just want to giggle. Bud speaks as if Significant Relationships were lying in wait on every doorstep—as if every time you sauntered down to the delicatessen for cat food, you could meet another "intimate connection." In theory it's powerful; in execution it all sounds so promiscuous and absurd. Where, for one small example, *does* he find the time? How does he do his work and think his thoughts and wash his socks and carry on all those relationships, making room for yet another whenever it appears?

The DeLeons speak, too, of ego strength as a requisite for success in their enterprise. I have been commenting to Bud and Marty (Donna is still interred in the kitchen) that in regard to jealousy and possessiveness, they are evidently in a more highly evolved spot than most strugglers on this path. Is that because they are committed ideologues? Or is it the triad structure? Or the stretch of years together? It's ego strength, Bud assures me. "Given that your mate might be struck by lightning or might leave you," he asks, "can you live through it? How much pain will you endure? A person with a solid ego knows he can stand alone. I think all three of us are individually quite sturdy entities. We don't feel like or treat each other like extremely perishable objects."

I know that there is something in the very nature of monogamy that makes partners become so interdependent that our egos are progressively weakened. Sometimes I think it's simply the force of habit and order. Or maybe we come to believe, more and more over time, that indeed we cannot live without our mate; perhaps it's guilt—we *should* be so chained to someone we love, and he to us. So that, after all, monogamy contributes to the gradual erosion of self-sufficiency, and we come to live in dread of being left. This, regardless of how we even feel about said mate.

Bud agrees happily, as expected. "Part of the tenet of monogamous marriage is that you two will be one, and the more needy and dependent you are, the better and closer the relationship is. I don't feel married in the conventional sense but a great deal more like a single person with all my freedoms intact. I don't experience myself like one half of a couple, or one third of a triad. Donna and I have a bond that's very important to both of us" (Note: he does not say "Donna and Marty and I have a bond . . .") "but that's not *the* defining thing in our lives. The defining thing is our own autonomy and capabilities, exclusive of one another." What a strong, enviable, irresistible state. How few of us, especially women, achieve such selfhood in marriage. But does an alternate form —like the triad—really bear a direct correlation to that state? I'm not yet sure.

Bud's axes about traditional marriage are ground incessantly, and what he spouts is not wrong but exaggerated. Traditional marriage, he emphasizes, does not exist between two people but between two well-defined roles, like the breadwinner/housewife stereotype, or the dominant/passive stereotype. Monogamy doesn't allow for privacy, he rails—although I cannot envision anything more smothering than sleeping three in a bed. Where do *you* turn to be alone? I beg.

"Privacy is a matter of being able to go off into your own head without somebody tapping you on the shoulder asking what's wrong. In an ordinary marriage every minute has to be accounted for; if you want to go off and read a book it must be because you're mad at your spouse. And the more dependent the relationship, the less alone-time is tolerated."

His ax is so honed that he extends the models of conventionality into nonsense. In the meantime, guess who still hasn't come out of the kitchen in forty-five minutes except briefly to set the table, guess who shops and does the laundry, guess who later will be interrupted frequently during conversation and whose ideas will be dismissed as if she were the family cocker spaniel?

Donna and Bud met in 1967 in the Berkeley library. She was going to graduate library school, he was selling the *Berkeley Barb* on Telegraph Avenue and doing research on the Huichole Indians of Mexico. Both were California natives, she from a family of Bakersfield conservatives, he the offspring of San Francisco attorneys. Donna had had only one lover before Bud and a low estimation of her attractiveness. "Even though it looked like I was liberal and bohemian at Berkeley, I was really into being a good girl and pleasing my parents all the time."

Donna's father to this day doesn't know the truth about the triad, but her mother does and apparently accepts it willingly, if not wholeheartedly. Donna says, "My younger brother and sister are dropouts, so she's really had to go through all kinds of changes with the three of us. I think she's the ideal American mother—realizes the world is changing and goes with it. My dad just blocks it all out." When Nicholas was born, Donna's mother came to stay with them for a week, and according to Marty was as concerned about *his* state of well-being as her grandson's. "She was really worried I might be feeling omitted from the whole cozy familial scene. I assured her I wasn't." I have no idea of whether he's telling the truth about himself or whether he simply has too much invested in the public success of his trio to admit failings.

Bud and Donna lived together for two years in Berkeley, New York and finally Los Angeles. Under pressure from their respective families to get married, they did. A strange twist: They were sexually faithful for those years before marriage— but never again afterward. "We didn't really start consciously examining our relationship," Bud explains, "and what we saw in other people's, until we made that commitment and started taking ourselves seriously. We wrote our own vows, which were all about maintaining our own identities and defending the other person's freedom and not growing together and losing ourselves." I had the feeling, as he spoke, that that wedding was possibly the glummest ritual since the Dreyfus trial.

Said freedom included sexual license. For Bud it was, is and apparently always has been an easy and untortured option. For

Donna, "I had a hard time handling it but I knew I wanted it. I had never dated in high school, and in college there was just Bud and this other guy, so I felt I'd missed out on a lot. I enjoyed sex pretty much but for a long time I didn't reach orgasm. So having more experience seemed like it would really help. And it did."

Marty erupts into dirty laughter. "Oh, she has 'em left and right now. You can't even look at her without her going off like a rocket." He is without grace, this man. Nobody flinches but me.

So they were young and faithful and inexperienced premarrieds until literally moments before they wed. Two weeks prior, they met a couple at a party, swingers. Donna recalls: "They were being real loose and turned on to us and assumed we were swingers also, because we're touchie-feelie kind of people and nudists and all that. So they gave us a copy of *The Harrad Experiment*—we'd never even heard of Robert Rimmer—and called us a few days later. Elaine, the woman, said, 'Why don't you celebrate your marriage by coming over and having an orgy with us?' We thought about it for a few days and somehow it seemed real fitting. So the night before our wedding we went to their house and did an orgy with them."

I should point out here that what they actually did was they switched companions and hid out in separate rooms at opposite ends of the house, which hardly qualifies as your hot sweaty bona fide orgy.

—How did it all turn out?

"Well," she says with some faint trace of melancholy, "it was a disappointment for me, although okay for Bud and Elaine. Al, Elaine's husband, was real nervous, and I'd hardly had any sexual experience, much less something this freaky, so it was actually pretty much of a bummer. We've been good pals with them since, but nothing's happened again after that one time."

But the die, as it were, was cast. Within six months of their marriage both Donna and Bud were dating other people regularly, mostly mutual friends—less menacing than mysterious strangers. Again: We do it with our friends, or we include our new loves into the family network. "I was finding myself attracted to a lot of the men we knew in common," Donna recalls. "It was the first time in my life I even allowed myself to flirt with men. But I wouldn't let it go any further. Eventually Bud said it was okay with him, so I started having casual sex occasionally. The only really serious affair I had, until Marty, was with Sam. That started a couple of months after we got married and lasted one and a half years.

—Who's Sam?

"Oh, he's Bud's best friend."

Donna had been having what she calls "these real good feelings" toward Sam for a couple of years, but they only became crystallized for her at her wedding. Sam was the best man. "When I told Bud that I really loved Sam, he said he thought it would be fine and nice if something happened between us, and it did. It was really an emotional, deep relationship. It only ended because Sam started living with Arla, my ex-roommate in Berkeley, and she was completely alienated to the idea of Sam and me and the openness of Bud's and my marriage. She didn't want to have anything more to do with us, which caused a lot of conflict all around. We don't see either of them any more."

I ask Bud if Donna's romance with Sam, enduring for a year and a half, really *was* "fine" and "nice" for him. "Oh, yeah, sure," he flips. "We were best friends in high school, roommates in college, so we'd shared a lot of things. When he was seeing Donna he was always at our house or we at his, and the three of us made love together fairly often."

"You weren't ever afraid she'd leave you for him?" I ask. This question for me is always instinctive. It seems to lie at the center of things.

"No. I don't know why, I just wasn't. I had a lot of confidence in the quality of our relationship. We'd been together for a few years by that time, and things had gotten better and closer. Donna and I were good friends. To go back to the friendship comparison, I felt as threatened that she would abandon me for Sam as I did that Sam would end our friendship if he formed a connection with somebody else." Utterly logical.

I ask Donna if she considered dumping Bud during that time. I am looking for a news angle, or a clanging imperfection at the very least. Things work too swimmingly with these folks for my taste. "Never," she replies meekly. "In the beginning with Sam it was really strong—new and different and real romantic—and I felt somewhat of a lessening toward Bud. But then it leveled out so it was more equal toward both of them. I realized that I really loved both, that between them I had everything I wanted in a man, even though I knew I didn't want to live with Sam."

It is so hard to imagine Donna, Donna of the lackluster manner and uncared-for body and bleak kaftans as multiple mistress, blithe courtesan. Bud credits their open arrangement with Donna's alleged "ego strength," little of which is in evidence to me. "When I first met Donna," he says, "she had a low impression of herself. But after being with a lot of guys who found her attractive and wanted to be with her and sleep with her, she developed more confidence."

How naïve. As if erasing lifelong patterns of self-doubt, self-hatred, were as simple and quick as accumulating fucks in the night. Donna, anyway, does not impress me as a candidate for a mental health poster.

Despite her own meanderings, Donna was torn in those years about Bud's extracurricular sports. "The strongest feeling in me was one of being left out. Even sometimes we'd be in bed with the other girl and I still had some sense that I wasn't a part of it."

Note: The DeLeons often speak of "being in bed with" or

"making love with" a third person. It never, I discover upon careful probing, signifies anything homosexual. They are quite rigid about that, in fact very unnatural given their predilection for three-in-a-bed. Why bother inviting the third? Enjoy the audience? Or a way, possibly, to keep the jealousy level down, the intimacy factor low?

She no longer carries anxieties about Bud's rompings, but suffers with Marty. Which is peculiar, since Marty has no outside relationships. But he is new and not totally predictable yet. Bud—operating via his mental processes and media persona—is determinedly, sternly consistent.

Marty Simon. Blend of brittle Sammy Glick and fretting poet, both sides of a Jewish dichotomy. His parents are Russian Jews from the San Fernando Valley, his sister a thirty-year-old Home Economics major at USC, "bound by her neurotic obsessions with food" he says edgily. He had never lived away from them until merging with Bud and Donna. Marty's conflicts are sharply painted—he's given his long-suffering parents the classic finger, in spades, and pays the price in being a guilt-ridden underachiever. Donna and Bud accept him, take care of him, don't bug him. Good, easygoing low-key *shiksa* mama with Jewish breasts but no hassle.

He was working as a messenger at the Los Angeles public library where Donna was one of the librarians. Very gradually they evolved a friendship, taking lunch breaks together and rapping throughout the day. As they never discussed the contract terms of her marriage, he had no thought that Donna was available until the morning she made a pass at him.

The first time they made love was in Donna and Bud's bed, in their cramped apartment in the middle of a weekday afternoon, and Marty was utterly frozen. Even as their affair progressed he was apprehensive about meeting Bud. But at the same time, Marty was acquiring a headful of alternate-lifestyle dogma which he quickly learned to spout in proper syntax. He has written, in one of his public statements: "Clearly Donna and her husband Bud had a very good marriage. The quality of our relationship couldn't have been possible without it. As our love grew so did my image of their marriage, and I began to learn and to believe some of their philosophy. You *could* love more than one person at a time, and not love either one of them less because of it. Jealousy *didn't* have to be part of a relationship. Their kind of marriage started making sense to me." As of this moment Marty cannot envision ever being trapped, choked and stultified in the strait jacket of monogamy.

Marty's narrative returns every few minutes to his family in Sherman Oaks. Mother, need I tell you, went bananas, a state in which she apparently thrives to this day. Donna was both a married woman and a goy—a moot point as to which is the blackest offense. "My mother doesn't understand why I'm not in a big career now," Marty reports harshly. "She knows Donna and I have sex and she doesn't understand why Bud allows this mischief to go on. When she calls on the phone, she won't talk to the others, she'll just ask for me. She's never invited all of us to her house, been here or seen Nicholas." He not only bears her no compassion, he has trouble hiding his mean delight.

Bud and Marty became friends, although it required many slow months of dancing around each other. During that period Marty would stay overnight frequently in the DeLeons cage of an apartment—sleeping with Donna in the living room while Bud slept alone in the bedroom. Then Marty's clothes started arriving and eventually the decision was made. Bud, he says, never had adjustment turmoil. This is, after all, what he Believes In and he is, besides, an uncommonly noncombustible man.

Marty traveled an arduous route of feeling omitted, feeling like an intruder—a competitor who could not compete with Bud and Donna's solid tie of history and legality. "When I first moved in I felt uncomfortably like it was Donna and Bud, and

Donna and Marty," Marty remembers. "But never the three
of us. It was incredibly hard for me, emphasized by the fact
that I slept in the front room and Donna joined me some
nights, and Bud slept in the bedroom with Donna on other
nights."

At the time of my initial dinner with them, the DeLeons
and Marty have been ensembled for about a year, but only a
few months in this house they bought, where they sleep three
together and have enough physical room for privacy. Marty
describes the year, in retrospect, as "full of adaptations and
intense feelings and emotional and sexual investment." He had
never, remember, been away from his family's nest before,
much less . . .

Admittedly, my most active conjectures center about
Donna's position in this constellation. She has it made, I think
reflexively when the conversation returns, as it often does, to
sex. With Bud she has the equanimity, the comfort of time and
trust. With Marty, the honeymoon. Then, too, she gets to
choose rather than waiting passively to be chosen—the classic
spot in which women perceive themselves to be shackled. She
controls a crucial area, the bedroom, and thus is less vulnerable
than most of us. The question of where is the power in any
relationship is answered by knowing who needs whom more,
and I imagine that Bud or Marty need her more than she does
either of them. One can leave and still she is not deserted.

But my mind then turns the dream over, looks at the under-
belly, at the business of having to accommodate *two* males'
myriad needs instead of one. It is so natural, so female, to lose
my own Self in the kaleidoscopic demands and appetites of one
relationship, so mechanical and unquestioning to view my own
existence solely in terms of nurturing others while denying Self.
With two men?

—Do you feel you have to equalize your sexual activities? Do
you think, God I've made love with Marty three times this

week and Bud only once, what does that mean? Should I run in and fuck Bud?

"I went through all of those in the beginning, even thinking I should have oral sex with Bud if I had it with Marty. And I'd feel doubly obligated to make love when I didn't want to do it at all. I used to get upset that I'd go through periods of being much more attracted to one man than the other. But most of this has just ironed itself out, with time and practice."

—Don't you ever just want to be left alone by everybody?

"I guess not. I'm just used to having loads of people around all the time. I like it that way."

Bud interrupts. "Our sex life has changed since we started sleeping in one bed. We don't have sex too often at night when we get into bed. Mostly it's during the day at different times, two of us separately. When the three of us make love together —which hardly happens—it's more recreational than intimate."

"Yeah," says Marty. "And whoever feels like it does the soliciting."

Bud has previously mentioned that Marty and Donna make love more than he and Donna. Is that a problem for anybody? I ask, gazing at each for telltale signs of A Problem. Donna shakes her head "no" limply; Marty merely shrugs; Bud answers; "Uh-uh. I get as much sex as I want or can fit into my schedule." Of course. Bud has Julia on Thursday afternoons, and now Barbara, and God knows what awaits him on his next trip to the laundromat. Bud is the sole member engaged in outside amours.

My questions about homosexuality are greeted with tension and sarcasm, dumb jokes flying through the air and collapsing like punctured balloons. Everybody seems nine years old on this topic. "Bud and Marty haven't made it together," Marty smirks, "and I doubt seriously if they ever will. I know it's probably culturally enforced, but I don't feel particularly sexually excited by the prospect of sucking his cock." Bud chuckles a little awkwardly and agrees. "It's okay being sensual or affectionate with Marty, but not sexual—and only when Donna is there." How potent that fear is among men, even men like Bud and Marty who have so conscientiously worked at junking our most pervasive belief systems and stereotypes. It is the only issue which they seemingly cannot dominate with their brains.

As I drive home on the freeway from Eagle Rock that night, my mind races. The DeLeon family triggers some deep distrust in me—the intuitive distrust of anybody claiming all the answers when I'm not at all sure of most of the questions. When we speak, for instance, about the raising of children in their scheme of living, they appear glib and irresponsible, Bud dismissing my concerns with: "If he's raised in an open household from the beginning, I don't think he'll have any trouble accepting it. Kids have a way of reconciling the differences between what goes on inside their family and in the outside world." But then, as happens so repeatedly to my mind, it peers at the flip side. Why not? I remember the Meyers' son Teddy, his unguarded openness. And I certainly have no evidence that the steadfast, Norman Rockwell, divorce-free families of my childhood produced any models for the aforementioned mental health posters, so what am I defending? Psychotherapy as an American pastime of the 1960's was spawned by *my* generation, and we know the rigor mortis of the family constructions in which *we* were bred.

Steve and Pat Meyer, as my first subjects, implanted some seeds of change in my mind, but neither convinced me nor drew me emotionally to their route. The foursome in Bethesda were either just too young, too plastic or too unlike me to make notable indentations. Donna, Marty and Bud are the first, so far, who could render me speechless, or rebuttal-less with their Truths, and those are moments for me of both exhilaration and panic.

Yet I don't really warm to them much. And I cannot imagine myself plunging into a triad. I make a mental note to myself this night, turning into my own safe driveway, to practice more rigorously the separation of ideas from personality. So what if they're slightly icky. . . .

But why, oh why, do they not seem to have, or admit to having, any problems?

I play in my idle fantasies with the notion of being in a triad. I create probable scenes and pursue them to their logical outcome. All end impossibly, like a film from which the director could not extricate himself and so tacked on a desperate, preposterous finale.

Fantasy One: I arrive home from the supermarket, expecting Rodney to be there alone. Due to the logistics of our triangle Rod and I have not made love for twelve days. And as Esmeralda, our third, has bowling league this afternoon, we have planned a glorious assignation. I leap into the bedroom, carrying a jug of Asti spumante and a plate of avocado dip, but instead of finding Rodney lying in wait, quivering in expectation, I find him plunged into Esmeralda, whose bowling match was canceled. They see me enter, he winks, she whispers a breathless "Hi, sweetie," and not a beat is missed by them on their ineluctable journey to the moon.

Do I curl up at the end of the bed and watch, noting how gorgeous the choreography and how splendid their fire for each other? Do I weep for the cosmic joy and love that vibrates throughout the boudoir? Do I think, nobly, I'll just go and vacuum the living room while my beloveds have their perfect moment? Do I take this opportunity to revel in my aloneness, deal with my subjective feelings of rejection and exclusion, seeing that I am choosing to experience the abandoned child in me rather than the autonomous adult, viewing this whole episode as a positive growth experience?

Or do I pick up a meat cleaver and dismember them both?

•   •   •

Fantasy Two: Horace and Myron and me. I am reading *The Female Eunuch* before the fireplace, solitary and content. Myron enters, throws himself bodily between me and my book. He has been yelled at by his boss for losing the Schlockhopper account. His head on my lap is ripping the pages. Two days ago he had a fight with same boss, went out and got plastered, came home and got sick. I held his head and cleaned up. I do the same thing, figuratively speaking, now. He's too upset to cook dinner even though it's his turn on the schedule.

Horace arrives home as I'm kneading the dough for the bread. He is exultant: He's just received galley proofs for his new book, *A Guide to Mailing Lists in the Mid-Atlantic States*, and begs me to read them, this instant. After I finish drying the dishes and walking the dog, I climb into bed with Horace's spellbinding 685 pages. Around midnight I fall into an exhausted sleep, only to be awakened by Horace's hands moving across my stomach. He's aching, as a completion of this landmark day, to have me go down on him. Myron turns over from his fetal position on the opposite side of the bed, removes his thumb from his mouth and sobs: "Me too, it's been the worst day of my life. Do it for me too!"

"CHECK PLEASE!!!" I bellow to the world at large.

Or do I leap into my performing seal act, filling their needs while they empty their overflowing cups?

Over a year after our time together I appear on a television show with Donna, Bud, Marty and Nicholas—a documentary titled *Is Marriage Dead?* Afterward, after the three have done their well-practiced tap dance for the cameras, we all talk and cluck to the baby and gossip. I ask Marty, who is bouncing fire-headed Nicholas on his lap, how it's going for him now. Predictions had been, you know, that after the baby arrived Marty wouldn't last a week. He absolutely beams, shelves his body-suit of armor for the first time since I've met him. "Shit, it's *terrific*," he says, grinning like a newborn himself. "Look at my kid, will you? What an incredible family we've got going!" The three adults hug impulsively, laughing, encircling Nicholas, and in that instant I believe it all. All the words, the rhetoric, the maxims, the logic. And I feel a tiny, surprising twinge of envy.

Something in me is beginning to truly turn around about open relationship. I have often flirted with it but then re-treated, embraced for an instant but then wiped out with a scoff. Now, in a mission that has from the onset been as much personal as journalistic, all my rock-bound certainties and my entire anatomy of living are beginning to quake. I am, for the first time, wobbling on my convictions. Something is moving under my feet.

VI

Jerry and Roberta Miller

The party where I meet Roberta and Jerry Miller takes place on a Thursday night in Evanston, a suburb of Chicago. It is a crowded covey of architects, urban planners, engineers and their wives. A respectable citizens' band, gathered in a comfortable glass and chrome home to hear the pleas of a young ultraliberal candidate, running for legislature in an upcoming Illinois Democratic primary. Roberta and I have mutual friends in Chicago, I've heard about her open marriage on the rumor mill and she has heard of my book, so we find ourselves talking vigorously within minutes. She introduces me to the man with her, Burt, whom I already know from the tom-toms is her most significant current lover. He's an especially handsome man about ten years younger than Roberta, gregarious and sensual, the rare male who likes and listens to women.

"What are you doing here?" I ask Roberta, realizing that the same banality could be put to me. "Well," she says, "you know Jerry's with an engineering firm, so we always get invited to this kind of stuff. And he's really interested in this guy, he's been canvassing for him." She points with short, peach-lacquered fingernail to her husband across the room immersed in avid conversation with the candidate and his stunning wife. On Jerry's arm, leaning and hanging the way one does when terrified at parties, is a pretty young Midwestern woman, scrubbed and chestnut-haired, skin without landmarks. That, explains Roberta, is Fran, Jerry's mistress for the past year. With her free arm, Fran waves at Roberta, smiling a tooth-filled lustrous smile.

Roberta and Jerry's story is one of success. They begin as a conventional, role-bound, predictable, monogamous and dissatisfied suburban couple. Married for twenty-one years, three kids, and adamantly bourgeois. They end—at least in the spot we now leave them—as outlaws, pioneers of a radical change in lifestyle. And content with their lives and each other.

I can identify with the Millers, not just scattered slivers of them—a thought here, a word there—but the whole of them. They are the first I wholeheartedly comprehend and accept without the nagging presence of skepticism, that grainy filter through which I've heard, reinterpreted and to some degree invalidated all the sagas so far.

After the DeLeon crew, I interviewed dozens more—triads, couples, a swinging commune. Some were making it, many were drowning. Most were humans either too alien to my world or too unconvincing to make serious lacerations in my own thick skin. I would wake up each day with a full-blown case of ambivalence that lasted for month after month. But then, from time to time I came across individuals like the Millers—and like the Jamisons and the Barrons, whom you will next meet —and I knew I had found what I started on this expedition to find. Options that truly succeed.

Roberta and Jerry Miller, like the Meyers, have an open relationship. They share the same classic credos: Being an individual is more crucial than being half of a couple; dialogue with one's mate must spring from an honesty that is total; one person cannot possibly fill all of another's needs for a lifetime.

They celebrate male and female equality, privacy, independence, expectations that oftentimes coincide with reality. The Millers exercise a quantity of personal liberty once thought indecent in the fable of American matrimony.

And they are a couple who, because of the catapultic shift in the formula of their marriage, have been transformed not only in their couplehood but as individuals.

Let's be clear: Open relationship may or may not, but almost always does, include sexual freedom. In fact, that *looks like* it is the point. In the upwardly mobile middle classes where all such lifestyle experiments are incubated, ideas such as "autonomy" and "space" are not argued. We understand these days that it is okay—no, it is *growthful* and thus mandatory—for you to take a flamenco guitar class on Tuesday nights while I study Szechwan cooking. We've tossed out, in embarassment, our matching LaCoste golf shirts and madras Bermudas. We work diligently at relinquishing control over each other's psyches. We say "we" as seldom as possible. The real business of concern, always, is sex. Is it all right for me to be physically attracted to somebody else? To have a date? A sexual encounter? A love affair? And, then, there is the question I myself face over and over through this venture: How important is sex, anyway, to justify all this hoo-ha about it?

The second time I see the Millers, the scene is a notable contrast. I've been invited to attend as an observer one of the sessions of a weekly Sunday night "couples group"—a combination therapy and coed consciousness-raising and marital-counseling workshop. The group is for people in various stages of the journey from standard, monogamous practice to open, and the Millers are participants. Actually they are the stars, the old-timers, the models, the ones we'll-get-to-be-like-when-we-get-our-shit-together. They've been at it longer than anybody here, two years, and are assumed to have all the kinks ironed out. It goes without saying that they do not, but I am impressed along with everyone at the vitality and frankness between them. The neophytes are thrashing around in bewilderment like ski bunnies their first day on the hill ("It isn't fair, you have all the advantages, meeting groovy women all day in your office; I don't find anybody exotic in elementary school teaching"), while Roberta and Jerry are positively Buddhist in their flowing serenity. With miraculous imperturbability and mastery of the techniques, they are like the ski instructors, *wedeling* while the children flop. They have seemingly licked score-keeping, jealousy, ambivalence, logistics. Near the end of the evening—a night leaden with self-revelation and duet-confrontation, Roberta shares with the group of ten: "I never wanted to leave Jerry, but I wanted an open marriage because I was miserable sexually. Now I find that I'm satisfied with Jerry, and sex is the least of it in my outside friendships. There's a lot of loving, pain and intimacy between Jerry and me, and I can honestly say that I've never been as happy with my husband as in the last two years." And for the moment the beaming Millers seem to all eager listeners like discovers of The Answer—the Duz-does-everything testimonial to having found IT. My Bullshit Meter, so spastically active at past statements of this grandiose nature, is still. I instinctively believe her words and respond to their way with each other.

In the North Side suburbs of Chicago, streets and houses tend to all look the same—flat, even, undistinguished. If you were to be plunked down blindfolded on Fallbrook Terrace, on the Millers' front lawn, and then released, you would have no idea where in America you had come to rest. You would know only that this is a place where imagination is missing, a place dependent for its life's breath on the automobile, since every driveway has at least two stationed there, and the Millers' driveway has three plus a Honda 360 motorcycle.

Jerry and Roberta are in back, lazing on the brick patio in redwood deck chairs, drinking apple juice, when I arrive this mid-Saturday morning. Their eight-year-old, Maggie, is playing on the front lawn with some pals and dogs; the two older kids are not present. Roberta has just returned, a few moments before, from last night's date.

At forty-one, in lace-up jeans and no-bra tank shirt, she is slender and fair, her neck-length straight blond hair sprinkled with gray. She is welcoming, relishes the prospect of regaling a reporter, and thereby the world, with how her life has been transformed. Like all converts, she bears that evangelical "yippee I've just started Transcendental Meditation let me tell you all about it" fervor with every thought that races down the freeway of her mind. Jerry is more reticent to talk, but that is probably because he is a reticent person. And, too, he looks upon his discovery of nonmonogamy as on some glorious secret restaurant which, if he reveals it, will be spoiled by too many tourists going there. Jerry is a ruddy forty-five, brown curly hair, not handsome but sort of adorable, with a large irregular nose. In tennis whites from an early morning singles match, he is fit and trim—a newly acquired physical state of which he is clearly proud. He wears turquoise and silver jewelry, a lot of it, and is proud of that leap in consciousness too. It is easy to spy the remnants of "straight" around his borders.

"How was last night?" Jerry asks of his wife. He is smiling.

"Terrific. We just grilled some hamburgers and walked along the lake, got a little stoned, listened to Mahler's Fifth and went to bed. It was quite lovely." Roberta too is grinning.

I leap in nervously. I'm not yet sanguine about these level-headed dialogues between mates about lovers. "The man I met at the party—Burt?"

"No," she says. "Somebody I met at school a few weeks ago. He's very dynamic, a wonderful pianist." Roberta is studying music composition at a local college.

The Millers seem finished with this exchange, while I have only just begun. I believe I'm seeing the character of their open bond displayed before me in this little interaction and I'm dying to go on. Isn't Jerry scared? I would ask. Doesn't he want to know more, to be assured that he is still on firm ground? Is Roberta really as tranquil as she appears? Who will this new man be in her life? We will obviously come back to this story, but first things first. Jerry wants to guide us back to the beginning.

"I always thought we had a wonderful marriage," he says laughing. "We never fought, we congratulated ourselves as our friends got divorced one by one. We'd look at other people and say, 'Don't they have a horrendous relationship? Too bad they don't have one like ours.' Of course I never thought too much about the fact that we were only making love twice a month." Roberta whips around toward him. "Once," she says, then turns her face back to the hot sun. "Let's keep the facts straight." Not anger, exactly, just a strong reminder.

That was *his* "wonderful marriage." Roberta's, as is commonly the case, was of a very different, more silently suffering nature. "I was the feminine mystique personified. When Betty Friedan talks about the unknown disease that afflicts women, that was me. I was tired all the time and not doing anything much, not even the basic things around the house. I didn't know what was wrong with me, so I went to the doctor and he just gave me amphetamines."

Your classic noncommunicating coalition, masquerading under the tinsel of the great middle-class fairy tale. When they wed, twenty-one years before, they knew their parts by heart: Jerry plunged himself into career aspirations, she into wife/mother/homemakerhood. All of his energies were loaded onto becoming the brilliant young civil engineer of the Midwest, so that by the time he returned to the nest at night he was burned out, wanting only to topple into vegetable unconsciousness in front of *Gunsmoke*. At the same time Roberta, minimally engaged in bridge, PTA, the church and three kiddies, popped pills and hungered. Must we go on? We know this tale so well.

They were unerringly monogamous, of course. A good and proper marriage meant fidelity. That it also meant a drab and infrequent sex life could somehow be ignored by Jerry, who admits, "My real life was at the office. I loved my work with this small, tight-knit firm that was like another family to me. It was an exciting place to be, more so than home. But don't misunderstand. I thought Roberta and I had something outstanding going. We always had a good time and we felt good together. We just didn't make love much. And part of the old conventional thing is that you just don't talk about sex, so I didn't regard it as a problem."

Roberta says, "I knew the sex part of our marriage was bad, but I thought everything else was so fine that I could do without the other. After all, how important is sex?" She swivels around to Jerry and they both chuckle—this being one of their common joke topics now that things have shifted so far. "And I never talked to him either, I was too embarrassed or ashamed. Women are not supposed to get horny, you know. I would try to entice him to be more turned on to me, and usually nothing would happen—he wouldn't even notice I was parading around wearing some garish Frederick's of Hollywood number. So after a while I got tired of being aggressive or conniving and I just withdrew. The only time we went to bed was if we'd been to a party and got drunk. When it did happen—at the full moon—sex was totally mechanical. I was not what you would call your blooming, sexually fulfilled lady."

She is surely sexy now, with a keen awareness of her body and an air of graceful availability. It's not easy to imagine the deadness she describes. Women like Roberta, in beginning to explore their long-buried sexual natures, are acknowledging themselves finally as being *at least* as sexual as men and thereby refusing to settle for mediocre, ungratifying or exploitative love-making. A recent *Redbook* survey of women found that 39 percent of the married women questioned claimed that they wished to have sex more frequently than they do now. It was the first time, says *Redbook*, that such rumblings of dissatisfaction appeared in their studies.

Unless one has been there, one is awed at the delusions and lies, the withholdings and dearth of intimacy possible between partners for so many years—even between those who consider their bond "outstanding." How frequent for "I want," "I need," "This is what's good for me" assertions of self to become deadened into "I really shouldn't make an issue out of that" or "I can't expect to have everything I want." Presumably, in a love relationship we should be able to express our needs more openly than in other places, in an atmosphere of tender safety. But in truth the opposite occurs: The more the continuance of the relationship matters, the more we tend to deny ourselves, bury who we really are and what we want in order to preserve the sanctity of couplehood.

In an open relationship that burial of needs won't do. Compromise, Erich Fromm's notion that "love is making a settlement with life," just won't pass muster any more. Sacrifice, accommodation, adaptation—the former keys to maturity—aren't courageous or self-actualizing enough. This is the Brave New World.

It is also part of the standard libretto for the Millers to have had an active sexuality during their early marriage. For the first year they made love religiously every night. Then, after their first child was born, the battery suddenly died. "We were in a one-bedroom apartment," Roberta recalls, "and the baby slept with us. I think Jerry felt pressed to the walls by responsibility. Also, I think I became a very boring person, since I had no outside life. But of the two of us, *I* always had the big sex drive, I never lost it for Jerry all those years. Although," she turns to him briskly, "you weren't so fascinating yourself. All you did was work and watch TV." He nods in agreement. When they speak of these twenty years, it is like they are reporting on two strangers whose story they happen to know.

I'm not sure I believe that the slate is now all clean of those old resentments.

After sixteen years Roberta became irrevocably conscious of the bleak void in her life with Jerry. She had an affair, her first. "I was on a committee at the church and I met a man there. Willy was married, and we saw each other for four or five months before we went to bed. Just like the Middle Ages, a terrific romantic love, gazing into each other's eyes over lunch, mooning and pining, but no sex. It was a very beautiful and agonizing time but I just couldn't bring myself to do it. When I realized my feelings for this man, and that I was starting to really come alive, I tried to tell Jerry without actually telling him.

"For the first time in our marriage I began talking to him about my needs—for touching and holding, to be really loved sexually and intimately. I remember this big weepy scene in a bowling alley when I told Jerry I was terrified I was falling in love with somebody else and would leave him if things didn't change with us. He said, 'Sure, I hear you' but promptly repressed it. Two months later he couldn't even remember the conversation!"

Jerry replies, "I remember thinking, 'Okay, we'll have sex more often, that will make things better.'" Says Roberta, "Yeah, so we increased it to twice a month." Jerry grins: "I'm *sure* it was three times a month." He is very self-mocking from his new vantage point.

People *do* have varying sex drives, a heavy burden in many marriages. And now, nobody wants to suppress his or her appetites any more. Nobody, as has been pointed out before, wants to be the wife these days.

With Roberta—and with many of the other women in this book—there's a strong correlation between open sexuality and feminism. In the old togetherness mystique, the wife paid the steepest dues, most twisted herself to be the perfectly controlled and dominated companion, felt most strangled and trapped. Her husband fooled around while she kept the kitchen floor waxed. She was property, and what was plainly owned was her body. Roberta never felt the right to complain, never insisted on being heard by Jerry because she bought that lie. When she released herself from the property ethic to claim self-ownership, monogamy seemed unappealing in its restrictiveness.

Roberta's *amour courtois* ultimately was consummated, lasting three intense months until Willy was killed in a car accident. During that time however, she became Lady Chatterley. "He made me feel important, adored. I thought I had a terrible lumpy body and no man could ever desire me, but he opened my eyes to being sexual and alive.

"We usually could only get together for one afternoon a week, but it was divine and I was grateful. After all, I'd been used to sex once a month, so this was like an orgy!" As her home fires received the spillover from all that glow, Roberta and Jerry's general association improved, she wanting to pour out her newfound bliss on the entire universe. Their own conjugal bed however, remained immobile. But Roberta no longer fretted, and Jerry, as he says, ". . . noticed her added affection, and I didn't feel all that former pressure to perform sexually, so I was overjoyed. If I'd had any idea what was really going on, I probably would have caught the next plane for Reno."

She never wanted to leave Jerry or to live with her lover, and the only taint on her joy was the secrecy. It chewed at her mercilessly until she felt, to use her word, "immoral"—"as if I were the only woman in the world sneaking around having an affair. The crazy thing is that Jerry really knew, because I had talked so much about Willy and I'm sure I *wanted* him to know. But he blocked it out, fooled himself, pretended it was platonic. One night we went out to dinner and Jerry asked me, "What's happening with you and that guy, what's-his-name?' And I shrugged it off, said I'd abandoned the thought of ever going to bed with him. And, God, that was the only reason I was getting up in the morning. I despised myself for being able to bring off the lie so well.

"After Willy died I promised myself not to do it again, the cheating aspect was so painful to me. But I was just starving. I could feel the drives in me and men could feel them too. For the first time in my life I was constantly being propositioned. After a year of abstinence I started sexual ties with two men within a week. I said to myself, 'I really need this, so why should I fight it? And I'll lie and sneak and risk being caught.' Part of it was that I was getting close to forty and I thought this was my last chance. 'If I don't do it now, while I still have some looks, I'll never have anything, after all these years of having nothing.' "

Midlife crisis, the newly arrived sense of perishability and time running out. Kinsey said if there is a time when women are most likely to have extramarital affairs it is in their late thirties. And, of course, there is the monumental disparity in sexual life cycles between men and women to consider: Males reach their functioning peak at age eighteen, while women arrive at forty. The authors of *Sex and the Significant Americans* have written of midlife, middle-class men: "By forty, a majority of American men in this social class are so emotionally crippled, confused, and generally neurotic about sex in their own lives that they are washed up." At the same time women like Roberta are bursting from their shells, coming exultantly, menacingly alive. What to do about such a crazy fresco?

Open sexual relationships, on the other hand, are most easily handled by kids in their twenties. Often—more often at least than we in our thirties and older—they have no concrete belief system about the holiness of monogamy. My generation treasured security above all else, thus we made the stolid decisions we did. For people maturing only one decade later, the true value is freedom. When older partners decide to make the large leap from monogamy to openness, they are bucking eons of entrenched conviction and habit; kids often begin a coupling with agreements of nonexclusivity.

My friend Jenny, thirty-four, has been going with Peter, twenty-six, for a year. They have an open relationship which is easy and clean-cut for him, hazardous and battering for her. She has accommodated because she wants him and because her head tells her openness is healthy. But she cannot bear knowing he is fucking anybody else, while he would like her to tell him the microscopic details of each of her encounters—in fact, it would arouse him considerably, he coaxes. Plus, he wouldn't at all mind playing group switchies on occasion or even watching Jenny make love to his best friend. It is doubtful they will last.

Whatever the generation, however, these are the New Romantics. Don't be fooled by their guise of cynicism, their "Love Is a Supermarket" appearance. These adventurers yearn to re-create the mystery, the irrationality, the illusions of romantic love over and over, to experience the ideal of passion forever. Intimacy greed perhaps being today's replacement for the sexual greed of the '60's, they may indeed be greedy. But they are not cold.

As Roberta was not cold. Confused and wretched, yes, but by the time she was five months into her second major affair, with a distant cousin, she couldn't tolerate the secrecy any longer. She loathed the furtiveness, the disconnection from Jerry. And she hated herself for what she considered a huge, profligate betrayal of trust. Still, she was unwilling to retreat into listless fidelity with her husband and tortured herself about what to do.

Right about then, in 1973, *Open Marriage* was published. If nonmonogamy was born as an inevitable product of sparks blowing through the culture—the Human Potential Movement, burgeoning divorce rate, sexual emancipation, the Women's Movement—it caught flash-fire with *Open Marriage*. The O'Neills' book, theoretical and Pollyanna as it is, seemed to speak to millions of Americans wallowing in stagnant pools, not knowing quite what was the trouble in their homes, just knowing misery. Or lethargy. Or, if things were not all that bad, knowing that plainly there could be more. They read the book in bed, late at night while matey slept. Having turned the final panacea page, they nudged the familiar old spouse snoring at their side, and fairly fainting in elation, proclaimed: "This is it! I want an open marriage!" One hears that same story again and again. That is exactly how it happened with Jerry and Roberta.

The book's premise provided an exhilarating alternative for Roberta: She would have Jerry and she would have liberty to pursue other interests, and she would have utter honesty in all camps. Her life would be clean and rich.

She dragged Jerry to the Wisconsin countryside the next weekend, and in a romantic hotel room by a lake she "proposed." From the bubbling spring of her own excitement she was unprepared for Jerry's reaction: "Okay," he answered, stunned. "Let's get divorced." He explains: "For about the past year I had begun to think there was room for messing around if I could get up the nerve. But I was as pure as the driven snow, which means I was scared to death and probably enjoyed being a martyr, feeling I was sacrificing for my family and my marriage. I never even came close to screwing anybody because I believed in fidelity and my inability to lie. So when Roberta brought it up I was just rattled to the core. I said, 'Why do you need to be married if you're going to do this? Why can't you just go from affair to affair?' I was angry and terrified, but part of me also admired her in a different way. All of a sudden she was standing up to me. What I believed —it was *always* what I believed when these things came up— was that all she needed was a good fuck. So for a couple of months I made love to her every morning and night, even though it was an effort for me to get out of the old habit of going right to sleep."

Roberta continues: "Every night that whole summer we'd

be up until 4 A.M., talking this all over and making love. I knew I couldn't go back to the old way, I had all these sexual needs and if it meant the end of my marriage I was willing for that. I felt really strong. That freedom was the only thing that mattered to me. I cut off with the two men I was seeing because I wanted to throw all my energy into Jerry and this new thing I was trying to create for us. After twenty-one years of pretense we finally began to talk to each other."

Roberta's bulldozer energy was beginning to galvanize Jerry. He could see the benefits of breaking out of his smothering cookie molds. He could start to envision working less, studying jewelry-making as he'd always wanted, joining a nudist camp, shedding his dutiful roles, having a lot of sex. Life was opening up.

It happens that the jolt from conventional to open relationship can be the most intense emotional experience a couple has ever shared. With self-disclosure, transparency, comes waves of newborn intimacy. Sexual drive is heightened by the rocking of the steady old craft. Jerry and Roberta turned on to each other as if newlyweds, twenty years worth of dark secrets gushed up in torrents as if from a buried well. They were discovering each other, they were communicating, it had all the earmarks of a new love affair. My God, the air was electric!

Open Marriage decreed the necessity for a treaty spelling out every rule, handling every contingency. Some couples' agreements resemble the United Nations Charter—beginning with the splitting of household duties equitably and ending with the testiest negotiation of all, outside sexual involvements. Jerry and Roberta's initial contract (it has been revamped many times since) took heed of Jerry's total inexperience in the adultery realm. He needed to catch up with her, so they agreed that Roberta would abstain from sex with anybody else until he could tolerate it, whereas he was assigned to go out and find one or more liaisons.

"I had a miserable time," Jerry reports. "I hadn't gone out on a date in twenty years, hadn't even made an effort to talk to women socially while I was married, and I certainly had no confidence that I was attractive. So I made some adolescent attempts, had a few disastrous dates. For the first six months I despised the whole thing. Then a friend of Roberta's called me. Jill had just been divorced and heard we were trying an open marriage, so she invited me to a party. We wound up afterward at her apartment making love. I arrived home at three in the morning, slamming doors, waking Roberta with 'HEY, GUESS WHAT HAPPENED!' I felt like I'd just gotten laid for the first time."

"I was really excited for him when he came home," Roberta says. "We always talked after our dates, and if a woman rejected him—a lot did in those days—I'd really get angry at her. I was delighted with the possibility of him finding out what it's like to be with other people." He continued seeing Jill for three months, and by then he had begun to blossom—taking down his hair and throwing away his spectacles. He was dating and making love to several women regularly; finally he told Roberta he was ready for her to join in on their open marriage.

An interesting feature in all of this is that Jerry and Roberta's sex, at the same time, became so radically juiced that her roving eye was considerably stilled, and she became content to focus on her husband—for the most part. Jerry, on the contrary, tried it and liked it so much he became like a horny pubescent boy, the stud of the Windy City. He began to feel, and has felt since, that the possibilities are limitless, that his cup of sugar is virtually unemptiable. The levels of irony in this turnabout are of a dimension that truly bend the brain.

"Why do you suppose your sex life together has been so revolutionized?" I ask them skeptically from the patio chaise longue. Behind my question are my own assumptions about the tricky maze that forms the nature of sexual response, and the irreversibility of long-established patterns. My preconception is that sex gets worse over time, not better.

Jerry's idea is that their staleness was really a matter of deep ruts, years of lifeless habits. Habits that were simply blown apart by the massive convulsion of the open relationship. "Roberta and I have felt like brand-new people to each other. I've become less absorbed in work, more concerned with just living. The trapped feeling, the sense of tedious routine and sameness has gone out of my life, so I'm never exhausted in the evening any more, just sleepwalking until it's time for bed. In fact, with all the things I'm doing and people I'm seeing, I can't even find any time to park in front of the TV."

"You've changed so much physically," Roberta says. "You started to dress differently, cut your hair in a hipper way. You're just more loose and sexy." Jerry says, "Somehow, in the involvement with other people, your flame for each other gets revived. Last week I stayed overnight in Chicago with this girl we both know. I had a nice time, but on the way home the next morning I was thinking about jumping into bed with Roberta and driving like a nut. I couldn't wait to get home!" Roberta leaps up from her chaise and settles on Jerry's lap seductively. "We went to Mexico a few months ago," she says, "and we were making love four or five times a day. It was unbelievable! I think I'm more alluring to you because you know other men find me exciting."

Before my expedition I would have found this case too simplistic, too much a "Can This Marriage Be Saved?" recipe from the syrupy pages of the women's magazines. Yet I've heard so many other couples report the selfsame dynamic that I've had to look seriously at it. Yes, there is something about open sexuality, extra alliances, that feeds the fires at home. Something that appears as fundamental as the freedom to do what one wants to do. "We don't take each other for granted any more," admits Jerry. "There's not this 'old shoe' thing that married people fall into any more. When we're together, every minute counts. In fact it's like we're dating again." Don't we all yearn to keep that "dating" high spirit in our unions, but aren't we also resigned to its being humanly impossible to sustain?

There is no question in my mind of the freshness and vitality coursing between the Millers this day. Whatever else they may be classified at this moment, they are not the stodgy settlers of their first twenty years. How much the change is *really* rooted in actual fleshly sex is a curious question. My increasing sense is that sexual freedom is in great part metaphor for the true grit.

After two years of adventure, Roberta and Jerry's contract is more flexible than ever. They spend one week night together, trying to be away from the kids, and stay home on the weekend from Saturday morning until Monday. Contingencies, such as wanting to go away for the weekend with another friend, are allowed. If one wants to sleep out—as Roberta did last night —the other must be home with the children. Lovers can spend the night at their home only if the partner is away, and neither Roberta nor Jerry will sleep in their own bed with another person. They have none of the Meyers' predilections toward sharing lovers, threesomes or bisexuality.

Most people have pacts, too, about the sharing of information. How much can you ask? How much are you obliged to disclose? How much is masochistic? Sadistic?

"We tell whatever we want to," says Roberta. "We tell each other when we've been to bed with somebody else because that level of sharing is very important to both of us. We want to know what the other is doing, and I think it strengthens our own closeness to reveal a lot. But we have some differences of opinion about just how much is kosher to talk about. I feel I have a private relationship with Burt, or whoever else I'm seeing, and it wouldn't be fair to violate that."

Jerry: "I tend to blab and tell every detail, so Roberta shuts me up when she thinks I'm going too far."

Nothing else will be revealed about Roberta's date of Friday night. Jerry has picked up his wife's subtle signals that she has no more data to divulge. And if he is uneasy, if quiet demon voices are plaguing him with "Is he better than me?" or "Is she falling in love with him?" they don't surface and he doesn't admit to them. Another irony of the Miller story: Roberta, the pathfinder, is the one who now has to deal with her own vipers of jealousy and possessiveness, as Jerry is rather deeply involved with Fran, spending increasing amounts of time with her, while Roberta is playing the field.

A characteristic of open relationships is their resemblance to old-fashioned extended families, a movement away from nuclear and toward community. Roberta met Fran first, at a women's workshop, and later Jerry met her at a party. She was recently separated from her husband, so she and Jerry and Roberta and both sets of kids began to do things together. They still do, like horseback riding or trooping en masse to the local nudist camp at which everyone in their new crowd hangs out. Last Easter's dinner guests at the Millers included Fran and her kids and Roberta's boyfriend Burt and his two kids.

"We don't do group sex or anything like that," Jerry assures me, "but we *do* spend time with each other's friends. That's one of the reasons, I think, that jealousy is at a minimum and we can work out whatever comes up. There aren't any skeletons in the closets, unknown people to stew over. I guess I'd rather see Roberta with Burt than imagine what they're like together." For Roberta, who has felt some pangs of being cheated since Jerry's tie with Fran, her solution is to have lunch with Fran, tell her precisely what she's feeling. Roberta doesn't think her marriage is threatened—why would Jerry leave her when he can have her and Fran and whomever may appear next on the horizon? And since everybody in this small private army is committed to struggling the good struggle, these new ways of confronting seem to work. In the old days, the aggrieved wife would have sneaked hemlock into the mistress' buttermilk; now they have lunch and "relate."

The principle of "primary" and "secondary" relationship is central to open marriage. In ancient polygamies, the first wife held a higher position than the others, sometimes she was considered the only *real* wife, while the others were concubinage. The same separation seems to be natural today. Participants have to keep the distinctions clear, so as to know where priorities lie. "Primary" is most often used interchangeably to mean "wife"—as in "What were you doing kissing my primary?"—but since the rules are shuffled here (monogamy doesn't allow for secondaries and tertiaries), "primary" may signify somebody else. In order for an open marriage to work, the theory goes, your mate is your primary kinship and the others are secondary. Even if that focus shifts temporarily, as in the fiery ignition of a new affair, it should ultimately swing back. If not, something is keenly amiss. Secondary links should enhance the primary, not replace it.

What all this means is that in the traditional modern view of marriage, the potentiality for permanence has been almost discarded. We live in what the sociologists call "serial monogamy," going from marriage to marriage to marriage. Paradoxical though it may look, given the emphasis on unrestrained latitude, practitioners of open marriage are often much more dedicated to the concept of permanent commitment to one primary partner. Jerry and Roberta's solution to an ailing merger was *not* to sever, not to toss out their twenty years like last night's chicken bones, and surely not to continue the barren duplicity of secret infidelity. Those are traditional choices. Commitment in *this* setup means something different, not sexual exclusivity or the control of one human over another, but an investment in working things out no matter how treacherous. Nonmonogamy is a solution of a different color entirely and arises from, among other drives, a compelling desire for one's marriage to last.

What about children? is the next obvious question. Most of these crusaders are either in their early twenties and have no families yet, or are older, with children that have already left the nest; those are the two periods of life when people are drawn to this style. The Millers and the Meyers are exceptions. "The big thing I had in the beginning," Jerry says, "is that I just couldn't see how the kids could handle it. I used that as a reason to protest." Besides eight-year-old Maggie, there is Neil, sixteen, and Tessa, twenty. "I had a talk with Tessa," says Roberta, "and gave her *Open Marriage* to read. She said she thought the whole thing sounded like a terrific idea. Kids her age are incredibly wise and sane about things like this." Tessa, it should be noted, moved away from home six months ago to live with a thirty-three-year-old man, in an open relationship. The night of the political party where I met the Millers, Tessa and friend were also there but she left with another man.

Another couple, married twenty-four years, told their teenage son about Dad's apartment at the beach, to which he escapes twice a week. Dad explained delicately about friction and fights and the need to separate a bit. The boy gave his instantly considered opinion that there are so many kids in his school with divorced parents that his folks' way might be a step in the right direction. After a moment's thoughtful pause, he added: "Can I use it too? You can hang a towel on the banister if you're there, and I won't come up."

George lives in Southern California with his wife and another man, and has three children under the age of eleven. He is one of the charter members of Family Synergy, the mushrooming nationwide club of alternative seekers. Although George and Hillary sleep together, and Frank, her lover, has a separate bedroom, Frank is home with Hillary during the day, and the kids see them in bed frequently. "But they've never said anything," George reasons, "so for us to go through an explanation would point out the oddity rather than treating it as normal. They now think it's natural, and I believe that kids are totally flexible as long as they're getting what they need."

I spend some time with Neil, the Miller's teen, some days

after my first trip to their home. He is one of those immensely articulate, attractive kids that convinces me the planet would be in different shape if my generation had been of his consciousness. He tells me that neither of his parents had exactly spelled out to him whether they were "screwing all these people that keep coming around," but that he sort of knows in general, and doesn't really care in particular. "My mother was afraid I'd look down on her," Neil says, "but I really don't. I don't think I have any romantic illusions about marriage, although I'd like to find one girl, not have a whole batch. But the important thing is that this open relationship seems to work for them. They're a helluva lot happier together than before, so I guess it's okay."

Roberta mentions that in her new way of being she's given up the task of Supermother, and with it the smothering dominion over her kids. Neil reaps the harvest. "I have a lot more freedom now to do what I want, she's not on my back any more." He also receives considerably more attention from Jerry than ever before; the two have just returned, in fact, from their first weekend alone together in over ten years.

The verdict is probably not in yet on the effects of open relationships on children. One wonders whether the offspring of such unconventionality will choose, later on in their own lives, the same emancipations. Or whether they will return, in classic rebellion, to old-fashioned monogamy.

If you ask most citizens whether they would select an open marriage or a situation in which they don't know if their spouse is adulterous, or they "know" but it is undiscussed by tacit agreement, most would prefer the latter two options. "I'd rather not know what he's doing" is the sentiment repeatedly expressed. "I couldn't deal with the anxiety, I'd just rather pretend everything's okay" from another blindered husband. We assume we can't swallow the thorns of candor, and so the damages of lying are more subtle. Yet, for the Millers, it was *only* this candor that has allowed them to grow and move as they have.

For instance, Judy and Mark Rose are a couple in their mid-twenties, in the throes of exploring an open arrangement. They thrash and fall back and persevere. Their marriage sometimes looks like a Grand Guignol. I ask them, "Wouldn't it be easier for you both to have secret affairs?" "Yeah, it sure would," Judy responds instantly. "But it depends on what you want from your marriage. If somebody just likes the idea of coming home and having a nice dinner on the table and watching TV and telling his wife he's going to a poker game on Wednesday when he goes to see his lover, and they're satisfied with that, that's great. But that's not what I want, *at all.* I want total trust that this person I'm living with and I know each other completely. *That's* what intimacy is. I guess, if your priority is pain-avoidance you'd prefer infidelity and all the bullshit that means. I can't live that way; it feels like death to me." At the same time, Judy could not abide the strictures of monogamy.

Something way beyond sexuality has been transmogrified in the Millers. Neither had close individual friendships before; now they do. Before, their lives were static, empty; now, blossoming and vigorous. They feel not only free but obliged to express themselves fully to each other, without reservation or withholding. Whatever one may think of the virtues or penalties of such thorough, merciless communication, at least no atomic stockpile of grudges accumulates, there is no sitting on needs for fear of hurting or being hurt. You can decry the selfishness or the narcissism or the plain foolishness of such blabbing, perhaps; you can't deny the particular kind of trust it inspires.

"The key is not so much that we're seeing other people now, but that we're involved with so much," says Roberta. Indeed, their résumé of activities reads like the dossier of the class

president. Roberta is studying music, training to be a leader of
therapy groups, starting a plant store with a friend; Jerry is
making jewelry, taking yoga twice a week, building a darkroom,
reading novels. They are a paid advertisement for open relationships.

Transforming a monogamous marriage is not ever a painless
process, and if Roberta and Jerry seem cavalier, it is only
because they have crossed over the threshhold. The rewards
now are more in the forefront than the costs. But it was not
always that way for them, and I have not met anyone for whom
the passage has not been perilous. Even Steve Meyer, the
dogmatist, ached during Pat's initial excursion. Jealousy,
possessiveness, fear of loss—an unabridged dictionary of
human emotions are called up and laid bare in this escapade
of open marriage. Those who don't make it across the tightrope
tend not to retreat into a closed, monogamous union but to
plunge to divorce. Those who succeed proclaim they have
found a higher form of relationship—not merely an alternative,
but something infinitely superior. The Millers have succeeded.

VII

Sara, Karen and Lloyd

Is it truly possible to love two individuals equally? DeLeon and Company insist yes, of course, without question. A more sardonic friend of mine says, "Sure, one from the waist up, one from the waist down." A trio in Charlotte, North Carolina, consists of a husband, wife and another woman, all in their sixties; the wife hasn't been turned on to her man for years and is delighted that ladyfriend takes care of that department. The two women are comrades and everybody adores everybody equally, effortlessly. They say.

The consensus of authorities is no, that we humans are not congenitally capable of loving—with all that that entails—more than one other, simultaneously and in exactly the same amounts. Bud DeLeon believes that loving seven or twelve is not only feasible but natural, if we could suspend the socialization that dominates us. But his defining term for love, remember, is "friendship," and for most of us that is quite unlike—even at odds with—our common yardstick called "intimate relationship."

I think of two dear women friends; I cannot know which,

if either, I love more. They are very dissimilar people, and so is my tie with each dissimilar. Judy and I share, among other bonds, our both being writers, so that we can phone each other at three in the afternoon to whine and commiserate over our mutual loneliness, agony, elation and the matchless insanity of our trade. There is nobody else I do that with, and I cherish it. Diane and I have a twelve-year history, a wide-sweeping knowledge of who the other is and was, and an amused interest in watching the disparate paths we've taken in recent years. Each friend touches different corners in me, corners that are not to be compared. I don't know to whom I would give the last seat in the lifeboat—if that's even a measure of caring. If my house were burning, would I save my manuscript or the dog?

I have never been in two concurrent love affairs that were of precisely parallel emotion and importance to me. One always prevailed, and although modulations may have occurred—from week to week or moment to moment—my instinct, physiology or acculturation, I don't know which, impelled me to make a choice always. And I was usually certain at any given instant which man would get the lifeboat.

Dr. Leonard Zunin, a Los Angeles psychiatrist, is one of the experts contending that the trio form cannot provide a deep love relationship for each of the members, and for the reason that we are unable to sustain several equal, intense alliances. "The nature of deep romantic relationships," he says, "is that they are never constant but rather they ebb and flow. All relationships in the universe are in a perpetual state of pulsing, of moving towards or away. Nothing is static. So to love two people with precisely the same intensity is possible only at instants. We can hang in a state of seeming balance for days or weeks perhaps, but life's personal crises which are inevitable, always require us to redefine our priorities, to flow towards one and ebb from the other. All intense relationships present difficulties, but in a triangle this process of motion has to create

massive compromises and stresses which make a sustained tria-
dic balance improbable."

Sara and Lloyd Jamison and Karen Cole live in Garden City,
a suburban town on the south shore of Long Island, about
twenty-five miles from Manhattan. Although they are cross-
country friends of the DeLeons, and carry a strong and unique
link, they could not be further apart. To assume that if-you've-
seen-one-triad-you've-seen-them-all—a preconception of which
I was guilty before meeting several—is no wiser than believing
that of all seven-year-old boys. Whereas Bud, Marty and
Donna are ideologues sculpting a lifestyle out of their doctrines, Sara and Lloyd and Karen are three adults who just
happen to be quite in love. By all my intuition, they defy the
wisdom of the authorities who insist it cannot be done.

They are the tribe I spoke of earlier, the family that stirred
such long-submerged yearnings in me for my own original ties.
You will not hear them spewing dogma, sound argument or
friendly persuasion; you will mostly hear them speak of their
feelings for one another. They are so alike in looks and manner
that frequently they appear to be siblings rather than lovers,
pups from the same litter. Similarly gentle in spirit, of discriminating intelligence, and with the same evenly white, un-
blemished skin that used to be romanticized as "alabaster."
When first I saw them I was reminded of the cliché about
people married a long time who so meld together that they do
indeed come to resemble their spouses. The connotations have
always been fiercely negative to me, speaking to that ingrown,
intermeshed surrender of identity that characterizes so many
marriages. With Sara, Karen and Lloyd, my sense of their
likeness was an oddly mystical one—that they were no less than
predetermined soulmates.

It could be Peyton Place, the small-town stucco plain on
which they live. Tupperware Country. Their rented, one-story

house sits on an elm-rimmed, dead-end street, a few blocks from Adelphi University, and so their neighbors are mostly young married students with children.

The most arresting feature of their living quarters is the way they have divided the space and what that signifies about them: There is just one bedroom but, as they all work at home, three separate office areas; as far as this trinity is concerned, sovereign space is required for work only. Their personal dominion consists of one king-sized bed, three unmatched dressers, a single big closet. And one bathroom bulging with tiny bottles. Crowded bathrooms always arouse the same choking concern in me, and I ask if they feel no claustrophobia. They do not. "But I certainly would if I didn't have my own room to work in," says Sara, the perennial student. "I need a ballroom to ramble around in when I'm studying or reading or writing." But not for sleeping or love-making or solitary private pursuits. No doors need be shut there against invasion. It is still a mystery to me.

They do look like they might be fraternal triplets. Sara and Karen are the same age, twenty-eight, of medium height, slender and small-breasted, bodies that are just a shade schoolmarmish. Their faces are pretty and pleasantly unglamorous. In high school each would have been attractive enough to make baton twirler but probably not cheerleader. The hair is austere brown—Karen's long and turned under, Sara's short and squared off at the neck. Their voices are so interchangeable—soft and high-pitched—that it is difficult to transcribe tapes and know who said what.

And their man Lloyd, thirty-three, is the male physical counterpart, except for the voice in its high-bred English accent. All three have exceptionally large, hazel eyes.

Professionally, they work on different branches of the same tree—child psychology. With a Master's in Counseling Psychology, Lloyd works with emotionally disturbed children;

Karen teaches in an alternative school and Sara, a Master's in Child Psychology, is writing, studying and "exploring." The grand master plan, one which consumes many reverie-hours for them, is to build their careers together someday. The huge dream is to have their own school.

They speak in the vocabulary and syntax of the Human Potential Movement, like so many citizens in this alternate-lifestyle sphere. That is, their communication is always staunchly personal, never abstract or cerebral, and by its nature implies an invitation to anybody in the room to uncork the dustiest of our own layered secrets. Creatures like these are generous or tolerant or—unlikely though it seems—genuinely concerned with even a stranger's ruminations, as long as they are "personal" and not theoretical. They would, I surmise, be delighted with Einstein so long as he expectorated his feelings; the instant he told them about this terrific new theory he was putting together, they'd yawn and look to the horizon.

Sara and Karen met in the summer of 1970 in a graduate psychology class at Adelphi. Recognizing the uncanny physical resemblance they bore, as well as some of the other parallels, they hit it off immediately. Both were twenty-three at the time, both had been married for five years, both wanted to be child therapists. They were Mahler and Agatha Christie freaks, loved to ski and backpack. The only difference of any consequence that they could find, in fact, was the quality of their respective marriages—Sara's to Lloyd was growing firmer all the time, Karen was on the edge of divorce.

Lloyd was in the class too, but Karen barely noticed him. For one thing he is quiet, nonintrusive, slow to speak. For another, "He was my girlfriend's husband, you know, and I just sort of ignored him. I spoke to Sara about everything I was going through with my marriage in the last rough days, but I'm not even sure I spoke to Lloyd at all, about anything, that whole summer. I remember one night a group of us went out drinking beer after class, and when we parted Lloyd gave me this long embrace and a heavy gaze into my eyes and I was just amazed. I hardly knew he existed at that point."

More about that hug later, a hug which for Lloyd was no less than an apocalypse.

In October Karen left her husband. She found an apartment about six blocks from the campus, ten from the Jamisons. One day she showed up on their doorstep and announced, somewhat shakily, "Hey, guess what, gang! I left!" And quickly they adopted her, became her surrogate family, nursed and stroked her. "They were my primary people to relate to," she says, "because all of my other friends were rather angry that I'd left my husband for the reasons I had, which were kind of esoteric reasons."

"What were these 'esoteric reasons'?" I ask, recalling a friend who dissolved her marriage because, after four years of committed joint vegetarianism, her husband went back to eating meat.

"We just had a conflicting value system," she answers dryly. "He was an up-and-coming executive, an engineer, a real comer, and I couldn't support what he was going. It wasn't that I actively resented it, I just wasn't interested in it."

On her own for the first time, Karen was both frightened and exhilarated. The Jamison house became her cradle and her sanctuary, the place where she took new boyfriends to test if they passed muster, and where she spent lazy Sunday nights over spaghetti and *The New York Times.* People in the single state often find such a warm nest, the chicken soup for an otherwise unsettling existence. There are few arrangements more soothing, less threatening, after a wrench such as Karen's.

But, as she became closer to Sara, she continued to obliterate Lloyd from her line of vision. "All I knew was that he made me uncomfortable. Several months went by during which I was getting these weird messages from him. He seemed to be showing too much interest, playing games with me, but never being direct. He meant nothing to me, and I sure didn't want anything which would jeopardize my friendship with Sara. Besides, in my heart I was a totally monogamous person. I'd been in a monogamous marriage and I knew someday that would be what I would have again. So Lloyd's presence just seemed to throw my head into a spin."

Small wonder. Lloyd, during those months, had fallen in love with Karen.

It had surfaced for him that night after class, at the bar. "We'd known Karen for about six weeks," he recalls. "I liked her, felt good about the thing she and Sara were developing. When we all left to go home, I spontaneously reached out to hug her. And it was the closest I'd ever come to experiencing bells and stars and rainbows. All of a sudden it was like this rush of feeling and I just did not want to let go of her. I wanted much more. It scared the shit out of me."

So those months moved on, months of Lloyd's all-enveloping fixation. "It was like being fifteen years old again and having a first crush on a girl, and you're afraid to tell her. Karen would come to the house—she was Sara's buddy, she was going through these upheavals in her life—and all the time I was absorbed in feeling all manner of things I couldn't even put names to. I just knew that every time I'd get near her I'd come unglued."

He never revealed any of it to Karen. He did, however, to Sara. To his wife he babbled interminably. Sara says, "We'd go somewhere with Karen and afterward he'd just rant on and on about her. At first it was fine with me, but then I realized I was an outlet for all the tension he was feeling, tension he was able to reduce by pouring it out to me. I told him he *had* to tell her what was going on. All the blah-blah-blah was just making him relaxed enough so he wouldn't have to confront her."

—Weren't you endangered by his feelings for her?

"No, I wasn't. The one clear thing was that I really valued

my tie with Karen, and I wasn't going to allow him to interfere with that. That's why I wanted him dealing with her face to face."

—No competition, rejection, no fear of losing?

"Really not," Sara says. "I liked Karen so much it was nice to think that Lloyd felt that way too. And, you know, the possibility of greater contact, of really bringing her into the house, was appealing to me. What wasn't appealing was to think that Lloyd might screw things up by playing silly games. And I was damned if *I* was going to talk to her for him."

Back two steps. How is it that Sara was so dispassionate, did not suffer as most people would, as I think *I* would, in such an imbroglio? I would be comatose, how could it be that she was as composed as a Revlon model?

The answer to that may lie in the fact that she and Lloyd had been sweethearts since childhood and married since she was nineteen. Maybe that allows for insurance, or at least the absence of a turmoiled history that makes many of us so wary and frail. Or it may be from their years at Boston University —Robert Rimmer territory. Late-night bull sessions on the ever-popular theme: What Do I Want from Life? In my college era, late 1950's, the axis of those dialogues turned on issues of Contributing to Mankind, Denying Materialism, Refusing to Become Marjorie Morningstar. We never thought to question Monogamy.

Lloyd, Sara and compatriots, mid-1960's, read *The Harrad Experiment, The Rebellion of Yale Marratt,* and sprawled on the floor in their Cambridge apartment eating grass brownies and examining Lifestyle and Relationship. "I didn't know what I wanted," Lloyd remembers, "but what I didn't want was a White, Anglo-Saxon, middle-class kind of married life with kids, driving to work day after day on the same highway. No way did I want that kind of routine.

"I think what those books did for me was to say, 'Hey, there's another way to go.' Not only didn't I know anybody who was into open marriage, I never knew it *really* existed. I just knew six people who had read Rimmer and sat around pondering if we could all live together. It was all very cheerful and safe. So Sara and I would speculate: 'What happens if I meet another woman I really get excited by? Or if you find a guy?' But it was all up in the head, a game. Nothing became a reality until years later when I met Karen."

Sara was more specifically dissatisfied with the topography of her standard marriage than was Lloyd. People treated her differently the moment she was somebody's "wife." They put her into a box with a label—and with all the restrictions boxing imposes. "I knew I didn't intend for our worlds to revolve around each other. When we lived together we had lots of outside friends, but then as soon as we got married, those same friends started acting as if I had suddenly become less interesting and valuable. In their pictures, wives were less interesting and valuable. And my male friends started to disappear, as if they could no longer have any connection with me in any way. I was very, very angry about that. I'd blame Lloyd, make him responsible for isolating me. I hated my life shrinking so."

Christmas of 1970, six months after Lloyd and Sara met Karen. It was then that what was originally philosophy, fantasy, ideas and imagination, became real and tested. Karen popped in one night to see Sara, who happened to be skiing in Vermont for the weekend. Lloyd drew in a long breath, and exhaled everything. How he felt about her, what he'd been putting himself and Sara through, what he thought he wanted.

Karen's first words: "Jesus Christ! Let me the fuck out of here!" What Lloyd wanted and proposed was for the three of them to be architects of a new relationship, a new form that would be whatever together they chose it to be. "It was not simply me bringing another woman in," Lloyd maintains. "My idea was that we'd each let everybody know where we stood and we'd create the thing from that. If what the three of us wanted was for Sara and me to be married and Karen to be a good pal, then that's what it would be. If what we all wanted was for me to swing with Karen and for Sara to find some other dude, then it would be that."

"It was really a gigantic risk," Sara says. "Not to have any expectations of what would finally be born. Or not to know if experimenting would splinter all of us apart permanently."

While Lloyd was exposing his hidden life, Karen was in shock. As much by the feelings being unleashed in her as by his words. In minutes she flew from ostensible indifference to mighty caring.

How often it happens that we believe we're in correspondence with ourselves, that we know the contents of our caverns, then suddenly a searchlight moves in, illuminates the blackness and what is there is not what we thought at all. It is sometimes awesome to greet the stranger in oneself.

"I realized for the first time how sensitive and vulnerable he was," Karen says. "He was almost in tears as we talked, and I guess his pain opened me up from all this denying and dismissing I'd been doing for six months. I started to feel waves of love for him. I was frightened, but after my first response I just listened to his words and I knew I wanted desperately to talk to Sara."

Lloyd, too, was fearful, after all this time of locked-up, safe speculation, conversations existing only between him and him. Then focusing on Sara, his wife, the only woman he'd ever been connected to, the ramifications buzzed through his mind like random electrical charges. Can I really trust that Sara won't leave me? How do I know that if I really try to include Karen, Sara will be able to handle it? Am I risking throwing away everything?

One possibility that was never an option for him, never even crossed his mind, was that he might feel compelled to choose between the two women. "That was never my intention, nor did the thought ever occur to me," he says firmly. "I didn't go into a relationship with Karen to get away from something with

Sara." Their long coalition was increasingly nurturing and communicative, grounded in trust. "We had bumps and grinds but nothing that we didn't eventually work out. There were never big secrets between us, or covert goings-on. If I hadn't had something solid and viable with Sara we all wouldn't be sitting here right now. Karen would have become the dull way out."

"Just in passing," Karen interrupts. "I think that anybody who goes into something like this as a way of solving a problem is nuts." We all nod agreement. The Fourth Commandment of Multiple Relationships. "To me it's no different than people who get married to solve problems, buy houses, have kids. 'Listen, we've got a lousy marriage, let's have two kids, that'll change things, or let's buy a new car, let's get another person in, that'll *certainly* do it.' That sort of thinking is devastating."

Lloyd's declaration was followed by an exploratory period of nine months before Karen moved in. The trio began to stretch, to congeal, to create a new organism. Luckily they are folks who dig probing, otherwise they'd undoubtedly have wearied each other to death. But, instead, this complex tapestry came to be, to unfold a rich new life and a tale of its own. One vital ingredient was missing in the early stages: For a long time Lloyd and Karen did not go to bed.

How is it that sex is sometimes so offhand a commodity and at other times so loaded and burdened down with seriousness? We pass through each other's beds and bodies, we rampant sexual libertines, like shoppers strolling down the aisles in the supermarket, grabbing off a can of this, a jar of that, mostly by rote. But then, on occasion, we make screwing so mountainous a thing, it paralyzes us with its very significance. So it was that these two potential lovers, two-thirds of a blossoming consort, rebels with a cause, could spend weeks picking through every infinitesimal niche of their psyches and evade the most obvious frontier for investigation.

Ultimately, of course, they did the deed. On a night when Sara was in class and Lloyd walked the few blocks to Karen's apartment. "It was like a courtship," he says shyly. "We made love finally, and no sooner was it over than both of us said hysterically, virtually in unison: 'What the hell are we going to tell Sara?' And again, for me, it was another crisis. Okay, so Sara's been able to tolerate me being affectionate with another woman, how is she going to stand me actually being sexual with Karen? Karen and I mumbled back and forth and just then the door opened up and it was Sara, as if on cue. She knew intuitively I was at Karen's, what we'd done, and she came right over."

"Were you carrying the sawed-off shotgun?" I ask Sara.

"Oh, God, I was so *relieved*. I felt like something had finally been resolved, and now we could get on with this relationship."

For those of us having trouble with Sara's cavalier position in all of this, a bit of background to illumine, if not thoroughly enlighten. She is from a little town in Maine, an unusual community where families are of the archaic extended type, where kids travel in clans from earliest childhood on through high school, and where the American urgency for pairing from the cradle does not govern. "I ran into my first trouble in college, when I'd be dating guys that girlfriends of mine were also dating, and I found out this wasn't acceptable to them. Everybody seemed to have mind-sets toward exclusivity and I never did. I know it's hard for me to identify with jealousy."

By the end of her freshman year Sara was nestled into an apartment with Lloyd, monogamously. So she never had the life experiences of rivalry, betrayal, hands-off-my-man, being left for the new girl in town—that leaden baggage most of us tote through our lives.

But family backgrounds don't necessarily provide us with explanations or even clues to one's later choices. Sara's parents have each been divorced twice, having separated from each other the day after she and Lloyd married; her only brother is also divorced. Karen's family, on the contrary, are religious West Virginia cops, with nary a kink in two hundred years.

During the early and difficult stages of their merger Karen
was seriously involved with another man, causing her no small
quantity of head-swirling. Trying to bring him into her new
life, she hoped a quartet would evolve from the mix, but he
wanted no part of the Jamisons. In fact, for all the months of
overlap he pretended they didn't exist—as if Karen were having a short-lived fling with the tennis instructor who would
vanish when the snows came. Instead, Karen shut the door on
him. "I made the commitment I'd been making all the way
along. It became clear to me that this is really where I wanted
to be. This is where the love was."

Now when I meet them, it is four years later. They are like
some married couples I have known, at that point in their story
when they are beyond the initial agony of adaptation, the
struggle for or resistance to commitment, but haven't moved
yet onto a plateau of tedium or accumulated angers. Couples
who are so comfortable yet so alive with each other that they
are delicious and restful to be with. The saviors you run to
when your own life isn't up for an Oscar.

The good will spreading through the Jamison household is
like Thanksgiving Day at Grandma's. They know each other
so well, are so tuned in, that they finish anyone else's thoughts
or sentences. Lloyd comments naturally on the irregularity of
Karen's menstrual cycles ("every ninety days or so"), Karen
speaks on Sara's shampooing regime, Karen tells me all about
Lloyd's Welsh cabinetmaker father, whom she has never met.
Whereas they argue all the time, without stop—guys "into
feelings" do that, you know—the arguments never seem to
hold rancor, cruelty, what somebody called "killer talk." They
are but part of the communications game.

Fierce work went into this meshing, surely more than in the
usual duet. Deliberate, repeated battling with the tigers of
dependence, independence, interdependence, fluctuating
from one condition to another, fighting to find a harmony.

Their essential problems, they say, are set in three categories, all diminishing as the years together speed on.

The first was Karen's sense of exclusion, her newness pitted against the Jamisons' long past. Names were dropped that she had never heard, families and friends entered that she had never met, liver prepared for dinner when she loathed liver.

For Lloyd the difficulties were sexual, the questions not surprising: Am I obligated to do it with her if I just did it with the other? How many times? What positions? What if Karen is sending out signals but I've only got eyes for Sara? The internal pressure to maintain high sexual recuperative powers made him practically dysfunctional for a time.

Least yielding to solution has been the continuing quandary of third-person omission. Common in most triads, the roots are usually sexual. So, it may startle you to learn that in the Jamison ménage the aggrieved party in this, their most raging conflict, has been Lloyd.

It is he who experiences crushing jolts of being left out, sensing in his two women a special rapport that often seems like a solid front which he cannot penetrate. "They talk in code," Lloyd says testily. "The other day I met them at a Japanese restaurant in Manhattan before we went to the ballet. They had been there for a while, talking heatedly, and I didn't understand a bloody word they were saying. I said, 'What's the *it* you're talking about, who's the *they?*'. . . When this happens, as it does a lot, it sounds to me like they're speaking gibberish."

Karen, in the basic therapeutic inquisition, asks, "How does that make you feel?" Lloyd: "Resentful, sometimes." Karen: "And abandoned sometimes?" Lloyd: "Bullshit, *sometimes. Always.*"

Sara says, in a tone mingling pleasure and vague guilt: "It's true Karen and I don't even use words sometimes, and we seem to relate to each other in a way that Lloyd will never be able to do." Lloyd interrupts her thought, turns away and addresses me: "I get furious when they congratulate themselves on this 'special' sensitivity they have." His co-spouses are stunned by these emotion-filled revelations from Lloyd. With all their self-searching and feeling-spieling, he had never before confided this gnawing state.

Sara and Karen are not sexually involved, only with Lloyd. Triangular lovemaking happens occasionally, always impulsively—a planned adventure is still too scary to contemplate. The women say they are relaxed with each other "sensually," by which they mean they can caress, touch—whatever—as opposed to actual genital sex. Karen views the matter as pure cultural conditioning. "God damn, you know, I've had years of socialization. I've grown up in a culture that says something is basically wrong with me if I find it pleasurable to even touch Sara. I do; she's a soft, warm person and I love her very, very much. But the breaking down of those rules without doing tremendous damage to my sexuality has been really difficult. I like being close to Sara, she feels different from Lloyd and that's very nice. But I'm a heterosexual person basically, and I need to have a man, physically. I wish I understood the differences better."

I remember an episode from my own life, which I repeat to them. Several years ago, at one of Steve Meyer's naked encounter-group hoopdedoos in Miami, we were doing some sort of hugging exercise with other groupies of the same sex. My partner was a young woman, large and large-breasted. We lay side by side on the floor holding each other very close—My, my, I wish I could remember the purpose of that sport!—and the emotion that came over me was remarkable. I'd never been in nude closeness with a woman before, and I can best describe it as a sense that I was holding myself. She was soft and round like me, and I kept thinking, Oh, so this is what I feel like, this is what a man feels when he embraces me. The familiarity of it, or the sameness, was not arousing to me but very, very soothing.

They talk of incorporating another man into the mix. It is

Lloyd who craves it, and the hunger must surely relate to his sense of being "other." Oddly, he is freer-thinking to investigate homosexuality than Sara and Karen.

At the same time, monogamy rules in the Jamison kingdom. In four years, nobody has strayed. Not that they are opposed to sexual liberty, or have a statute about it on the books. In contrast to the average American twosome, who would be morally outraged by the Jamison household, the Jamisons actually *practice* fidelity. Sara says it best. "My intimacy here is at a very deep, energy-emitting level. And so far I just don't have it for sixteen other people, or even for one other." The freedom is there, the desire absent.

I have commented to the trio that I find it curious, even contradictory, that they are monogamous ("biogamous" is the correct word for it in these circles). I don't really, but once again I'm playing devil's advocate. Karen, in response, turns to me sharply. "There's something you're obviously missing. I've been very attracted to men. But I am never outside of this relationship—I don't see myself as a separate entity out there. If I find a man I really like, my first reaction is to bring him home. See, I *am* my relationship. I carry the love, the support, the caring outside, and I know I'm not going to find anybody more out there. But maybe what I find out there can broaden, enlarge us here."

Several men have entered the sanctuary, none have stayed. One man, a friend of Sara's, was hanging around for some months, sniffing them out while he was being sniffed. He left abruptly. Is it the unorthodox configuration that is perplexing to potential joiners—the unknown, unconventional, untried? Or, deeper, is it the very nature of their synergy, that which struck me at times as incestuous, a tighter rope than mere man and wife?

"I can't imagine a relationship with Lloyd without Sara in it," says Karen lightly, and my head swivels in disbelief. Well, on short second thought, that could be logical. Sara was her first and primary kin, and she has never known Lloyd apart from Sara. For Karen, her triad has been the only unit, now after four years erected on its own particular foundations. What is quite strange to me is that Lloyd and Sara—together for a decade—are unsure whether, should Karen leave, their relationship could continue. "It would be very hard," says Sara quietly, "to let go of the intertwining between us, the background, the 'history' we now have, and to go backward. I think it would feel empty." Lloyd says: "When I think of being without either Sara or Karen, I think in terms of being without both of them."

I'm fascinated by this tidbit; my mind returns to it from time to time, as to some delectable unsolved mystery. It certainly speaks to the truth that a relationship is not just two individuals or even the combination thereof. But instead becomes a third, totally new *thing*—like a newborn child— with elements of the parents, but acquiring a life and essence and substance of its own. To scramble the pieces of the Jamison admixture, or to change the fittings, may alter the chemistry irrevocably.

I check back with Sara, Karen and Lloyd a year or so after our first meeting and find that dazzling shifts have occurred. They have just returned from a summer trip to India, with funny stories of trying to get hotel rooms for three in Calcutta. Lloyd and Sara have divorced, she has reverted to her maiden name, and he has married Karen. Sara was maid of honor at the sunrise wedding on the sands of Jones Beach. No omens or dire implications in these events. They have done it first for tax reasons—Karen has the biggest income and was getting hit badly as a single woman—and secondarily as a ritual affirmation of their pledge of unity. Sara and Karen have started a weekly women's consciousness-raising group, and Lloyd is feeling even nuttier on the subject of his exclusion. The three are co-writing a book on child psychology.

Well, most important news: Both women have recently ceased using contraception, and Lloyd is currently reveling in his grandiose new role as Johnny Appleseed. Whoever gets pregnant first, the other will retreat to the pill. These uncommon logistics have been engineered because nobody cares about maternity per se, they just know—as a family—it is time to have a child, and destiny will handle the details. No, it isn't exactly that nobody cares, but rather that both women *know* that they will each be the child's mother.

It is merely a question of who gets to have the belly and buy the new wardrobe.

VIII

Dorothy and Charles Barron

In the winter of 1975 Dorothy Barron fell in love. Vehemently, grandly, preposterously. Like an adolescent for the first time, or like Madame Butterfly. Teenagers, movie stars and other true believers are being struck by such global passion every instant, even as you read this, all over America. The only reason that Dorothy's case may be of special interest is that at the moment she catapulted she was fifty-eight years old, a grandmother, a very solidly, contentedly married woman. A woman with a richly woven life that others coveted. A recognized painter, talented cellist, maker of jewelry—all rewarding hobbies—and, professionally, one of the most respected psychotherapists to be found around San Francisco. Her husband, Charles Barron, sixty, is also a therapist, so that among other deep and lasting bonds they share one as meaningful as the creation of children: They work together, in teamwork that nourishes each and both of them daily.

Their Mill Valley home is usually full of friends—many are patients as well—music, wine, liberal politics and growth groups; their pool is kept, year round, at 95 degrees for midnight naked swims, and their land is high enough to spot the ocean. They are beautiful looking, healthy, vibrant, younger than springtime. They adore each other and have an unquestionably triumphant marriage; indeed they are paradigms to their friends. The Barrons bear the fruits of lives well-lived and learned from. Lives to be envied. "I want what you have. Everything. Exactly." I once overheard a patient say that to Dorothy. I have felt it myself from time to time.

Then Dorothy, at fifty-eight, in the prime of her days, fell in love, like she had never been in love before, as if it were the very first time.

The Barrons' marriage is not merely—merely!—an open one; it sits right up there with the fistful of really gorgeous and inspiring relationships I've ever seen. They reside in an elegant state of grace, a state of commitment, respect and freedom that is rare in any couple after sixteen years together—and almost nonexistent when they have hang-glided over as many cliffs as the Barrons. Air pockets and current changes that have wrecked other families have only tightened Charles and Dorothy. They veered from conventional to open marriage seven years ago, before the O'Neills gave a name to what they were doing. Like Steve and Pat Meyer they had no models, no *Gray's Anatomy,* and that they persisted is one of the heartening signs of our times.

Their success may explain why a large portion of their joint career is dedicated to helping other twosomes who wish to make the broad jump. It may be, too, why they personally view nonmonogamy as a supreme state. At the same time they never seek converts to the cause; they know this business is anything but a frisky romp in the old swimming hole.

I have known the Barrons for three years, known about them for somewhat longer. Charles' reputation preceded him: swinger, purveyor of free sex, fanny grabber. It was said of him that a casual hello kiss from Charles was veritable foreplay; it was also rumored that he promoted orgies in his home and slept with his patients. That he was Rasputin-looking—black-gray curly mane and rabbinical beard, the piercing-eyed sensual Semitic analyst—certainly didn't subtract from his image. Charles was your new order of West Coast shrink, cloned from the old-fashioned '30's Jewish middle-class radical and the California sunlit hedonist. But the most curious aspect of Charles and his naughty "rep" was that nobody I knew had ever known anybody who'd actually had an in-the-flesh affair with him. Before meeting him, I began to think he was an example of American press agentry in action.

Dorothy is my good friend, sister, mother, playmate, sporadic shrink. I found my way to her office a few years ago while commuting to the Bay Area and while caught in the center of a cyclone: A previously described love affair attempting to be open, but instead being slowly mangled by pummeling, blasting winds that we could not control. I had heard that Dorothy was the best female therapist in the city, that her specialty was man/woman maelstrom and open relationships. Over the next six months, while I floundered and suffered and raged—wanting only to chain my love to the bedpost or, better yet, to surgically graft him onto my side, a six-month period when the word "freedom" carried for me the same connotations as the word "leprosy," Dorothy spoke to me at length about her own marriage. What it was in the early divisive years, how it had metamorphosed, how warmly satisfying her union with Charles, how marvelous the rewards of this new way of loving. "If you two can come through this trying time," she said often, with compassion, "you can have a finer relationship than you've ever imagined."

I believed her. It made good sense, I knew she was right. She herself was the perfect flagbearer; in her mid-fifties, she was vividly sexy, a pixie Simone Signoret, a loving and generous earth spirit whom every man I knew, regardless of age, wanted to go to bed with. There was nothing old or dry or brittle about Dorothy, no sense that the best had already gone and little was left but waiting. That, for me, was the most seductive part of her open-relationship rap. Her own aliveness. For me to get to where she was, I thought, I just needed to have a face-off with all the myths I'd grown up with, fairy tales of fidelity and togetherness, impossible idealized expectations, self-defeating old notions like if-he-wants-to-fuck-somebody-else-it-means-I'm-nothing. I needed to penetrate to the inner sanctum of jealousy and dissolve its power. I had to learn that my survival was not really tied up with my man.

My head was sure, decisive. My intestines were being chewed away with fright and grief. That particular battle was not won by my logic, it was rather the spiraling ring of pain that eventually triumphed and led me to flee. I could not, then, be Dorothy.

But Dorothy, in 1975, fell in love. The outburst of it made for the baldest challenge her relationship with Charles had faced in its sixteen years. Oh, she'd been enamored, infatuated before; this was different, heavy, heavier than anything. That the Barrons endured, no—not just endured but grew closer— has to be testimony to the viability of an open marriage. There is simply no other way to look at it.

If Charles is the prototypical libertine sybarite, Dorothy is the nineteenth-century romantic heroine. With rare exception, all the connections of her life have been of the volcanic, *Weltschmerz* variety. "Show me something intense," she chides herself, during the first of our many interviews for this book, "and I can't get to it fast enough. When I met Gordon I was ready for this kind of love affair, one that was potentially more serious than I'd ever had," she admits. "I have some soul needs that aren't filled by Charles, never have been."

—What are they, what is the something missing with Charles?

"It's in the general area of poetry, turbulence, high drama," she tells me, self-mocking a bit, but not harshly. She knows herself well, and is kind to her foibles.

"That's true," says Charles, who during this candid dis-course is sitting right next to his wife—while she speaks easily of what's lacking between them. "I don't have this ardent romantic drive that she does, I never have had. She and Gor-don are both grand opera types, which is certainly one of the reasons they fell so madly in love."

We are lounging on carpeted platforms in Charles' office. Dorothy's office is next door, connecting entrances yet quite separate. Like their relationship. Both rooms are designed for group therapy sessions, with varying levels of platforms covered in thick carpeting, one or two comfortable chairs, several big batik pillows. Hers is quiet off-white, paintings and pieces of sculpture scattered around. Charles' is in lush earth tones, flamboyant and Mexican. I can see the San Francisco Bay and Alcatraz from their windows.

I've been given permission, by Dorothy, to say or ask any-thing in front of Charles. There are no secrets or evasions between them. She has just returned, a few hours ago, from a weekend with Gordon, and her spirits are so fevered that the words will hardly come without accompanying tears. She has never felt this deeply for a man but she will not minimize it for Charles' benefit. That is not their contract. Dorothy shares this affair with Charles as if he were her best girlfriend. I've never witnessed such frankness between partners, and for most of this interview I squirm. When Dorothy rhapsodizes of her sexual fire with Gordon, of his infinite erective abilities, I want to slither from the room, with embarassment for what I assume to be Charles' distress. Soon I realize these are my bugaboos alone. I've seen couples who employ "honesty" as one of the more deadly strategies of modern warfare ("But you told me you wanted me to be open and authentic, darling . . ."). But Charles and Dorothy do not play a sadistic game, I notice. Tender consideration stands beside the truth, and they are always sensitive to the other's threshhold. It's that their thresh-holds are not like most of ours. So it's only I who writhe.

•   •   •

Dorothy met Gordon at an educational psychologists' conference in Los Angeles. A guidance counselor, physicist and academician, he was conducting a workshop in existential psychology, which she attended and found to be the only vital event of an otherwise arid weekend, and his the only mind that sparked her. After his seminar they talked for hours with an instantaneous and exploding rapport; they agreed totally on ideas of psychotherapy, on ardor for political radicalism (Dorothy had once been active in the movement to free Morton Sobell, convicted conspirator in the Rosenberg case), on love of Chopin. He electrified her mind, she hadn't found such a sympatico brain-mate in five, maybe ten years. But she wasn't attracted to him. Gordon, also fifty-eight, was physically nondescript, and Dorothy had an incontestable history of heroic-looking men. Gordon was short. "I never liked short men," she says. "I remember thinking, that morning, 'It's too bad I'm not attracted to him, he's so exciting.' And then, later, when I became sexually interested in him because I liked him so, thinking, 'He looks like he's not very good in bed.' "

Gordon had been married for eight years to Laura, second marriages for both. Since neither wanted to be locked into the monogamy that had ruled their previous marriages, they had the license to make outside alliances. Yet so far neither had done anything beyond occasional fleeting encounters; they were well content with each other. Laura was present at the conference, then in the workshop where Dorothy first connected with her husband and, later that night, at the party where Gordon told Dorothy that he was sure he loved her.

I happened to have lunch with Dorothy in San Francisco two days after she returned from that life-shaking weekend. She told me she had met a man and suspected, from the bolts of lightning between them that this was going to be a significant chapter in her life. I believed her and was worried. What would happen to her marriage? To Charles?

This was evidently not to be a cute dalliance, this was *lightning*. I told her my concern but she shared none of it. "I told Charles all about Gordon and he seems to feel fine. He said he was delighted for me—it's so rare to find someone you connect with like that—and he encouraged me to pursue it. I don't know when I'll see Gordon, it may not be for months, and as far as I can see Charles has nothing to be threatened about."

It is usually not possible for me to identify with Charles' tranquility, to fathom his strength—if you will. Or composure, at least. I spoke with him often over the next eight months, as this extravaganza grew daily, and for the most part he seemed placid. Charles is a very intellectual man, reminiscent of Bud DeLeon, and he is ruled more so than many of us by his precepts and principles. One of the core principles of his life is sexual freedom. He believes in it as others believe in God or Jogging.

There is that to explain his sanity in the face of a situation that would provoke madness in most of us. Then too, there is the commitment that Charles and Dorothy made to each other, years ago when they opened up their marriage, to remain together for life.

Nonetheless we, their friends, worried about the Barrons and whether they could withstand the onslaught of Dorothy's affair. In June, at the height of a tempest that made Héloïse and Abelard look like a marriage of convenience, the phone lines from Berkeley to Big Sur buzzed with anxious fretting. "What will happen if Dorothy's *folie* continues?" we asked. "Poor Charles, how he must be suffering." "Poor Dorothy, she's so swept up in this thing." Everybody in the Barrons' *haute bourgeoisie* orbit became engaged in this production number. The whole question of open marriage was suddenly up for grabs. If the Barrons fell apart, who the hell could stay adhered? If *their* nonmonogamy tumbled, well—my God, it meant this whole experiment of which they were the gurus was a crashing failure, an impossibility, a crock of shit. Dorothy's affair echoed through the Bay Area Human Potential community like a hot stock tip moving through Wall Street. We watched it daily for signs of zooming or hints of a sharp drop. We needed to protect our own investments.

Dorothy was forty-two when she met Charles at a party. Divorced for eight years, her two daughters grown and about to leave the nest, Dorothy had sensed for some months that she was ready to get married again. She recalls that when she spied Charles across the dining table, knowing nothing about him except that he was some local hotstuff psychologist, seeing only a tawny leather jacket and a forest of black curls on his head and face, she knew he would be her husband. As she got ready for their first date, two weeks later, she found herself muttering to the mirror, "Mrs. Dr. Charles Mitchell Barron," as one used to do in high school. Dorothy—a woman of great steadiness in most departments—has always been your total marshmallow in matters of the heart; it is one of her most endearing features.

On this first date Charles announced firmly that he did not want to be seriously involved at this time, with her or anybody else. He had had some wrenchings in his history, including the recent demise of a long live-in association, and he was skittish. Moreover, he informed her, he most certainly did not subscribe to or practice sexual exclusivity. After this staunch declaration of independence, he kissed her good night at her door and announced, "I'll call you tomorrow." For the next three and a half years they saw each other almost every day until after prodding, jousting and maneuvering, he permitted himself to be "dragged with classic male reluctance to the altar."

Their relationship, for the years prior to marriage and for five years after (until they opened it) was rooted in the Big Lie. The lie of pretended fidelity that underpins the majority of orthodox American marriages. Don't misunderstand. On the surface and for three inches beneath, it was blooming. A charming apartment on a mountainside in Sausalito, interests in common, loving friends and good dinners and fine sex. Dorothy ran through a stew of careers, from managing a gynecologist's office to catering parties; Charles disappeared every day to his cloistered analyst's tower. Their children were gone, they were free; the divine twosome, everybody loved to be in their atmosphere.

But the Big Lie poisons, corrodes, corrupts. Even if they were then unaware of why things were not exactly glorious between them, why intimacy was not running deep nor trust high, the answer is, in retrospect, obvious. Charles was and had always been screwing around, since the day they met. He had never ceased and had no intention to. Dorothy was faithful and believed that he was too, thinking his chatter and periodic rantings on the topic were mere bravado. The most basic communications gap of all. Even now, in the face of an openness between them that others might consider immoral, they are confused about the reality of those years.

Charles: "I've never been monogamous with anybody, oh, maybe for six months in my first marriage. But I've never had a mind-set that fidelity was an important thing. I always looked at it as a prison kind of agreement. It violated my own drives and my gut feelings that I'm attracted to a lot of women. But I always assumed that Dorothy knew. I thought we had an understanding that I had interests in other women and that since she didn't want an open marriage, it was okay for me to play around as long as she didn't know. Which is what I did, the whole time, whenever I had the opportunity."

Dorothy: "I thought you were faithful to me. I don't have any memory of an 'understanding' like that. When we were going together we saw each other all the time. And then all of a sudden, on an odd Wednesday, he wouldn't call and I wouldn't see him. That was very painful to me and we had a lot of fussing about it, but I didn't assume there were other women. I just thought he was trying to prove to himself that he wasn't attached to me. After we were married four or five years I began to wonder—he was away at 'meetings' so much. But, you see, I was this incredibly romantic person who needed to feel I was the one-and-only, the most important person in the world, and I just couldn't let myself accept the fact that he might be turned on to somebody else. Funny, now I can accept that easily—I *know* I'm the most important person in the world to him, and it has nothing at all to do with his attractions for other women."

Charles' position on monogamy is unequivocally negative. "I don't think it works for anybody, or ever has," he asserts. "I also think that the way it's practiced is utterly sexist—the stereotype of the woman playing a subordinate role, sticking close to the kitchen, the church and the kids, while the husband philanders secretly.

—Is there anything biological, innate, about a desire for a monogamous alliance?

Charles is adamant in his "No. I'm sure it's just a custom." Dorothy is more tempered, always, than he in her pronouncements about human behavior. "I think," she says, "that any framework that is supposed to fit for everybody simply can't work, because there are too many differences in people. For me, the way to live my life is for me to determine at any given moment what's right for me. And when society or tradition says 'This is the way to live,' it's impossible for us to be up to date with ourselves, existentially. As to whether monogamy is natural, I think there's a human impulse for many people to be attracted only to one person, involved with one at a time. What I observe with friends, myself and the people we work with in groups is that I may fall madly in love and be focused on one male *for a period of time* and then . . . It's not for ever and ever, sailing off into the sunset. It's never that."

Dorothy and Charles were married for five years when she found herself getting restless, depressed. "There seemed to be so much we weren't sharing, although ostensibly we shared everything. But we never really connected. There was a lyrical, poetic quality I wanted in a love affair that I'd never gotten from him. When I looked at Charles it was as if there was a veil over his face, and I couldn't tell what was underneath." This must have been, in part, an expression of the enormous untruth festering between them, the alienation and unsafety that must create. Charles remembers his state during those years with words whose harshness amaze me. "My life was a drag until we opened up our relationship. What was missing for me was the freedom to do what I was doing anyway, but without guilt or the fear of detection." Dorothy responds with a characteristic compassion: "I think what was missing was that there was so much of your life that you felt you couldn't share with me, and so there you were living in a marriage without having a marriage.

"For me," Dorothy continues, "the ultimate intolerable sin is lying. And I know that most married people do it and find it quite acceptable. People who would point their fingers at Charlie and me for not living in the expected way, respectably." Where would they be today, I ask, if they hadn't opened their marriage seven years ago? Dorothy answers without hesitation, "Divorced. I was getting bored and not realizing it and Charles was living a lie. We couldn't have gone on that way too much longer." No wonder she is fervent about non-monogamy; it has been the penicillin that saved them.

You will probably find some contradiction and irony in the following tale of the Barrons' plunge into open marriage. It contains some elements so illogical and puzzling that I have returned to the players three times for further elaboration. Follow closely. Humans will not be squeezed into molds of logic merely to simplify a plot.

Dorothy in those years, before launching her own demanding career as a therapist, dabbled in a scattering of activities, like many women with boundless energy who cannot take themselves very seriously. While working on an American Civil

Liberties Union committee she met a man, a composer from New York. "He came on very strong to me just at the right time when I needed a lot of loving and attention. We were arranging a benefit movie premiere and reception and decided not to get involved until after it was over. I followed my pattern, the same thing I'd done in my first marriage when I'd had a couple of affairs—I magnified them out of all proportion to justify my being unfaithful. I told myself they were grand passions, bigger than both of us, no way to resist. By the way, I think you're much more likely to lose your husband or wife in a conventional marriage, where the outside sex is hidden and you tend to make it more significant than it really is. And eventually you *have* to choose between your mate and lover.'

"The night of the premiere Paul, the composer, was there with his girlfriend, a gorgeous, lanky Swedish blonde. A bunch of us went out to dinner afterward and I felt Charlie was attracted to her. I put it out of my mind, and Paul and I started having an affair. I felt quite guilty and disappointed in myself, yet I needed it. I liked him, sex was pleasant, and for a while I concocted a lot of intensity, but when that wore off there was nothing else. Occasionally in bed he'd joke: 'You know, I think Charles and Pia are sleeping together,' and I'd say, 'Don't be ridiculous, Charles wouldn't do that to me.' A few months after I ended the thing with Paul—the spark had just completely died—we were having a Christmas party and I wanted to invite him and Pia. Charles just ranted. 'She's a drunk, why do you want her here?' I said, 'My, my, you seem to have a lot of energy for a girl you barely know,' and then I remembered Paul's jokes. I asked him if he was having an affair with her. It turned out to be a question that changed my whole life."

Charles takes over at this point. "When she asked me I thought she really wanted to know, that she was ready to hear —since she'd never, ever, brought up that subject in all the years we'd been together. I was dying to be unburdened from the secrecy and I simply said, 'Yes, I am.' "

Dorothy had not wanted to hear, of course, as none of us do when the answer is 'Yes, I am.' She was not ready to confront awful, stabbing truths, betrayals that had been going on for nine years, lies that had formed scar tissue on the ligaments of her marriage. But life, as it does, hurled her against itself. She asked Charles if there were others and he said yes, always, even while they were going together. He revealed everything and insisted he would not, could not, stop. As much as he loved her, to cut off his sexual interest in other women would be for him a living death.

"I went crazy, berserk, off-the-walls insane for ten solid days," Dorothy says. "I threatened divorce, mayhem, suicide, breakdown."

But, I point out—and this is where confusion overtakes— she had been having an affair too. How can she justify her indignation?

"I can't," she laughs now, light-years later. "I was just nuts. I wanted to play the hurt and injured wife and I probably enjoyed it immensely, on some level. I walked around in this lunatic state for days until my thirty-year-old daughter grabbed me by the arm and said, 'Mother, how can you rave on like this when you've been screwing Paul and Charles doesn't know anything about it?' Then I confessed to Charles, very sheepishly, as you can imagine. He thought it was hilarious and was relieved, although not pleased about whom I'd picked. 'How could you?' he said three times. 'My God, that guy looks arthritic.' It was my taste he was upset about. But I felt my entire world was crashing down on me."

There was no way to go back or recoup. Go back to what? Certainly not to deception, nor to a sexual fidelity that was San Quentin to Charles. The next six months were armed warfare for the Barrons. He pressed for an open marriage, she mostly thought about divorce or homicide.

Her first terrified attempt at the new way, a way Charles promised would liberate them both, turned out to be a nightmare. She agreed to go with him for dinner to the home of a woman he had been seeing for a year. "I was demolished on sight," says Dorothy. "She was twenty-five to my fifty, skinny, dark, creative. Her husband was out of town, and I managed to smile and choke my way through the chicken. Then I asked where the bathroom was and Charlie answered, automatically, 'It's down the hall and on your right, through the bedroom.' And I freaked out. 'I can't live this way,' I shrieked, and we left immediately. In the car going home I was wild. 'We're too different from each other, I can't take this. Let's just break up.' When we got home he wanted to make love and I bellowed some more. He literally raped me and it was incredible, I had orgasm after orgasm, the best sex we'd had in years. Charles and I saw her a few more times together, still trying for something, and the more she saw us the less she wanted to be involved with him. She was cheating on her husband and she thought Charles and I were really suited for each other and what was she doing there?

"How did you get over all the misery?" I ask. "How did you come to *love* having an open marriage?" Knowing where they are now, their security and serenity, their virtually limitless freedom, their glorification of this architecture, it is hard for me to imagine those stormy early stages. How can such grandiose reformations occur in the human psyche? Dorothy is the least possessive, least anxious person I've met on my entire journey. How did she get there?

"Therapy, lots of it, a lot of primal screaming, and the willingness for both of us to deal with everything that came to the surface—no matter how crazy or hurtful. I went through many months thinking I'd kill him or myself, and also sure that I'd lose him. Finally, when I began to quiet down, I looked rationally at all the alternatives and knew I wanted to stay with Charles. I confronted, with immense difficulty, every notion I had about faithfulness and one-and-only, all the stuff we've all grown up with. I took it apart and examined it, piece by piece.

I remember a friend once saying to me, 'Why are you getting so upset about his putting his penis into somebody's vagina?' That one question helped to reduce the whole issue to reasonable dimensions for me.

"Charles wanted me so much during those hellish months that I could have made him agree to any terms, I knew that. But I said to myself, 'Now that I know who he is, what would I have? A bird in a cage, trying to get out all the time.' I realized I simply had to accept him as he is. It was at that point that we started building."

"And it's been pure trial and error," Charles continues. "We've tried all kinds of agreements—like, you can only see other people when we can't be together, or we can only be involved in foursomes, or total looseness with no rules at all. We discuss everything and renegotiate whenever we need to. What I've found since we opened our marriage seven years ago is that I have much less desire to be with other women. I was able to relax as soon as we agreed upon the freedom. As long as it was forbidden I *had* to screw around to prove I was my own person." For Dorothy, too—at least until the advent of Gordon—the license was enough. "We've almost never chosen to spend time with someone else when we could be together. Our lives are so busy and full that we almost have to make an appointment to see each other."

Their viewpoints about sex are amongst the Barrons' widest disparities. "I'm interested in everything concerning sex," Charles says. "Casual sex, orgies. Long affairs or short. I think it's all positive and healthy." His ideas coincide with those of Wilhelm Reich on the body's requirement for orgasm in the maintenance of mental and physical well-being. Ideas that form the intellectual spirit for West Coast hedonism. In the East, citizens are still locked into mere mind; we bordering the Pacific live for the pleasure principle.

Not coincidentally, Charles has never become seriously entangled with another woman since he met Dorothy sixteen years ago; his need is for fleshly play, new and kinky invigoration.

She only falls in love. Oh, there has been the infrequent one-nighter but that is much more Charles' style than hers. Before Gordon—who was Dorothy's height of heights—there were two other prolonged kinships, both of the love letters/flowers/tragedy school. But once Dorothy made the gigantic adjustment to a new and sexually loose union, she was never again challenged by Charles' sporting life. "Because I get terribly involved with people and he doesn't," she reports, "I feel much more secure with him than he does me—now that I've been able to accept the truth of his sexuality, which is bigger and more driving than mine."

A few times in these years, very few times, the Barrons have fallen into group sex. I say "fallen" because as Dorothy describes these episodes each had the selfsame ingredients of their both being very high on wine, and the event being unpremeditated. In each case it was Charles and Dorothy together with another woman, always somebody she liked very much, twice very close friends. "They were very lovely experiences," she says, "but not something I feel free to do very often. It just has to sort of happen." She has reached the airy, incredible place where several times she has watched Charles make love to another woman and truly found it beautiful, even felt loving toward the female. But that cosmic cool has only evolved for her after years, after work, after reconditioning. "Early on I remember watching him once and I started pounding on him and the woman while they made love. I just died."

As open relationships go on over time, each experience seems to bring a diminishment in shock and torture until—the reports are universal—people *do* indeed become unruffled, delighted even in their mates' escapades. After he's had six affairs or nine orgies or you have watched him fucking your sister for the third time, the very marrow of jealousy, its seemingly impregnable power, subsides and even disappears. The Barrons, like many others, have conquered it for the most part. Through time, endurance and stalwart effort—and the repeated acknowledgment that involvement with others does not mean, as most of us assume, the loss of everything we treasure.

Witness Charles Barron during Dorothy's tempestuous merger with Gordon. We, their friends and backers, found far more danger than Charles. You could say (we did say it, naturally) that he was repressing, unable to deal. You could also say that while he admitted to twinges and stirrings and broke out in a skin rash at the onset of the affair which did not leave for many months, he knew something their friends and allies did not know. He knew their commitment was and would always be indestructible, a fortress that might be approached, entered but never demolished.

We should have had more confidence in that fortress. A month before Dorothy went to the conference at which she met Gordon was the Barrons' twelfth wedding anniversary. As celebration, they decided to get married again before all their friends and family, on the hillside next to their home. I flew north from Los Angeles for the occasion, a day- and night-long festival overflowing with love, dancing, food (everyone invited —eighty-five strong—contributed their favorite home-prepared dish) and a tidal wave of champagne. Dorothy wore her original twelve-year-old wedding dress ("one of the high points of the whole thing was that it still fit me"), and this golden couple reaffirmed their vows before us and each other. Vows that spoke not only of their long, growing connection and caring but of freedom and supporting each other's freedom and the commitment to be together for life. Even we weary cynics and tarnished romantics were moved. Not only to reflexive wedding tears but to some new peaks of optimism, maybe even courage.

Dorothy did not see Gordon for four months after their first meeting. But they spoke often on the phone, corresponded voluminously, exchanged cassette tapes of her cello playing and his random musings, sent their papers and poems and journals back and forth across the state. Although he lived in La Jolla, a hilly coast town north of San Diego, less than two hours' plane flight, there were good reasons they stayed physically apart. For one thing, they were wary of the fierceness of their attraction. Wary to carry it farther lest it overwhelm their lives, and on the opposite shore, afraid they might be disappointed and this luscious long-distance obsession disintegrate. High passion thrives on yearning and noncompletion. All true romantics know that what one wants is better than what one has —that after the first consummation something definitely is lost. Thus they try to prolong foreplay forever.

Then, too, it became impossible to get together. Two months after the conference Dorothy, during a routine gynecological checkup, found out she had cancer of the uterus. A hysterectomy was performed immediately and although the prognosis was excellent—the malignancy had been contained in two small tumors—the effect on Dorothy and Charles was stunning. Charles had lost his sister and mother through cancer and was terrified, frail; he said to me the morning of the surgery, pathetic and childlike, "Everyone I love gets cancer and dies."

Dorothy was as buoyant and philosophical as I have ever seen her, as worried about her husband's fear as her own life. The day following the operation I phoned her in the hospital to ask if there was anything she needed. "No. But I wish you would be willing to go and sleep with Charlie for a few nights," she answered half-seriously. "He so hates sleeping alone." I was not willing.

The shock of cancer, a hysterectomy, of her own perishability, escalated Dorothy's thoughts about Gordon until they became gripping mania. This probably would be her last chance. As soon as she was able, she launched into a program of strenuous exercise to reshape her body, began a spartan diet from which she would not budge and, in general, behaved like a downhill racer in training for the Olympics. She and Gordon planned their first assignation a month ahead of time, as if it were a junket to the Far East instead of four days in a motel in Big Sur. It happened finally, this momentous fusion, and if Darryl Zanuck had been in charge, the shooting script would have called for cymbals crashing, stars exploding and the theme music from the *1812 Overture*. She had anticipated every possible emotion and happening except for the hunger and ferocity they had for each other physically. In fact, most of the long weekend was spent in bed, after which Dorothy said, tearfully, "I never knew or imagined that I had the kind of sexual capacity he's touched in me. I'm so happy to know I can feel this way at this time of my life." For a long time after, she would cry every time she remembered.

Afterward: More letters, including one from Gordon's wife expressing to Dorothy her dreads, her difficulties in dealing with her husband's newfound rapture, her longing to find a comfortable position—after all, she too is an open-marriage proselytizer. Dorothy sculpted a bronze key-chain ornament with the words engraved, "You are my love," for Gordon's birthday. Laura, his wife, drove his car one day, noticed the bauble and practically crashed into a Mercedes stopped at a light. Charles developed a rash in the genital region, making sex with Dorothy difficult. Charles wrote to Laura, his comrade in this cellblock. Dorothy was no longer able to keep Gordon out of her speech for more than three minutes; she began turning her journal entries into a book. Charles told me she would come home from her office, play Brahms on the cello and weep.

The next time Dorothy and Gordon met was about a month later, when he and Laura flew up to Mill Valley to spend a weekend with the Barrons. This was Gordon's idea, as Laura was having surging anxieties over the seriousness of her husband's feelings for Dorothy. She was, from the beginning of the affair to its finale, the only member of the quartet who truly feared her marriage to be in jeopardy.

They arrived on Friday afternoon. Although the Barrons' modern home is spacious enough, Laura and Gordon had reserved a room in a nearby motel. It was Laura who, during a cordially stiff hour of Scotch sours and cheese and chitchat, suggested that Gordon and Dorothy might like some time alone together before dinner. So they sped off to the motel and returned three hours later, blissful. Then the four of them went to the Barrons' favorite French bistro for a leisurely wine-filled dinner in which the conversation became more intimate but, curiously enough, stayed away from the key topic, the topic which brought them here in the first place—The Affair. For folks whose *modus operandi* is self-examination and confrontation, it seemed particularly odd to me that virtually none occurred in these forty-eight emotion-drenched hours.

Driving home, Charles suddenly uncorked what everybody had surely been thinking. "I think it would be good for us to consider whether we're sleeping with the people we want to tonight. For instance, Laura, I'd like to spend the night with you. How do you feel about that?" Laura agreed happily, having felt a keen attraction to Charles since their arrival that afternoon. Dorothy, from whom I hear this tale, says she fell in love with her husband anew at that moment. "He was such a *mensch*, saying what *he* wanted, not taking the obvious and easy way out, which would have been, 'I'm sure Gordon and Dorothy would like to be together tonight.' "

I think it's fascinating that most people, even in the loosest of marriages, have bed taboos—that is, they will not sleep in their nuptial bed with a lover. That was true, you recall, for the Millers. It must be that the bed represents sanctuary, an inviolably intimate shrine. It's okay for you to make it with my husband, just don't do it in our bed. His body's not sacred, the bed is. It is the place where we share our deepest mergings, our most treasured privacy, our sleep and dreams, a place beyond fornication. Dorothy, typically, could not sleep in her own bed with Gordon, so they drove off to the motel to spend the night. Charles, a pragmatic man, held no such stigmas. When Gordon and Dorothy returned the next morning Laura was in the king-sized playpen with Charles, nestled in his arms, laughing and light. And Dorothy felt, somewhat to her surprise, absolute equanimity at seeing them naked, cozily tucked together in her very own bed. She was delighted that they liked each other so well; it seemed to take away some burden from her . . .

In the afternoon, as the quartet lounged nude by the pool, sunning and reading, Laura suggested a group massage. Dorothy thinks, in hindsight, that Laura wanted to promote group sex because it would be easier, safer, than was her husband's previous disappearance to the motel with Dorothy. But Dorothy would have none of that, and in the course of Gordon's tender, sensuous massaging of his lover, his wife became upset and stormed out, causing the first of many jealous crises that would eventually overwhelm Gordon with bewilderment and guilt. Laura's crises would be responsible for killing the affair.

The quartet was never to be repeated, logically enough. But Gordon and Dorothy had many subsequent weekends together —three days at Pismo Beach, for instance, after which Dorothy cried for a week. Not unhappiness, but ecstasy, peak fever, soul longing. Then a nasty letter from Laura followed by two weeks of Gordon's withdrawal due to pressure from his frightened wife.

I ask Dorothy after the Pismo Beach weekend how Charles is bearing up, what things are like between them. She answers solemnly that she has every hope this would do good things for Charles and her. "He's reminded how precious I am, and I'm loving him dearly because he's been so incredibly supportive to me. The better my sex gets with Gordon, the better it also gets with Charles. I'm just turned on all the time."

Then I ask her, with no small trepidation, if she has considered breaking up her marriage, if she and Gordon talk in these

terms. I'm relieved at her response. "No. I've never had any
intention of leaving Charles, nor Gordon Laura. If he lived
here I don't know how it would develop, since the dynamic
would be quite different. But we're both such grand opera
characters that probably this intensity is at least somewhat a
function of the physical distance between us." It's perfectly
apparent to me that she doesn't want a day-to-day familial
domestic thing (it's what she has, in happy harmony, with her
husband), but rather the high-wire thrills of An Affair. If they
lived together in wedlock he'd belch and get polyps in his nose
and it's so long, Madame Butterfly.

I think that the most interesting figure in all of this is
Charles. What is it like watching your mate of sixteen years
caught in a tornado for another man? What ancient stirrings
are aroused? Charles and I talk for some hours one afternoon
in his office; Dorothy, at that very moment, is locked in hers,
writing a long love missive to Gordon. "I have had some minor
to moderate pinpricks of jealousy," Charles admits, "but bigger
feelings of possessiveness, both of which I'm working on in
myself." He sees the difference between the two states distinctly, possessiveness being the philosophy of ownership, and
jealousy the subjective way that he experiences the loss of his
rights as a slaveholder. You can see that there is no self-pity in
Charles, no sense of being the aggrieved, cuckolded or abandoned spouse. Dorothy is not, in his view, doing it to him; he's
the victim only of his own antiquated hangups and beliefs.

He knows everything about Dorothy and Gordon. "It's a
very deep love bond," Charles says. "Very involved and stormy.
The positive and negative factors can be reassuring to me,
because it's hardly idyllic. Possibly I might feel jealous about
a loss of her time if he lived here and they continued on this
level, but I'm not experiencing a loss of love from her. Dorothy's wanted the *Sturm und Drang* of a highly romantic affair
for a long time. We never had that, and I have no need for it;
in fact, the only equivalent in our relationship was after we'd

gone together for four years and she wanted to get married and I didn't. So she sold her house and ran off to Europe for three months to see if I'd miss her and marry her. I did. It was quite theatrical for a short while. She loved it; I despised it."

Things between *them* are heightened at the time we speak. Routine has been disrupted, new stimulus, tension poking at the glands. Understandable, perfectly. "She doesn't describe stroke-for-stroke sex," Charles says, "but I feel free to show curiosity, and if I don't want to hear, I tell her. My sexual interest in her is increased lately. When she talks about their sexuality while *we're* in bed, I'm likely to get turned on and we'll wind up having intercourse. My fantasy life about her is certainly enriched right now." Charles' voice softens in extreme loving gentleness, as he says, "I feel closer to her now than for a long time. I'm sad when she is, I feel her pain and her love for him. I felt a great deal of empathy when he drew back from her. In fact, I suggested she take the initiative and call him."

It is not, please note, that Charles is of a different species than you or I, that he is indifferent to jealousy. "I used to be extremely jealous by nature," he reflects. "I remember, about twenty-five years ago, crawling through a laundry-room door in my girlfriend's apartment building to get to her apartment to see who she was sleeping with. And when Dorothy and I first opened our marriage I recall dragging her against her will to a weekend nude marathon in Palm Springs. I was devastated to see how many men were turned on to her. She proceeded to have the most beautiful weekend of her life, and I had migraines. But I've spent a lot of time and concentration working on freeing myself from jealous and possessive feelings, because of my philosophy about open marriage. I have no doubt, you see, that open sexuality is the only way for a primary relationship to blossom and grow. If we had a closed marriage, there would be a much greater chance that Dorothy would leave me right now."

It ended as it began—at a tempestuous pitch. Laura was

overcome with fear, and Gordon, forced to choose, retreated from Dorothy. It took her, then, more months to recover than the affair itself had consumed. In fact it is questionable, given her periodic inexplicable bursts of weeping after some wine, whether she is yet finished with it. She has always understood the mythic elements of her connection with Gordon: Her own father left her when she was eighteen months old and that specter of desertion has never been buried, the search to re-enact and rewrite that tragic scenario has always propelled her. Gordon was supposed to be the symbolic daddy who would fill those gnawing spaces in her, but of course he disappeared as did the First Man. Obviously, Dorothy has never had that particular primordial linkage with Charles.

We were all probably relieved when Dorothy and Gordon broke up. A hidden relief, naturally, as we also suffered for her and with her when it was over, during those long months of her mourning. But her affair demonstrated in spotlights a truth that we do not want to glimpse in our own relationships: that indeed we cannot get everything from one person. Giant, gaping voids exist even in the most abundant of marriages, primal needs aching to be met. Dorothy, despite a life that she treasures, skated through her days with a throbbing vacuum that pressed to be filled. When she met Gordon, it burst out.

What Charles and Dorothy have together is big. What she longs for in her softest and darkest spots is also big.

I think often about what the Barrons have that has made their open marriage a victory, while so many have gone down in flames. A devotion to growing, moving, stretching, changing—the keynote of the constellation in which they orbit. And their conviction that open relationships—with all their inherent stresses—are a noble goal. Above all, they have what only a scattering of relationships can claim right now: a commitment to each other as firm and fertile as a great forest, around which things shatter and crumble while it just goes on and on.

Charles talked of this rare commitment during the stormy

days of Gordon. "We made the agreement to stay together for the rest of our lives in the process of forming an open marriage seven years ago. And our relationship is closed as far as this commitment is concerned. Of course, I know that a pledge is minor compared to the kind of atmosphere we have; I know that all commitments are subject to change at any time."

"What does commitment mean to you?" I ask Charles. "To me," I have to admit, "it has some torture-chamber quality, like no matter how hideous things are we'll stick it out, do or die, until the grave." Like my family.

"I understand the implication, since that's what commitment used to mean, and still does to a lot of people," says Charles. "What we mean is something quite different. A deep emotional investment to work out problems and sustain the relationship, not to put up with a daily nightmare, but to insist on growing and challenging and being totally truthful with each other. If you don't have a monumental amount of this an open relationship won't work, you'll just split when the going gets rough."

"The most committed people we know," Dorothy adds, "are the ones with open relationships. The fact that I know I'm going to sleep every night and wake up every morning next to Charlie gives a stability and richness to my life that I cherish. I can't imagine life without Charles."

Unfortunately, I don't know very many humans, together for so many years, who could or would express such sentiments.

Now. What about me. Can I execute such a daredevil maneuver as an open relationship in my own jumbled life . . . ?

PART THREE

It's hard to be faithful.

—Marcia Seligson, 1977

It's just as hard to be unfaithful.

—Marcia Seligson, 1977

IX

Ruminations

The Dream

I am a creature of my times. Of broken myths and dreams that haven't panned out and a shocking residue of romantic hopes that defy all experience and persist. I still believe, for example, in some secret and embarrassed corridor of my soul, that someday my prince will come and on that day my life will make it.

Oh, because I'm too wise and worldly for that, I allow as how we'll have to work hard and really communicate honestly and give each other lots of "space"—my favorite mid-1970's gospel—and not lay yokes of expectation on the other. We'll each have to be whole, centered people, brimming over with self-esteem and the ability to live now and not yesterday or tomorrow. We'll both be immersed in our own vital work and won't need the other to survive. We'll have a range of like passions and dissimilar interests and bring to each other a battalion of splendid friends and new hobbies. We will not be insane nor destructive with each other. He will not be a sexist.

Our sex will grow and grow. We will make love in the bathrooms of 747's, spend whole Sundays getting stoned and massaging and fucking and taking baths together; we will leave restaurants in the middle of dessert to speed home. We will never be predictable, routine, pretending, familiar, obligatory. Our love-making will cover a spectrum from the richest love union to hilarity to "rape" through unafraid explorations of our most hidden animal natures. This fierce connection will be our secret that we carry everywhere, always. We will have no need for anyone else.

I have never, must I even tell you, found this prince, this union. Each time I fall in love, although I assure myself I'm being "realistic," I really start out believing—or praying, to be more accurate—This is It. It never is. Or at least so far it hasn't been (which very statement, please notice, illustrates my point that I am still ever looking). And then, at some point, after some time, and for a bucket of good reasons, I move on. Because I want everything, I often come up empty-handed. Just waiting.

When I'm happily linked to a man, as now, the dream is buried and still. But it never dies. It surfaces, in a flash, when we're up against walls. I'm not seeking a replacement, you understand; it's more subtle, more insidious than that.

A few years ago I was lounging in a girlfriend's living room; we were drinking wine and complaining about this and that. "How's your marriage?" said I. "Oh," she answered thoughtfully, "it's like going to the bathroom." "Sounds fantastic," I said. "What the hell does *that* mean?"

"Well, I just do it every day and don't think about it too much and some days it's terrific, so I notice it, and some days it's awful, so I notice it. And that's about the way marriage goes. It's just there."

"Yuccchhhh," say I. "Not for me, thank you. I want a lot more than taking a daily crap."

"Listen, dummy," my friend railed. "Haven't you gotten the

picture yet? You're in a relationship and it's got lots of garbage and trouble and pain, and it's like being on a roller coaster a lot of the time. And he's not the *most* fabulous in bed and you hate his friends, so eventually you leave. And the next one's definitely a tiger in bed and plays bluegrass banjo but he doesn't make you laugh and can't express his feelings and smokes in bed. Don't you get it? All relationships are shitty in some ways, and when you run from one to the other, you just exchange one pile for another. You just aren't ever gonna find that prince."

The flip side of me: I am also a creature of the cynicism of my times, or the pragmatism—however you look at it—and I certainly know that princes only exist on tobacco cans, and that future shock has mightily invaded all our cells. And yet I yearn for my romantic storylines, am woefully bitter that they never, ever, turn out the way they're meant to, and I still feel betrayed that they don't. I long for a perfect marriage, I am too terrified to risk the imperfect, I believe anyway it will all turn to shit . . .

I am a classic model for Maslow. The Theory of Rising Expectations. The Grumble Theory ("Whatever one yearns for, when achieved, one then yearns for more. The whole process repeats itself throughout life . . ."). How can one be reasonably happy under the Grumble Theory? One can't. We won't even look at the trivial, the obvious—the Cadillac didn't do it, let's get a Mercedes. That's crass, and besides everybody hip knows that doesn't work. Some of us have sat in lotus position and done *est* and know where the sixth chakra is, so I know that fulfillment lies totally inside ME, not in anything the slightest bit external. Guess what? I've had moments of *satori*, as we say in the fulfillment business, of splendid completion where I knew that I was the entire Cosmos, and then—grumble, grumble.

I usually think everybody knows how to have a marvelous relationship but me. And the corollary: I couldn't make the last one work, I'm scared blue of this one, but for the next one I'll definitely have all the answers. Just ask me then. I'll be happy to tell you everything.

I get restless in love. Sometimes I just don't want to be in love any more, don't want to pour out the continuing, merciless river of energy into somebody else, don't want his burdens atop my own cargo. Sometimes I want to be more in love than I am, smothered by it, encapsulated in it. Sometimes I want to fuck someone new, just for fun or for serious. If my mate wants to, of course, I go crazy.

I'm a creature of too much greed, too little patience, too big appetites, too imbedded fears. Too many body-blows and too little faith.

I know too much. Or too little.

The Coward

I sometimes tell myself that I'm a noteworthy coward. What I mean is I like guarantees with no risk, I want to know the ending before the beginning has even begun. I'm always looking for the deal that will make me rich, the investment that will triple in three months, but I only have to sink a fraction of my savings in it and it has the surety of Chase Manhattan. I play poker the same way, folding fleetly if the stakes are big. I can never quite understand why I can't just keep betting quarters on a full house (you never know, you see, who might have a slightly fuller one) and go home wealthy. I *do* understand, naturally, it just doesn't seem fair. My aims are very high; I just hate danger.

Love? Need you ask? My mate says I have One-Foot-Out-the-Door disease. My suitcase is never completely unpacked and stored away in the cellar. I leave it under the bed. My white Fiat convertible, if not quite left in drive with the motor running, is always ready. Like the Green Hornet's. Primed for getaway at briefest notice.

The escape route in my brain is rarely inactive for long, and that is really what I'm getting |to in all of this. There are those who think that open relationships are about nothing more than cowardice.

He and I have a terrible grinding disagreement that goes on and on. Not of the sudden eruptive kind that is ventilated and then over, the kind where we shriek, want to murder, sleep at opposite hemispheres of the bed, but within a day or two it's gone. That's not the kind of feud I mean. Nor the sort that can be ironed out civilly or nit-picked until it just expires of terminal tedium. I mean the crushing, slashing kind that doesn't seem to have a resolution and threatens to continue on forever. No sight of welcoming shore anywhere on the horizon, just black sea everywhere. It threatens to slaughter us, this Big Problem.

It's about his two children. My connection with them, theirs with me, with him, his with them. All four of us are Oedipal, demanding, self-righteous, guilty, baby trying to be adult, grownup yielding to our own interior infant. The wiring of one to the other in this highly charged quartet resembles the telephone system for the city of Detroit. We can't untangle it easily, maybe ever.

On the one hand it feels like the real gritty stuff of life, growth from tribulation and all that, one of the major challenges to handle and win, thereby making me more of an adult, wiser, evidence of my increasing mastery over things. But I want only to escape, like the Green Hornet, and disappear into the night. Who needs this?

Maybe I'll get drunk or stoned, I think at particularly desperate moments. No. Maybe we should have an open relationship. (Is that just a hipper version of maybe-we-should-get-a-divorce?)

So my mind jumps to lovely fantasies about calling this man Michael, this married man who pursues me, adores me without really knowing the awful pieces of me, promises only jolly times between noon and two-thirty and let him and *his* wife worry about the stinking kids. I want to play, not work. I want music, not muck. I especially don't want to be drained or short-changed. I'll just tiptoe backward from my love, just a few steps, he'll never know. Just to divert myself from this dismal quandary that pushes against us, this fever blister that will neither erupt nor heal, nor surrender to any known miracle drug.

Most crusaders say the drive for open relationship is about not getting everything we need or want from one mate. Or about wanting to "experience" more. "I can't fathom my life without him," one hears, "but he doesn't turn me on enough . . . doesn't go down on me in quite the right way . . . comes too soon . . ." That's what they say.

For me, it's not about those things, it's about hedging my bets, borrowing from Peter to pay what's his name. The Great Escape. The desire for many rising from the terror of one. Whatever else they are, open relationships are the coward's own special brand of opiate.

The Truth

Dear Dick,

I want to have an open relationship. And I don't want you to have one. That may sound somewhat unfair to you, but the truth is I can handle it and you can't.

I won't let other men, other carings, other love-making interfere with us. You will. You'll get guilty and confused and nuts and destructive, and you'll lose control of yourself. I know you will.

You'll let it screw up your life and our relationship, rather than enhancing them. You'll start calling me "Abigail" in your sleep. You'll start forgetting our dates, or messing up who you're supposed to take to the opera next week. You'll be disorganized and chaotic and you'll make me absolutely bananas.

You'll keep score. You'll pit me against all the others. You'll tell me how much more Stephanie gives you than I do. You'll compare me to all the rest in bed. You'll fall in love with the first woman who doesn't give you any static about your drinking. You'll be too tired to have sex with me some nights. You'll promise to take Trudy to the Rams game after you've already promised to take me. You'll be in Mexico with Evelyn some romantic weekend while I'm home knitting you a sweater. You'll make caring gestures to Mary Lou that you don't to me any more. Like buying her turquoise earrings. Where the hell are *my* turquoise earrings? You'll have long phone conversations while I'm at your house. You'll be moody after you've had a fight with Elsie, and you'll want to ask my advice. You'll become infatuated with a new woman once a week and think about leaving me. You'll manipulate me to death.

I won't do any of those things, as you well know.

I really want *you* to have an open relationship too, as soon as you're ready. But for now, we both know you'll fuck it up. So let's just forget the whole thing.

All my love,

Paradise

It is ten-thirty in the morning and I am in Big Sur, in bed with Dick. Our hotel is high on a bluff; from our bed I have a spectacular view of the redwoods, the sugar pines, the Monterey cypress, the voluptuous green hills, the sea and the sky. Each of those, here, is more majestic than anywhere else I have ever seen them. There is almost total silence except for a faint but constant rustling that may be the wind or may be the ocean. The morning is cold and faultlessly clear.

Inside, I am aching. We have been in Big Sur for two days. At this splendid retreat with a fireplace across from our bed and an outdoor hot tub where you soak, then lie naked on the deck looking at the stars. Our first night we smoked grass in the tub at one in the morning. We were the only ones there. It was so quiet that every word we spoke seemed too significant; I listened carefully to all our words to each other.

We have planned a special trip—a getaway into this paradise. We will forget his two children who live with him, my book deadline, Los Angeles. We will fuse into each other as the cliffs fuse into the beach, the rocks into the sea. We will lie nude in the November sun, give each other long massages, look at each other's bodies as if they were new bodies. We will make deep, slow, frequent love. Where else, if not in this place?

Those of you who know about Life know where this story is headed. His ulcer is acting up, his secretary calls to whine long-distance. Last night, he fell into a cacophonously snoring sleep watching Monday-night football on television, while I hid under the quilt, and tried to give him his space, tried not to slip into fury or desperation or the impulse to flee. I failed meanly.

We have made love twice since we arrived, for eleven minutes each, and neither time did I even come close to coming. Earlier this morning, when I was still more angry than melancholy, he reached for me and I froze, catatonic until he understood and withdrew. This afternoon we will drive to Carmel, visit some galleries, have lunch at the General Store, continue on to Monterey and fly home.

This is not—and I need to tell you this—a deadly, empty, rageful attachment. If it were, Big Sur would somehow be simpler, the choices would be sharp. There are special moments here, enough spots of sweet juncture and laughing that we continue on. This is the best man I've ever known.

But, oh. Oh . . .

Do you know what I mean?

I am thirty-seven years old and I still yearn. Some times more than others, surely in some splendorous places more than others. Places that, by their own perfection, reach down inside me into that well of dream and myth and memory and hunger. Day by day, in the ordinary course of things, that corner in me is still. As it must be.

I peer out over our terrace, past the cliffs and the rocks, the Santa Lucia firs, out into the endless Pacific. Does it exist, somewhere out there, anywhere in all of that?

Ecstasy

How important is sex anyway? Since that's what this book is about—maybe—I ought to know the answer to that question. I don't.

But I think about it much of the time, so I'll just let you in on those thoughts. They are like fireworks flares that burst out into the darkness and then disintegrate, mutually exclusive of the one before, no pattern or network to them. No consistency either.

A love of mine from long ago asked: If we had to give up fucking together or laughing together, which would you choose? As it happened, we had both very fine fucking and very fine laughing (those were, incidentally, our only virtues), so it was a decision on my part that required serious deliberation. I opted for relinquishing sex.

My pal Annie is horny all the time. Not only can't she find a good man to love but she has trouble getting laid. "When I'm having sex regularly I don't need to eat much, I work better, I can concentrate on anything I put my mind to and I have limitless energy. I could make love every night and every morning but I can't find any man these days who wants that too." Annie's whole purpose in sex, she says, is a good orgasm or five.

Grace thinks sex is a pain in the ass. A distraction, a waste of time. "At night I feel I should be going to sleep, in the morning I want to be getting up for work." So there you are.

Me. Sometimes I'd kill for a spectacular fuck.

Sometimes I'd rather watch the late movie.

Sometimes I don't even think about it for days at a time, as if it didn't exist. The same way I don't think about skydiving. And other times I can't drive on the freeway or read or write without obsessing about it.

Sometimes I feel like I've fucked everybody in the world and other times like I want to.

And sometimes thinking about it is better than doing it. Like when it's somebody you've been hot after for a long time, and you've imagined every single stroke, minute-by-minute, and while you're imagining the whole scene, including the dialogue, a delicious throb/hum/flutter/itch thing, that incomparable pleasure, is rising down there in your pants. And one day you finally get around to doing it. Only he's not nearly as funny or flattering or muscular or carnal or GREAT in the real bed as in your own head. It's all over much too quickly, and in the final moments you have this really horrible, frightful recognition that you've done this before. That every fuck of your life has been, in some key central way, like every other fuck of your life. After all that anticipation, it's over. And so goddamn what?

But then there are those times when sex is the only activity that matters at all. I understand those instants less than anything.

We know that our age has made sex so critical that it is almost impossible to be happy in bed. It isn't only that the standards are so preposterous, which they are. Multiple orgasm, Matterhorn peaks, Nobel Prize longevity, positions executable only by Nureyev. But more misery-making: How do I even know if I'm having a successful sex life? I used to think one big rolling crying orgasm was sensational, the heights. Now there's a voice buried somewhere inside me that squeaks, so quietly I can't even locate it for combat,

"One, only one . . . ?" Whatever I do or feel isn't quite enough, competent or pleasureful or meaningful or supreme enough. I've been promised Ecstasy by my era, which is all nifty—except what the hell is Ecstasy?

I chuckle a lot about the silly and abysmal state of things. I'm a "cultural observer," so I don't have to be sucked in with the rest of you. Yes.

Yes, but when sex is not great—whatever that means—such a rumbling of discontent begins to be heard in my depths, starting its inexorable journey to the surface. When love-making is merely adequate or tiresome or bad it's as if I'm not fully alive—the deprivation I feel is actually physical, like starving. It takes a day sometimes to recover from poor sex.

Then, I have had otherworldly, transcendent fucking with men I didn't even like. And the opposite.

I know too much. Or too little.

Death

Dick and I are driving home from an evening of dinner and the movies. I have sensed all night something wrong in him. I suspect it relates to Paula, the lover from whom he's been separated for two and a half years. Recently, I have felt her presence in subtle ways, felt her a threat, felt a bond between them that I did not perceive when I leaped into love with him six months ago, trusting that he was free, available to me, believing that they were just "friends," passionless friends. Whenever I bring it up, he tells me I'm nuts, manufacturing crisis. But I know what I know.

"Something is going on, isn't it?" I ask. Please say no.

"Yes, honey. It's about Paula." He is very grave, the doctor announcing terminal illness to the patient.

"Tell me quickly," I say, my stomach moving. He takes a deep slow breath, makes dramatic pause. The bastard is enjoying this, I note.

He tells me Paula called him that day, asked him to take her to lunch. They have not had such dealings in nine months, since they stopped "dating," supposedly gave up the hope of reconciliation. He takes her to a French restaurant. Why not the Hamburger Hamlet? She says she wants him back in her life—not *back*, mind you; she would never say that exactly. She has been immersed in group therapy and uses the correct language: "I would like us to explore finding a space for each other in our lives," she says. I say, "How did you react?" "I experienced her differently than I ever have before," he confesses. "I was very moved."

At that moment, I have already written the end to this tale, and it goes: "I'm sorry, Marcia, I thought I loved you, I thought I was finished with Paula, but now I find I just want to be with her." And in that instant—waiting for him to say those words to me—I can only think to describe my feeling as death. I am dying. He has killed me. I am dead.

There is shock—"I can't believe I'm hearing this." There is the desire to grab the wheel and turn his Mercedes over and over. There is the impulse to clasp my hands around his neck and squeeze the motherfucker to death. There is an oddly gleeful self-righteousness: "Aha, I was RIGHT, he *is* still tied to her. I'm *not* crazy." There is numbness, in which only my mind is operating; I analyze the stupidity of his choice, calculate the quantity of his self-destructiveness. And there is, thank God, a physical sense of steel armor rising up to envelop and save me.

But not save me enough. Because the emotion that triumphs, stripping me of all others, is simply "I am dying." Everything else is canceled. I can't even hear his next words: "But I don't love her; I just want to stay with you." I've already been told I'm dying, and I can't hear the doctor's reprieve.

The Game

A thoughtful man said, "Having a relationship is like climbing mountains or being a nun. It's very, very, very hard. And probably should be left to very few people. The rest of us have to find some other way to occupy ourselves."

The problem is, as has been proved time after time, that relationships are the only game in town. How else to explain the ridiculous truth that we keep failing and trying, failing and trying, in a never-quitting cycle.

Frequently we try new people, sometimes we attempt new forms or combinations or sculptures, each time thinking MAYBE THIS IS IT, THIS IS THE ANSWER! Marriage isn't It, maybe living together is It. Recently I've decided that since living together clearly isn't It, the answer is Not Living Together.

Each time I invent a beautifully concocted logic system, infallible, perfect. And each time that isn't It either. George isn't It, maybe Arnold is. Monogamy doesn't work, maybe open marriage, or a trio, or nine or fourteen or A HUNDRED AND EIGHTY-SIX!!! Or celibacy, or girls . . .

The obvious point, I guess, is: There aren't any answers. Nothing is It. Still, we keep searching, we never say The Hell With It with any long-range serious perseverance. We just keep hoping and trying, the hope that it will work always overruling the fear that it won't. Beautiful, I say. Without that, there's no game, nothing to do, nobody to play with.

X

Sexual Jealousy

You remember jealousy. It's what made Othello strangle Desdemona. It's the thing that's responsible for a large proportion of what the police call crimes of passion: husbands shooting wives, wives shooting husbands, husbands shooting wives' lovers, and so on.
—Karen Durbin, *The Village Voice*

. . . the kind of jealousy that would once have precluded any non-monogamous relationship is hardly salient at all today. . . . It doesn't seem important enough to precipitate much popular discussion.
—Jessie Bernard, *The Future of Marriage*

O! beware, my lord, of jealousy;
It is the green-ey'd monster which doth mock
The meat it feeds on.
—William Shakespeare, *Othello*

I am combing my hair in the bathroom of his apartment, when I happen to look into the wastebasket next to the sink and see the wrappings of a Tampax. No. Of course I don't just *happen* to gaze there. I'm searching for traces of another woman.

It isn't my Tampax. At first I think, my self-protection rising reflexively, as if warding off a blow: "It's the maid's." That does not hold up for five seconds. Then I fasten on to the truth—what clear, inescapable, treacherous truth—fasten like a shark on to its dinner. And I will not, cannot, let loose, until I've shredded it, and myself, into a bloody mutilation.

We look for ways to torture ourselves. As if Life itself didn't have weaponry in the arsenal to do the job, enough of its own shocks and griefs waiting for us in the wings. We don't have to step outside the house looking for torment, thank you very much Life will drop it right at our feet. Just wait a few minutes.

But we do look. We create jealousy. And it is unbeatable, indestructible, a slow-acting poison with no antidote. Fatal every time.

I ask him, finally: "Who was it?" But in that act of asking —more like thinly disguised pleading—who am I? I am the woman who fixes on old Tampaxes in the garbage. Very lovable. Dignified. I am the one who is helpless because he can inflict hurt on me so easily. I am out of control: Do I really want to know whom he fucked last night? And isn't that only the first question in the series, and doesn't this horrific interrogation spiral downhill rapidly, zooming into Deceit, Betrayal and Insupportable Injury? And isn't the tiny paper tubing, tossed so carelessly by last night's lady, suddenly the harbinger of those things said that cannot be erased or retracted, ever? And can't I predict he will freeze and spit, "None of your goddamn business," as he does? But could I have predicted that I would be so crazed as to pick up a piece of valuable ceramic sculpture and hurl it through the valuable plate-glass window, as I do?

Damage is done irrevocably. Trust—so tenuous to begin with, so hazardous to build—is undone in a word or two, in a rageful gesture. Walls spring up where yesterday there were none. We are suddenly strangers, my lover and I. An agreement has been broken, THE critical agreement. Fidelity. A commandment, in fact, in its psychic weight. No, we're not merely strangers. We are enemies. He is capable, this loved and dreaded one, of destroying me with a Tampax.

There have been four occasions in my life when I felt that I was dying. Once was indeed when I thought that I had a terrible illness; the other three were when I was jealous. Sexually jealous. My man had slept with somebody else, and there was enough material in that one act to stir in me sensations of my very life being taken away. "Cruel as the Grave," the Song of Solomon says of jealousy—that emotion or conglomerate of emotions, that *thing* as potent as any feeling force we humans possess. People regularly murder for jealousy. In polygamous Fiji, women lost control and cut off the noses of their husbands' other wives from jealousy. It is jealousy that often keeps us monogamous (if I do it, then you'll do it), makes us secretly adulterous, and it is the biggest single factor responsible for the failure of most attempts at open marriage.

Jealousy, in truth, is the key required course in the curriculum of open sexuality. One can't, either as student of or player on this gridiron of unconventional forms, understand or evaluate anything, really, without plugging in to the heart of this matter. Jealousy is the matrix.

According to Fraser's *The Golden Bough*, jealousy has been "one of the most fruitful causes of dissension and quarreling, of secret murder and open war among mankind." On a less elevated plane, it's the number-one reason swingers drop out of swinging. Next to grief it is the most gripping, searing and cankerous emotion in our repertoire, but while grief frequently has its source in reality—the actual loss of a loved one—jealousy is, much of the time, either anticipatory or fantasy-laden.

There are two distinct schools of thought on jealousy, on what it is and where it stems from and what to do about it. One school claims it is instinctive, legitimate, healthy, an emblem of loving, poetic, morally imperative and unconquerable. William James held this view, as did Victor Hugo, Freud, Kinsey, Carl Rogers and Robert Ardrey, who saw it as a natural concomitant of the territorial imperative (This is my space and you can't come into it unless I let you). It is a view that, if correct, certainly defines some of our major limitations of behavior, since everybody agrees on the volcanic power of jealousy. If jealousy is biologic, then it probably cannot be erased or even significantly reduced, so we must create systems—like monogamy—to pay court to its sovereignty. To the degree that we believe jealousy is a badge of loving and the more jealousy we exhibit the more we love, it becomes rather an exalted state, somewhat like the glorification of war to applaud patriotism.

The other school insists that jealousy is conditioned by history and the culture, that as sociologist Kingsley Davis believes, it is an "institutional prop" of monogamy, and that it is infantile, sexist, capitalistic, small-minded, malignantly destructive and supremely *un*loving. With conscious work and commitment, this catechism goes, jealousy is eradicable. The sages of the alternate-lifestyle trend insist that there is no such "feeling" as jealousy. Merely behavior for which we have created a convenient label to disguise the true emotions of anxiety, anger, sadness and so on. They have reduced the mysterious monster to a mere set of stimulus-nerve responses. Pavlov and the conditioned dog.

The mood in America, these years, has swung—courtesy of the various human liberation movements—totally toward the latter approach. Jealousy today is considered wrong, a character flaw, a political crime, an error in logic, an immaturity.

I am—by nature or culture or some mix of each—an intensely jealous creature. I'm not sure how to measure myself against others, as these things go; I do know that often I confuse jealousy with some essential distrust of men, and almost always the feelings are ruled by anticipations of the future rather than truths of the moment. At its worst, jealousy engulfs me like some ancient, demonic possession, blinding and invincible.

On the spectrum, I can have a mild tweek of *something* uncomfortable if my dog seems too entranced for too long with somebody besides me. I define it as jealousy. More discomfort if a close woman friend is spending "too much time" with another female, but slightly less if it's a new man who's consuming her interest, since that's expected and presumably doesn't challenge her loyalty to me or my worth to her. Approaching the far right of the spectrum, the side that connotes not just twinges but the real center of the issue—stunning agony—are those people and incidents that surround my mate. Anything that implies a lessening of his energy, time or interest for me provokes virulent sensations I have learned to call "jealousy." Like, if he chooses to spend a Sunday with his son instead of me. Or if he has lunch with a former and undesired girlfriend. If there is any serious jeopardy, any possible loss of love or end to the relationship, the jealousy needle runs amuck on the meter. Sexual jealousy is the most treacherous and crushing of all, and to examine its nature is to find clues to the truly profound features of love and its kinship to sex.

And still, we live in a funny time, a time of both honoring and exploring our innermost emotional life on the one hand, and demystifying it into dust, on the other. We believe that we should love one person, passionately, persistingly. But without jealousy and possessiveness. Thus I am embarrassed by my jealousy. (I say "my jealousy" in the same way I say "my allergies"—something unattractive and tacky that I tote around with me, helpless to get rid of. Baby fat. Everybody has conquered it but me.) I find myself apologizing for my nature the way I used to when hip friends would find my John Denver records on the shelf and look at me with astonishment and a little scorn. "I'm sorry," I would say defensively. "But I like him. That's the way I am." And I hoped they would look at

my incorrectness, my lapse into square, as an adorable idiosyn-
crasy. "You want to hear something *wild* about Marcia?" I
hoped they'd say. "She's jealous. Oh yeah, and she likes John
Denver. Isn't that cute?"

It's not painful enough to suffer from jealousy. Now we have
to feel guilty about it.

It begins early, in our original relationships. The nuclear
family is tiny, limiting, a tight little island with one mommy
and one daddy, each indispensable to our survival. We quickly
develop the fixed idea that love is finite, and that simple notion
dominates our later life: "In order for me to be loved and
valued I have to be your one-and-only." When a new sister or
brother arrives we don't anticipate that the space will expand
to encompass and nourish everybody; rather, we see the horrible danger of being replaced, less doted on, less special. Deprivation and the possibility of abandonment are literal menaces
to our childhood survival. Thus, we learn very early to make a
connection with possessiveness and our life's-breath. My
brother, ten years older than I, developed severe asthma the
week I was born, bearing it until he left home for college.

For the newborn, entering a family with other children
means a battle to assert rights of importance in an already
closed corporation. That's the essence of sibling rivalry and
Oedipal drives—to be the one-and-only. In the world of the
child, everything breaks down into "my" and "thy." This is
mine, get your hands off, but I will do whatever I can to get
yours. Give one child a cookie and you cannot possibly get away
without giving one to the rest. The narcissistic way a child
visualizes life—given form and celebrated by the nuclear family construct—is the breeding ground for jealousy and possessiveness carried throughout life.

What we do as children is to make an association between
the arrival of a new family member and our own nonvalue and
unlovability. If I'm so terrific, why do they need him? What's

the matter with me? Every incident of supposed inequity, of his getting three cookies while I only got two, becomes a crisis in self-esteem.

And here, exactly, are the two prevailing elements of sexual jealousy: I'm afraid that I will lose you if you are turned on to/sleeping with/someone else. And furthermore, what's wrong with me that you are desiring/needing/doing this awful thing? I look at or think about this other woman, this intruder, and she becomes a signpost of my flaws; she is younger or thinner or more exciting or less difficult. It is a validation of self-doubt, of those parts of myself that I despise.

Then, after childhood, we become slaves to American romantic ideology and begin the search for the perfect prince or princess, the *one* magic person who will provide everything for us forever, like Mom and Dad did or should have done. We remain as hungrily possessive and nervously jealous as adults in a love relationship as we were as children; the dynamics, in fact, have hardly changed at all.

Let's talk first about jealousy that isn't sexual. With Karen, Sara and Lloyd, the trio from Long Island, fierce problems arise from Lloyd's sporadic sense of exclusion by his two women, and yet there is nothing sexual in the females' bond. He is not endangered by potential desertion. He is just—JUST!—left out on occasion from conversation because he's unable to share some special female correspondence. But he is relentlessly plagued with resentment and hurt, which he terms Jealousy.

Antoinette is a pleasantly married woman. Her best buddy, Allen, is a homosexual man with whom she plays tennis most afternoons. They have in common a variety of things she cannot share with her husband, including a passion for gardening, and gossip about the New York theater life, from which they are both expatriates. Jerry, the husband, is secretly, guiltily jealous. He confided his "aberration" to me: "I'm not afraid she's going to leave me for him, naturally. And she's not taking anything away from us in terms of time or energy. But I *do* sometimes compare myself to him, and I feel lacking—like I don't play tennis and I don't know who all those show business people are. And then I can slip into nutty stuff like 'She's only staying with me because he's gay' or 'Yeah, someday she'll find a man who's just like Allen, only straight . . .'"

Did I mention that jealousy is irrational?

The most beautifully married couple I know—they have what we would all like but believe to be impossible—have been joyously together for fifteen years, unfalteringly monogamous, frequently congratulating themselves on their rare fortune. Nedda has flashes of jealousy if they bump into an old college girlfriend of Barry's on the street, Barry is peppered with uneasy rumblings if a lover of Nedda's from seventeen years ago phones his wife to say hello. They laugh—know it's ridiculous —nonetheless knot-in-the-stomach anxiety pops up unexpectedly for either of them, as if it had a life and will of its own. Impending removal of love or reduction of self-worth is not at stake—they are remarkably secure individually, and precious together. It is something neither can define and I hesitate to do it for them. "I'm jealous of his past, before we knew each other," admits Nedda. "Of everything in his life that I can't be a part of. Even the fact that his mother died before I knew her." The freedom travelers will crucify these two for what reads like suffocation, unctuous togetherness. It is not, I promise you; they are autonomously functioning individuals, with strong goals outside their union.

At the best moments of love, I have experienced similar naggings of—well, call it jealousy. Feeling magnetically connected, in tune, indestructible with my mate and reaching for a fusion so utterly complete that I am resentful and envious of every crucial experience in his life before me or without me. Included in that satchel is a prickling desire to meet his ex-wife, and a vague rivalry with every old lover, no matter how fleeting and unimportant. That he went to Acapulco for a weekend five years ago with somebody, before I even knew him, rankles.

None of these instances has much to do with sex, unless we stretch the point. Thus none falls into the crushing riptides of violence and suffering for which sexual jealousy is so justly renowned.

The fact is that sexual jealousy wires us into the oldest, most treacherous of our fears—abandonment and helplessness. It jolts us back instantaneously—side-stepping our mental ruminations and mature rationality—to our most primitive states. You might remember that when you last experienced it, sexual jealousy began with a stab of shock that coursed through and took charge of your body, leaving your brain in impotent chaos. You probably became an infant right away, the overlay of calm and reasoned adult functioning gone, your life in danger. At those times I have been known to howl as if struck in the gut, or to rage like a taunted bumblebee or to run away faster than my body knows how to run. It must be biological, this jealousy. How could emotions so wracking and elemental be mere "social conditioning"? How trivial, out of sync with the anguish. That's what I tell myself.

What is it all about? Why, as somebody once asked, am I getting so upset about his putting his penis in somebody's vagina?

I dread losing him of course, and loss is implicit in the act. We all know, yes, that sex can be meaningless, disaffiliated, exploitative, unloving, even dreary and lonely. But if *he's* doing it, or did it, it is not that way. My self-torturing mind does not conjure up pictures of him falling asleep midfornication, fatigued from the drabness of the deed. No, to me she is Bitch Goddess, and together they are Adam and Eve. He will certainly desert me for her, my conniving brain says, I am nothing, she is everything. Whoever she is.

There it is. Self-hate and Insecurity. Bud DeLeon, the drum major of rational nonmonogamy, has said that if you like yourself, you will not be bothered a wink by jealousy. I suppose that's true enough. And utterly beside the point. I don't know anybody all that solid.

Roberta and Jerry Miller, two models of open marital bliss, recently had a predicament. Jerry became impotent with his wife. Only her, not his girlfriends. Roberta, who had been grateful and excited for his burgeoning social life, suddenly became violently "jealous" of those other women with whom Jerry could perform. In her view, his impotence was her fault: She wasn't sexy, exciting, feminine, good in bed. Her self-worth collapsed like a punctured beachball, and the expression of it was jealousy. Obviously, the truth of Jerry's impotence lives on a more intricate grid. But Roberta could not grasp that.

Beyond insecurity, beyond I-can't-compete self-stabbing, people in the throes of jealous agonies sometimes report a sense of being invisible, of no longer existing. The power of *that* must be galaxies above even the dread of losing the loved one. The feeling that your very Being has been obliterated is the stuff of nightmares and madness.

Vicki and Joe Maxwell are a young Manhattan couple grappling with an open marriage. They agree with its tenets, view it as the only way to salvage their troubled tie. And they are mostly like gladiators doing regularly scheduled combat, if not with each other, then with their own dragons. I saw them for the first time on a Thursday night and their joint tremors set the room aquiver. It seems that Vicki was leaving the next morning to visit friends in Vermont for the weekend. Joe was staying home and had a date to spend all of Saturday with Sharon, of Sharon and Ted, their closest friends. Everybody assumed Joe and Sharon would fuck, since they had always wanted to; the opportunity was there (Ted was, coincidentally, going away skiing) and it seemed a fine laboratory assignment for both couples' Open Marriage Project. But they were four virgins entering a whorehouse. Vicki had written every conceivable script beforehand in her head and none soothed her; there was no denouement that portrayed her as a victor. She imagined that she would stew all weekend about what was happening at home, thus ruining her own days. Then she projected that she would arrive home Sunday night and insist

Joe reassure her that she's Number One, and make wild love to her. "He'll have to reestablish our relationship, I think," Vicki admitted, "convince me he loves me the most, I'm the one he's chosen to be with." This, by the way, was her invented outcome even if Joe didn't go to bed with Sharon. If he did? "Then I freak out. Then I scream and cry and fume and rave."

She and Joe had spent hours of evening prime time debating and dissecting the potential climax of Saturday night, figuring what they will do and say if . . . We can assume that Sharon and Ted had done the same, so you might notice that this whole adventure lacked a certain spontaneity. They were virtually obligated to fuck in order to justify all the conversation and be true to the Cause.

I called Vicki on Monday morning. She was frantic, in a whirling confusion that radiated over the wires. "This is the worst pain I've ever had," she whispered, hardly able to speak. "All weekend I had constant fantasies of them in bed together, laughing, playing, being intimate. I started to feel like I didn't exist, the world was just the two of them. I knew they weren't thinking of me and my pain at all. I've never felt so invisible, so uncared for and alone." When she found out the truth— Sharon came over at three, they went out to dinner, lit a fire, took a shower and made love—it became unbearable. *Nothing* Joe said provided reassurance. She had been betrayed, by her husband and her best friend. She also felt she'd been betrayed by Open Marriage.

Like so many others, Vicki and Joe—in a quest for nuptial remedies—had read the O'Neills' book, with its peppy so-you-wanna-have-sexual-freedom approach. They had bought the package, its romanticized ease, its merrily achieved salvation. They had jumped in exultantly, unthinkingly, like beach mutts galloping into the surf to frolic. And then they had hit the rocks. The O'Neills had prepared them for everything about open marriage except sexual jealousy.

—Virtually all the studies of communal living report that

when the members are monogamous or platonic, the setup can work. When they begin playing with unrestricted sexuality, disintegration of the commune occurs in short order.

—Helen Gurley Brown, editor of *Cosmopolitan*, told me that her husband, film producer David Brown, lives for half of the year in California, while she is in New York. He spends easily as much time with his partner, Richard Zanuck, as he does with his wife. That is okay with Helen, in fact coincides with her own absorbing, career-filled existence. "But if he spent so much as one night in bed with another woman," she says candidly, "I'd go absolutely crazy."

—A man told me he bumped into an old girlfriend on the beach, walking hand in hand with her lover. He wasn't interested in her. In fact, he had curtailed their affair after a few months for a lack of interest and he was currently happily in love himself. Yet he felt a sudden zing of jealousy in seeing them. He astutely attributed his pangs to egotism, not loss of the woman. Yet it was sexual jealousy nonetheless.

I interviewed my mate Dick, setting up hypothetical cases for exploration of his responses. In one story, I go out to dinner with Len, a platonic buddy of mine; I come home and report, sheepishly: "We got stoned and made love, it just sort of happened, it was nothing." What does that tale trigger in him? "I can't compete with him . . . Sex implies total release and opening . . . There's a limited receptacle, and what you give to him isn't there for me . . . He can have you whenever he wants you, pick up the phone and snap you away for two hours and I'm powerless . . . My ego is raped . . . He must be magic, you and I are doing this work and commitment and he just has to pick up the phone . . . I'm being made a fool of, you're humiliating me, betraying me . . . The whole story validates my assumption that I can't trust women . . ."

It's even heavier, this scenario, if he doesn't know the male. "Then he's Albert Einstein and Fred Astaire and has a Maserati and a fourteen-inch cock." And my man feels like a cuckold, that age-old literary symbol of the ultimate male schnook.

He is unforgiving, merciless, in these fictions. I set up another case in which Frank comes to California from New York for a few days and we spend the weekend together. Frank was, in fact, a two-week fling immediately preceding us, a highly charged African vacation jaunt. He now lives with a woman, and we are periodic long-distance telephone friends. "Fuck you ever after" is my love's unequivocal projected response. "Everything you've told me is a lie. There's no way that 999 percent fidelity has any relation to 1 percent infidelity, or even one fall from grace. It's absolute betrayal . . . Not operative to say, 'Because I'm close to you for 999 nights, it's okay for one night off.' It's the only area where there are no bargains and no trade-offs."

Implied in sexual jealousy is a loss of control over the other person. Fundamental possessiveness. As we believed we owned our parents (and they us), so we think we own our mates. A man once said to me of his wife: "I own that space in her that my penis enters. I want to control her, her actions, so that she doesn't have the opportunity to do what I suspect she'd do if I let loose, if I didn't keep tabs or keep her on a leash." A San Francisco psychotherapist extends the idea to the very core of our American capitalistic system, "built on competition and property rights. It's the acquisitiveness of Western values; this is my coffeepot, this is my Oldsmobile, this is my human being. I own you, so I'm entitled to determine what your behavior should be."

"Jealousy can occur only if one person regards another as a mere body to be possessed or if he thinks love can be coerced," writes James Winifred Bridges. "To become angry or quarrel over a woman is to deny her the right to choose a lover and determine her own happiness or misery. It implies that she is a chattel rather than a person." The sexist innuendos of possessiveness are obvious, in fact they are the reason that some feminists have taken up nonmonogamy as a political *cause célèbre.* The truth is that the principle of I-own-you is neither relegated exclusively to men nor to capitalists. What is most engaging about the thesis is that it favors the Jealousy-Is-Cultural argument; if it's only that and not instinctive, we can alter it through reconditioning, programming ourselves to new patterns of thought.

For me, jealousy is not exactly an exercise in possessiveness. I don't want to own my mate, for the simple reason that I don't allow him to own me. I want clear and frequent separation for both of us—space and distance, among other benefits, keep our vitality flowing. I want him, as I do myself, to have exciting friends and gratifying interests, a whole distinct life. I just don't want him to fuck anybody.

The evidence is that sexual jealousy is not the same for men and women, and that it is a more devastating experience for men. To the degree that one partner assumes the other to be slave, views the spouse as object rather than person, function rather than Being, to that degree is he or she up for severe shock when the fixed positions are changed. Usually the slaveholder is *he,* so that if his wife strikes a blow for autonomy by sleeping with somebody else, many pieces of him are attacked, not the smallest of which is his station as all-omnipotent Lord of the Plantation. To discover that his woman is not dependent on him as on a tank of air under the sea is supremely castrating. The only way he can keep her, he believes unconsciously, is as a prisoner chained to him for her lifeline. In fact, he often experiences jealousy in a direct hookup to his cock.

"I imagine his is bigger than mine," said a man when explaining to me his torrential rages at unearthing his wife's current infidelity. "He's probably better than me in bed and turns her on in a way that I can't. Whenever I visualize them screwing, I just can't stand it. I want to murder him." That is typical: The main source of his self-demeaning jealousy is egotism and pride. He never spoke of losing her, although there was a strong possibility of just that, and he knew it. Not that he is willing to be deserted by his wife for another man, but it's a matter of priorities. Which hurts most, my broken leg or my broken cock? His vital organ is under armed assault—*that* is the site of his battleground. "It is not usually the assumption that women are promiscuous which provokes male jealousy in our society," writes Germaine Greer in *The Female Eunuch*, "but rather the assumption that they are merely acquiescent in sexual relations." If he sees her as a passive receptacle, not an active participant, it naturally follows that the biggest, most agile and creative penis that happens to find its way into her waiting frame will be able to steal her and win the booty.

For women, the wellspring of sexual jealousy is a dread of losing the relationship. Greer says, "If men regard women's fidelity as a necessary prop to their ego and cuckoldom as the deepest shame . . . women are prepared to tolerate infidelity because they so badly need actual security, and not apparent security. They suffer torments of jealousy because they are terrified of abandonment, which seems to them mostly to be all too probable. No man expects to be abandoned until he is faced with evidence that he is being cuckolded or left."

Greer's observation illuminated for me a phenomenon I have long noticed and never before understood: The most busily adulterous men *assume* their wives are faithful. One would think guilty projections would rule—my God, if I'm doing this, imagine what *she's* doing all day alone in that suburban nest with nothing to do and nobody to check up on her. But they don't think that way. Men are stunningly naïve and trusting about their wives' chastity, while foxlike in their own connivances. They *know* their wives are dependent on them—that's the covenant. Slavemasters are always electrified when the serfs revolt.

In a study of swingers and patterns of jealousy, sociologist Duane Denfeld observed a distinct variance in males and females. Men exhibited considerably more jealousy than did their wives, but for entirely different reasons. The husbands tended to be jealous of their wives' popularity, endurance capacity, general sexual performance, and worried that the wives might be having more fun than they. For the women, jealousy related to fear of losing the mate. "These findings," says Denfeld, "suggest the influence of the double standard; the emphasis for the husband is on his pleasure and satisfaction, whereas the emphasis for the wife is on the maintenance of the marital unit."

Sexually, women experience the "loss" or withdrawal of the penis all the time, every time. It may account, to a large degree, for our lifelong preoccupation with abandonment.

What are the components that make up sexual jealousy? Hurt and anger, universally—the quantity of anger relating to whether furtiveness and deception are involved. But jealousy is not a state that yields to reason, so we can feel extremely betrayed even in the most aboveboard of situations. When a woman in an open marriage told me of her agitation at her husband's making love to somebody—what a violation, what perfidy it was—I was puzzled. "But your agreement says that's okay, right?" I asked. "There are 'legal' provisions," she snapped, "and caring provisions. He had no right to do this because he knew it would upset and threaten me." Self-pity usually finds its way into the catalog of jealousy. So does a conviction of being mistreated and deprived, sadness or grief, despair, helplessness, humiliation. Fear of loss and self-loathing, as we've discussed, and self-righteousness to the heights. The experience of jealousy is always a physical one, manifested in either symptoms of anxiety (churning in the gut, lump in the throat, sweaty palms) or those of depression (headache, low energy, insomnia).

Some authorities say that because of social protocol we act out jealous behavior even when we don't feel it. "Much jealous behavior does not come from strong feelings but is the habituated or expected response in that situation," writes Larry Constantine, author of *Group Marriage*. He goes on to quote sociologist Jessie Bernard: " 'People . . . feel jealous because the norms of our monogamic society teach them to, expect them to, *force* them to.' "

Ah yes, some see monogamy as the villain, the perpetrator. Jealousy, claims psychologist Albert Ellis, is the result of the conflict between romanticism and reality. "Monogamy then," he says, quoted in *Open Marriage*, "not only directly encourages the development of intense sexual jealousy, but also by falsely assuming that men and women can love only one member of the other sex at a time, and can only be sexually attracted to that one person, indirectly sows the seeds for even more violent displays of jealousy."

A Chicago psychologist and student of open relationships goes even further. "A lot of jealousy is phony," he told me. "We *love* it, it makes us feel intensely alive in a way that we don't most times. It stirs up all our juices. It can also remind us how much we care for our mate or it can give us a *false* sense of caring, just because our pride is put in hazard. It brings back the exciting element of conquest into our primary relationship." As an illustration he tells of his patient who was having an affair with a woman in an open marriage. During that period the woman and her husband had a rebirth of their atrophied bond—they never had so much sex or frankness as when the other man was in the picture. When that man decided to end the affair, both the woman and her husband came to him independently to plead with him to continue.

I am as much of a shameful romantic mystifier of sexual jealousy as anybody, and I don't want it taken away from me, reduced to banality. We have few enough big emotions left to us these days, and I resist pop sociology and psychobabble trying to decimate one of the remaining grand gestures. If, in order to buy the notion that jealousy is essentially conditioned, I have to accept explanations that in their simplicity make See

Spot Run read like Kantian dialectics, I am lost.

However: A few months ago at a party, my mate flirted outrageously with a good friend of mine. He did it in front of me and several others, telling her that if he weren't involved with me he surely would want to have an affair with her. I agreed aloud with his fine taste and thought the incident charming; in fact, I thought no more about it at all. Two days later, I exploded. In that time voices in my head had repeated over and over, "How dare he?" "What a slap in the face," "I should be furious, insulted, humiliated, scared." I became all those things—and intensely jealous.

With all its tragic outbursts, its association with violence, its "jaundice of the soul" as Dryden called it, jealousy is more virulent a state than we even admit. That is to say, we keep many of our tendencies concealed, from ourselves as well as others. Los Angeles psychologist Carl Faber is convinced that every time we walk into a party with our mate we survey the scene for danger. If there is a gorgeous blonde over in the corner we become tense, begin to concoct The Script. We do this, he says, all the time, in an instinctive and purely animal reflex of self-defense. But the fears are so pervasive, primitive and shameful that we do not let them surface into our own awareness until something really happens to menace us. Until our mate actually sidles up to said blonde or she to him, we keep the anxiety suppressed—it is so uncivilized and unaccept-able. We are dominated by jealousy in our key relationships and always looking unconsciously for cues. Yet we loathe its indignity and force.

Since Dr. Faber and I talked of this, me recoiling from the unattractiveness of such a proposition, I've become unwillingly awake to its truth. I notice often that when we go to parties I have partial consciousness, for all of the evening, of who and where the smashing women are, where my man is, and if the two forces are coinciding. Like a giant battle plan with me as the commanding general, I need to know where the enemies are hiding, what are their weapons and strategies. There is a certain fundamental and humiliating distrust in this, both of him and of the assumed predatoriness of my sisters. And I feel petty, ugly. What I would most like to do—validating Faber's idea that we deny these emotions—is march over to where he and she are merely chatting on the couch, and grab him away, bellowing to her: "Hands off, bitch. He belongs to me." Obviously, I do not act out such barbarism today in sophisticated America.

Do we really love? Does "love" have any place in the afore-mentioned fantasy? Is it love that drives us to imprison those closest to us, to limit their growth and experience and joy? Jealousy, says La Rochefoucauld, "springs more from love of self than from love of another," and love theorists like Erich Fromm say the obvious: In real love, you want what makes your mate happy, you care as much for his well-being as for your own, you answer "yes" to Greer's question "Do I want my love to be happy more than I want him to be with me?" The best definition that I know of love is the following: Love is giving people the space to be exactly who they are, and exactly who they aren't. How many of us can claim to be loving in those terms?

In a provocative, intelligent book, *Love and Addiction*, author Stanton Peele sets up an engaging premise about the way we love. He began by observing drug addicts and then saw the metaphor which became his book. "Relationships which supposedly entailed some notion of growing together," he writes, "were really based mostly on security and the comfort of spending as much time as possible with someone totally sensitized to one's needs. In those cases, loving another person actually seemed to bring about a contraction in the scope of one's life. What made such relationships stand out for me was the feeling that there was something fundamental in their nature that made them this way. I could think of only one word to describe it: addiction. The individuals involved were hooked on someone whom they regarded as an object; their need for the object, their 'love,' was really a dependency."

The parallel that he postulates between lover and drug addict is quite literal. The comfort and reassurance provided by the "drug" becomes all-consuming; other nonrelated activities atrophy as the addiction grows larger. Satiation is impossible. The purpose is to take away the pain of living, to escape from oneself and to fill up the empty internal spaces. The drug, or relationship, "offers him a solace that contrasts sharply with what he finds everywhere else, so he returns to it more and more, until he needs it to get through each day of his otherwise stressful and unpleasant existence. When a constant exposure to something is necessary in order to make life bearable, an addiction has been brought about, however romantic the trappings. The ever-present danger of withdrawal creates an ever-present craving."

We are speaking of survival. Not choice. All those lyrics from generations of songs, about if-you-leave-me-I'll-absolutely-die, are not exaggerations, poetic license, but speak directly to the life/death crisis from the potential end of a love affair. Is there anything more acute, more fearsome to an addict than the real or threatened withdrawal of his drug supply?

What all of this means is that jealousy is as much a vital ingredient of addictive love as is the anguish of needing a fix to the junkie. The situation that provokes our jealous response is not an annoyance, an inconvenience, even a deep wound. It is not even in the category of intensely felt passion. Rather, it is simply death-dealing desperation, nothing less. What is at stake is our survival. One's life *is* threatened, and because we don't "care" for the other person ultimately, it becomes us or them—I'll do *anything* to keep you from destroying my life. At that stage of the game love, by any definition, is not an operative mechanism.

We are all love junkies, please understand; it is just a question of degree. And, hopefully, we all manifest some health in love, some true concern about our mate's unique value. In contrast to the experts whose view on jealousy is that it is nothing but pathological, many psychiatrists see it as, to some extent, natural and worthwhile.

Carl Faber talks of the rare "real relationship" (as opposed to the addictive) in which there is empathy and caring and an immense vulnerability. "If you start from there," he says, "if the relationship has any history, you've gone through one or more very difficult, painful and confusing relinquishments of defenses. When you bring somebody into your life you open yourself up to include that person, and on each level that you include him—counting on him, letting him see your hurt, sharing responsibility—you have to break through your own armor. The essence then is vulnerability. By definition, when you're vulnerable you're going to get hurt before you can defend yourself, there's just no way to protect yourself. So the longer a relationship like this goes on, the deeper and deeper the jealousy. When you're afraid of him being involved with somebody else, one reason is that it alters the deal, your connection. In the moment that you anticipate the worst, or you actually discover it, a spasm comes from the vulnerability that is just like the doctor saying, 'You have cancer.' You are being hit on all levels.

"But the better a relationship gets the more the vulnerability. Jealousy can make you aware of how valuable the other person is to you and you can share it, as a communication. An intense connection requires periodic bouts of jealousy as a vehicle for expressing emotion. It's an outlet for tapping the richness of feeling. In fact, I would say that no jealousy means no relating."

Sexual union, as the most intimate expression of love and vulnerability, naturally heralds the most thunderous attacks of jealousy. I have let down my armor, let you in to me; we have an unspoken covenant of exposure and safety, and if you make love to somebody else you're devaluing that, damaging and

violating it. The sense of treason that jealous people unanimously express is not just from the lying and secret conniving
of adultery. Folks in open marriages feel betrayed too, although
they know its incorrect and are usually apologetic. Essential
trust may be the issue at stake, trust that your lover will not
use the immense, awesome power you have given each other
to do damage.

I do not know whether sexual jealousy is, at its root, innate
or cultural. Neither does anyone else. The open-sexuality crowd
always refers, in its writings, to a tribe called the Todas of
India, who apparently lived in jealous-free, mate-sharing ecstasy; many anthropologists, however, claim sexual jealousy
pervades in all societies, even the Eskimos'. At any rate, I don't
think the biological vs. conditioned question is the pertinent
one. Acknowledging the global breadth and might of sexual
jealousy, the question is, for me, is it conquerable?

We know that it is. All the pathfinders in this book have
whipped it, which is why their experiments can flourish. They
do experience the rumblings, but jealousy, or the fright of it,
does not govern them as it does most of us.

"The only cure I've ever found for it is to accept one's
jealousy. I've never seen anybody beat it by fighting it or
repressing it. Never." This from Werner Erhard, founder of
est. "You expand your bounds to include the jealousy, you
allow yourself to have this lump in your chest, electrical sensation in your arms, and feeling of panic. And finally, it's like
what the Chinese did with their invaders. They spread out
enough until the invaders disappeared. If you let it be enough,
accept it enough, it seems to disappear. For some people it
doesn't, but they become less controlled by it. They know they
won't perish from the lump in their chests, they're able to
operate with it. Jealousy is mechanical totally, and if it's reduced to that kind of simplicity it gets to be less of a horrendous problem for people."

Such demystification seems to be effective. Getting the suff-

erer to look at *exactly* what underlies the jealousy, challenge
such beliefs as "I'm worthless," "You're shit" or "I can't survive this." It is important also to examine to what degree the
threat of loss is real or unreal, to separate out the elements one
by one—loss of status, pride, lessened control over mate and
so on.

One psychologist, convinced that jealousy is a totally conditioned response, uses behavior modification techniques in his
therapy (which information inspired me to ask if that means
I get an electric shock if I'm jealous and a piece of cheese if
I'm not. It doesn't). To simplify a slow, long-term process, he
has the client imagine the most pleasant and benign scene of
his own choosing—lying on a deserted Caribbean island with
his lover, say. Then to visualize a scene which causes him
minimal jealousy. Then go back, immediately, to the island
fantasy with its happy emotional stimulus. They proceed up
the torment ladder, each fantasy becoming more acute in its
jealousy-producing plot, then returning each time to the beach.
Until, like the famous dog-and-bell example, the automatic
jealousy response has been programmed out and replaced.
These techniques are used similarly in diet therapy and in
attempts to stop smoking.

It is difficult for me to accept that what seems like a bucket
could stop a flood. But another client of this same therapist
reported to me an even simpler strategy which has worked for
him repeatedly. Josh has been in an open marriage for nine
years, somewhat against his will, but Greta needs to be free.
Several years ago, when she was involved with another man,
Josh was having severe bouts of jealousy and saw the therapist
for help. The doctor had him fantasize the most distressing
scene he could concoct and describe it and the feelings it
engendered, in exquisite detail. The scene was always the same:
Greta in wild prolonged fucking with her lover. Along with the
torture of it, Josh became aware of experiencing a kind of
excitement, a rush of energy, an aliveness. That was valuable

information; he came to see what he was getting out of all his pain, the rewards for him. Then he could stop resisting it. Now, over the years, when jealousy erupts, he re-creates this same fantasy while understanding how he's "enjoying" it, he moves through the emotional content, and the pain always disappears.

The evidence is clear that over time jealousy subsides, like all emotions. "The longer a relationship lasts, the more secure its participants are likely to be," reports *Group Marriage*. "We believe this to be the explanation for the decrease in reports of jealousy from longer-lasting groups in our study and for similar results in the Kinsey surveys and in clinical studies."

True believers in open marriage cope with its storms better than those with shaky stomachs. And, too, sexual jealousy is more easily handled and less damaging in arrangements that are open than in orthodox marriages, where the whammy is a double one—illicit sex *and* deception.

The quality of the relationship may be the most indispensable ingredient in the recipe, communication and good will underlining everything. And then, compromise, negotiation, reassurance—and cosmic patience.

XI

Final Days

The Sandstone idea is based on a belief in complete personal
unity. We hold no dichotomies, mind and body we are one
and whole. Our goal is a process of continuing growth.
. . . We will continue to explore the nature of personal
freedom within alternative, intimate relationships in a therapeutic setting while keeping available the Sandstone option
for open sensuality in a congenial social setting.
—from the Sandstone brochure

Again, I am in the back seat of a car, heading up the
Topanga Canyon mountain on a chill night in winter. It is
December of 1975, almost four years after my first expedition
to Sandstone, and I have not been back since then. And again,
I am taut and armored, wondering in desperation, "What the
hell am I doing this for?" This time I know the answer but it
doesn't help. I'm doing this for research, going back to the
launching pad of this excursion, my cross-country star trek that
has consumed the last several years of my life. Going back to
see how it feels now.

So this Saturday night I have to store away the malaise that
dominated my evening then. I have to be a smart, observant,

quick-witted reporter; I can't afford hysterics or withdrawal. Knowing that, why is my stomach behaving like it just hit an air pocket?

I've commandeered different troops for this mission. My mate, my anchor and support, who has never been to Sandstone; my friend Larry who has been there, under unpleasant conditions which I will get to in a moment; and my friend Audrey who is also a virgin, if you will. She will be Larry's "date," due to the couples-only rule. They have never before met and we're all aware that for a blind date this is a tough scene. The only way both would agree to go was with no expectations, completely free to go their own ways once they enter the premises.

Dick and I have made the following contract: Although we have an open relationship of sorts (we will move to monogamy a few months after this night) we will not go off with anybody or flirt or in fact do anything to cause the other anxiety; we promise to be especially sensitive to each other's low thresholds for jealousy. Anyway, it's a laughable matter for me, since I'm quite worried about whether I'll even be able to *talk* to people to get the material I need. Sex is about as far from my mind tonight as the ongoing crisis in the Mideast.

Purposely, we four have gotten slightly drunk on champagne before we set out. It hasn't helped. In the car we compare trepidations. Larry remembers his one previous Sandstone venture, which took place under much the same circumstances. He went as consort to a woman he did not know. Although their arrangement was similarly loose, no pressure or demands, she was attracted to Larry and wanted to make love. He was busy eying another woman and it was all about as free and flowing as midnight in the singles' bar.

"I also had terrible performance fears," he confesses, a common male state. Men at Sandstone, I have noticed, tend to become focused on other men's penises; comparing and inevitably finding themselves wanting, they become sure they will never be able to get an erection, and even if they do, it's so much tinier than that stud's across the room, who will notice or care or desire, anyway? The opposite fear also prevails: What if I have an inappropriate erection, they think—like during the mocha mousse, while discussing the fiscal problems of New York City? Larry's fantasies are directly tied to high school. He is still thinking tonight, "How do you get the beautiful girls? I want the prom queen but she doesn't know I'm alive." What ancient but still-nagging sting in that one, that early bruise from which we never seem to completely recover. Larry, thus burdened, has no intention of partaking tonight.

Audrey: sculptor, poet, sensualist, mid-forties divorcée, feels increasingly nauseated. "I'm afraid somebody will come up to me and touch my breasts," she wails. "What exactly is the dread of that?" I ask her. "I'm afraid of the animal in me. That I'll get aroused and lose control and just want to fuck blindly, everybody, all night long. I've never done that, but I sense I have that urge buried somewhere and it terrifies me." She has deliberately left her diaphragm at home.

As for me, I am more than anything apprehensive of the sexual tyranny of men—that without those rudimentary social constraints provided by civilization I will be assaulted, abused. Like Audrey, I have some awe-filled sense of the dark core of my own nature, some fear/desire for its release. Unlike her, I cannot anticipate that happening in a subway station.

Dick has mixed feelings. "Part of me thinks they're a bunch of depraved nuts, part of me thinks 'They're okay and I'm not.' I fantasize talking with a woman and some guy walking up to me and kicking me in the balls for being with his wife. Then, I'm scared of the conflict of being turned on to someone and you"—meaning me—"watching from the corner. And what if you meet a guy and disappear into the woods despite our agreement? I'll be devastated."

So, you see, we are not exactly the jolliest nor most confident regiment of hedonists trudging through the hills this night.

• • •

I am near the end of a long locomotion, one that began as a quest for Big Solutions and often, en route, raised more puzzles than it solved. During these past few years friends would sometimes beg me in urgency, "Well? What's the answer? What works?" "I don't know yet," I would usually say. "Call back in three months." I figured that eventually I'd know something about this awesome topic of Relationships. And, now, finally, I believe I do.

I have passed through the homes and lives of scores of humans, absorbed them into my own tangled pursuit. Despite my trepidation as we approach the Sandstone Ranch, a feeling I recognize from the last unnerving voyage, I'm not the same. I can hardly recognize myself in that woman of half a decade ago . . .

Sandstone. The headquarters. On this night in December 1975, it exists in three parts: the club, the center and the community. The center functions like all growth centers which run daily or weekend seminars and workshops. These are open to anybody, not just members of the club, and feature your usual touchie-feelie smorgasbord, with a dutiful emphasis on sex. Seminar titles like "Enriching Sexuality Through Hypnosis," "Sexuality, Self and the Outside World" and my favorite title, "Responsible Hedonism," fill the brochures. The center has so far attracted mostly middling names on the growth-leader circuit—the Esalen hotdogs haven't found their way to the Topanga hills yet—and workshops are often canceled for lack of a quorum.

The club is the most visible part of the total experiment, and the membership is, at the time of this visit, much smaller than the owners would like, not the least explanation being that the yearly rates have soared from the $280 per couple at which it began to $740. They now require commitment to the Cause, not just recreation, and in our society money is usually the symbol for serious commitment. "People are much more reluctant to misbehave now," says Wally Lyons, the club's manager. "They don't want to be thrown out and lose their investment." Misbehavior, by the way, means smoking dope, drinking liquor, or exhibiting aggressive or abusive sexual behavior. In the old days, all that was common. Sandstone undoubtedly shocked more people then than now, and booze or dope would soften some of the jolt. The times have altered that.

The Family currently consists of twenty residents, we are told upon our arrival, although the number is flexible and the cast seems to change with some frequency. They plan and produce all the Sandstone functions. Some just work at the ranch, others have jobs in the outside world but devote considerable time to Sandstone. One is in the arduous process of becoming an *est* trainer. Six residents are alone, five couples are in primary relationships, two are monogamous. Pam and David, for example, have been living here for four months and still are sexually exclusive, but heading toward an open relationship. This was their goal in moving here from the city; Pam claims nervously, "It could happen at any moment."

There are two curious facts about the Family, more revealing than any gospel. 1) No intergroup sexual minglings occur. They view each other as brothers and sisters. And 2) you rarely see Family constituents fornicating with their spouses in the public rooms. When the downstairs fiesta gets under way, they usually retreat to their private nests.

Wally Lyons and Ann Factor are the sole remnants of the original Sandstone Family, their combined jobs being the management of the club. Wally, a man who has perhaps never been seen wearing clothing, vows that "God is my tailor;" Ann, a lithe young blonde with a beautiful and solemn face, claims— with pride—to have starred in a rather busily explicit feature film called *Sandstone*. Wally and Ann have persevered together for four and a half years, in a relationship that could indeed serve as a paradigm of the future—should the future propel in the astral direction predicted in these circles.

Wally, now thirty-three, had been in a monogamous marriage for several years when he and his wife, Janie, went up to Sandstone. "On my first visit here," he recalls, "Janie and I were hiding in a corner, afraid to talk to anybody. An older woman, very earthy and warm, came over, took my hand, said, 'You look a little nervous,' then marched me downstairs to the playroom and balled me. That was the beginning. I was sold." Shortly afterward Wally and Janie moved to the ranch. After a year of turmoil and stress, but increasing dedication to the principles of free loving, they separated and Janie left Sandstone.

It was just a few weeks later that he met Ann, who came to Sandstone for the day with a friend. "From our first conversation until this moment we have been involved in the most intense relationship of our lives," Wally has written. "We agreed immediately upon everything," Ann tells us. "We both said, 'I think I could spend a long time with you, but not exclusively.' "

Which is precisely the way it's been for the ensuing four and a half years. I am still, even after this journey, enthralled by those individuals whose programming is clearly and thoroughly unlike mine, unlike the culture's in which they were spawned and bred. How did they escape? I will always wonder.

A few months after Ann and Wally met, she decided to move up to Sandstone to be with him, whereupon she was forever ostracized by her friends and temporarily by her parents —middle-class Jews from the San Fernando Valley—who, in all the four and a half years, haven't been up to the ranch.

The quality in them as a couple that most strikes me is their insistence on not backing away from discomforting situations and their good-willed openness in handling them. They are confronters, not avoiders; they will risk pain to face truth rather than denying that what is there is there. As Americans we have lately come to deify the avoidance of discomfort, we have means to tranquilize or evade or obliterate every one of life's inescapable stings. And the price we pay for our cowardice, our anesthesia, is to often feel not quite alive. I know now that one of the messages to be found at the sexual frontier is that of taking risks.

I have known and spent relaxed time with Wally and Ann for a couple of years. But tonight, as the three of us cluster around the welcoming fireplace, I learn new data about them. Before, I had always assumed their bond to be tranquil. I was wrong. Now they tell me that they, like the rest of us, suffer acute bouts of jealousy; they get crazy, they need to repair and consolidate and come to blows with each other and their own monsters.

Ann can erupt if Wally is with a woman she can't stand— but also if he's with one *too* terrific, *too* beautiful. Recalling one incident, she describes it as an illustration of just how nuts she has gotten in her time. An incident in which, to me, she seems perfectly sane. One Saturday afternoon, several months ago, Wally met a marvelous woman on the lawn, a woman whose qualities seemed a major menace to Ann. After some hours of their enchanted mutual discovery (What could be more joyless to watch from the lonely sidelines, we all agree) they ambled downstairs. "I was very upset," Ann says. "This woman has everything I don't." Our most dire prospects coming true.

At the same time, a car started to smoke and burn in the parking lot and nobody was around to handle it. Ann took the opportunity to bolt downstairs, interrupting Wally midfellatio, screaming, "I want to talk to you right now," dragging him upstairs, bellowing about the burning car as if he had caused it. In psychiatry that is known as displacement.

Wally handled it ("It was only overheating," he smiles), after which Ann apologized weakly to him and his woman. "I'm so sorry I disturbed you," she said. By then, of course, the mood was broken and sex was over. She now claims to feel "absolutely awful" about her uncontrolled outbursts.

What glues Wally and Ann, I suspect, is their overweaning commitment to this kind of life, and the effort and investment they have made in the process. That kind of commitment must be the foundation for an open relationship to thrive, of that I'm now sure. Without it, there is no ground under the feet.

Ann is no longer fearful of losing him, which plainly eases the pressure of watching him turn on to another woman, even a woman "who has everything I don't." Jealousy for women is essentially about being abandoned, and Ann has happily moved past that primal fright. "If we have a good relationship going," Ann says, "it's not likely we'll manufacture a hot infatuation to destroy it. Infatuations don't just happen by accident. People create and use them to get out of the relationship they're in." Unfortunately, life doesn't always yield to Ann's lucid logic. And unfortunately there is no way to guarantee what she —what all of us—want desperately to guarantee, permanence and absolute safety. The question is, Does Wally and Ann's form of relationship minimize the dangers or heighten them? And, in any event, do we want to navigate our lives solely to the aim of eluding danger?

Neither has been importantly involved with anybody else in the four years, although God knows if there's a milieu with ample opportunity Sandstone is it, and when asked to compute how many men besides Wally she regularly has sex with, Ann responds, "Probably five a month. If it's a good month." Nevertheless she and Wally wisely retrench in bad times, withdraw to each other during periods of tension, and become faithful. I have seen some open-marriage twosomes reflexively run for open pastures—and the waiting herds—when their own going gets rough. The odds for their survival are bad.

For Ann and Wally, it is only when their union is sturdy that they reach out. When they are most close is when each can watch the other make love to somebody and as Ann says, "be thrilled with the beauty and joy of Wally being intensely together with a woman." I have repeatedly heard many other afficionados make such proclamations. I used to think "Bullshit," but tonight I merely nod in unempathetic wonder. Then there's the commonly heard theme which Ann now offers, the one about Ann and Wally being happiest and most relaxed when their beloved has tied in with a spectacular friend. I will probably never fathom this one: If my man has to sleep with somebody else, I'd just as soon she be as homely and dreary as possible.

There are 120 members of Sandstone at this moment, all adults. Because one can join either as a couple or alone for the same $740 a year, the number of men and women is unequal —73 males, 47 females. There are 24 married couples and 65 unmarrieds; 7 men joined without their wives (5 of whom confessed their wives don't know about it). Four members are black (3 of them men) and one is Oriental. For the majority of married couples, it is their first marriage and is over five years in duration. The mean age is thirty-seven.

It is not surprising, in looking at the demographics of Sandstone members, to find an education and income level far above the general population. The quest for self-actualization —if one is to believe Abraham Maslow and assume that is what Sandstone represents—is a function of leisure, affluence, consciousness and the prior fulfillment of lower-order needs. Even if Sandstone is not so solemn a venture but merely a playground for zippy sex, sport fucking is still a luxurious pastime. Lifestyle radicalism usually finds its breeding ground in the middle and upper classes.

The mean income, I learn tonight, is $21,000 for singles, $30,500 for married couples. Interestingly, in surveys of swingers and members of the California Sexual Freedom League, the figures were much lower—around $15,000 per person. Sandstone appears to attract the middle-classier folk, which could be attributed to its higher fees, but more likely to its higher ideologies, transcending the baser goals of swinging.

Fifty-four percent of Sandstone tribesmen are college graduates, 23 percent hold advanced degrees. Occupationally, the highest number are in business. To me the most revealing statistic is this: 25 percent of all Americans seek psychological counseling at some point in their lives; that figure, for the Sandstone population, is 71.7 percent.

I am told that these figures have been compiled throughout 1975 by Richard H. Rice, for his Master's thesis at UCLA. He has worked via questionnaires completed by all the members, and one area pinpointed was motivation. When asked to state their reasons for joining, 64.2 percent claimed for "relationships," 33.3 percent for "growth." "Freedom" and "fun" were other big items, but nobody admitted attending Sandstone in order to screw. "Growth within my primary relationship," or "having more social contacts" or "to explore and experiment with my relationships" are acceptable motives; getting laid is not.

And yet that is exactly the feature setting Sandstone apart from a nudist camp or resort hotel, cruise ship, or the local country club. At swimming pools all over Los Angeles, tanned and trim citizens convene every weekend to drink Mountain White Chablis and Perrier, to pass around a little $70-a-lid Colombian Red, get "mellow" and talk earnestly about what they're "into" this week. When things get mellow enough, off come the bikinis, on come the records and the poolside bumping. And a few phone numbers are exchanged surreptitiously, a few "business lunch" dates, made in sotto voce. If that's not "freedom" and "fun" what the hell is? Why do we need Sandstone, for Lord's sake?

Because somewhere in our sybaritic souls, we are still schizophrenic Puritans. We worship the orgasm, but at the same time we need to deny the pursuit of it, cloak it in terms allegedly resting on redeeming social value. So far, up until my second caravan to Sandstone, I have not heard anyone say unashamedly that he or she takes the long route up the mountain to ball as many mammals as the body will allow, to act out lifelong fantasies, to make into reality what has only been read in dirty books, seen in dirty movies, imagined in randiest dreams. And yet my biases so far have told me that that is precisely what Sandstone is about. I wonder if I will carry the same perception at the end of this unsettling evening . . .

Our Master's thesis researcher was led to some additional saucy conclusions. For instance, although it almost always is men who do the initiating—both to get their wives to join, and to begin miscellaneous sexual contact while here—it is women who feel more liberated once they *are* here. Men expressed a great deal of distress at actually viewing what they had always suspected: women's unquenchable appetites and superior endurance. These same twosomes reported that pre-Sandstone, of the number who had engaged in either free sexuality or clandestine affairs, the women found those experiences more positive than the men.

A common report was the one that goes: After a weekend at Sandstone sex with my spouse is better—fresh and thrilling—especially if we tell each other the details of our other screws. Some say they fall madly in love with said spouse after lifeless years. It's hard to know what to make of such information, or how seriously to take it. Analysis is facile and often fraudulent; observation seems more accurate.

Saturday night at Sandstone. As in the rest of America, it is big party night; they have not abandoned that particular powerful ritual. When it's warm, you can spend the entire weekend here. You sleep on the waterbeds and mattresses in the playroom or park your sleeping bag anywhere on the property. During the winter months the action starts at about 6 P.M. on Saturday night. It is, incidentally, a rather expensive frolic. The guest fee for us is $60 a couple plus $15 for dinner.

One may come up alone during the daytime, on Thursday nights when they show movies, Friday nights for the consciousness-raising groups or to any of the seminars at the growth center. You must leave or acquire a companion for the Wednesday and Saturday night soirées.

Except for New Year's Eve (Don't ask about New Year's Eve at Sandstone . . .) there is no planned entertainment. "Everything just flows," says Wally Lyons, the affable head counselor. Oh, occasionally a serendipity appears, like the night somebody showed home movies of his wife giving birth to twins. But mostly, Saturday night "just flows," as it does tonight.

Contrary to Wally's Zen-talk, I have both times found Sandstone quite formalistic, as if somebody is blowing a silent whistle every few hours which moves the assemblage from one activity period to the next. Sandstone's resemblance to a summer camp has never escaped my attention. Here's the schedule, this night, as before. Six to eight P.M.: "Getting acquainted in the living room." Could also, depending on your degree of skepticism, be known as "sizing up the action" or "preparing to score." Eight to nine: dinner in the living room; more getting acquainted and closing in on desired prospects. Nine to ten: Jacuzzi. Ah, here's where the good stuff finally gets off the ground. At the weekly kissing parties in high school, this was the part of the night when you solidified who you were going to be with later, for the no-fooling-around necking. By the end of this activity period, if you weren't paired off with somebody you'd better slink off home; if you'd somehow gotten stuck with a loser you were in big trouble, since no more switching occurred. Well, Sandstone's kinkier than South Side High School and a lot of switching and jostling and transplanting transpires. But for the first preliminary round of sport, the Jacuzzi hour is when you settle your initial match.

One can't stay immersed in steaming-hot Jacuzzi water too long. For one thing it enervates you, for another it makes your

skin look like a dried apricot, which is the last thing one would
want tonight. So you sit in it just long enough to get to feeling
tingly sexy—they have these bubbling jets, you see, which if
you're a lady you can manage to squat over in just such a way
. . . If you're a man they don't do much for you, I'm told.

By now you're loosey-goosey and sweet-smelling and sensual,
so you head downstairs, either with the cohort of your choice
or by yourself, in which case you hope for an invitation or you
just sort of lie around waiting for something to happen. In very
short order, it will.

My first large surprise of an evening of considerable surprises
is that I truly enjoy Sandstone tonight. From the instant we
enter the living room and naked Uncle Wally rushes over to
greet us with enormous warmth, I feel safe and—more to the
point—at home. Sandstone appears very cheery and low-key.
The fire-bathed room sheds high spirits, welcome and no discernible hustle. Maybe Sandstone has reformed, as many have
claimed, from the early frenetic days of my first visit. But, more
accurately, it's probably I who have changed in four years, and
the Sandstone planet no longer shocks or offends me. Suddenly
I understand what seekers find in Sandstone—besides and beyond fornicating.

The crowd is small. By seven-thirty about fifty revelers are
scattered around the house, getting acquainted. A few are
nude, most wear robes or kaftans. Sexy, revealing ones, not your
Granny flannels. The talk is quiet, and the word that best
describes the atmosphere is "pleasant." And that startles me
more than it does you.

Around the room, a few tapestries strike my fancy: The
pretty young woman posing rather self-consciously before the
stone fireplace, bare breasts obviously siliconed (you can tell by
the angle of horizontality), wearing nothing but those day-of-
the-week underpants I used to own in junior high school. I
ponder why she's got on "Tuesday" tonight. On the sofa sits
a couple; she looks like Mama Cass and wears a blue work-shirt,

unbuttoned. She focuses intently on the ceiling, as if searching for ants. He raps intently to the guy on his left. The entire time he is kneading her large bare bosoms. On the dining room love seat is another duet, he lightly kissing her unshaved armpits. Later, in retrospect, I will consider that the most porno visual of the evening.

As before, I still catch myself chuckling or sneering at some of Sandstone's denizens. Marilyn, for example, is twenty-three, single, one of the few unattached female members. Working as a bookkeeper in the garment center in downtown L.A., she studies fashion design at night and spends all her weekends up at Sandstone by herself. She has a frosted blond Afro, a striking face that seems sad and lost. The very closest Marilyn previously had been to emancipated sex was some work as a nude model for art classes. Then a male buddy brought her to Sandstone one Saturday and she signed up on the spot. She works five hours each weekend in the kitchen in partial exchange for her membership.

Is she looking for a serious alliance up here? I wonder. She says no, she's not ready for that now. But if she were, which she isn't, it certainly wouldn't be a monogamous one; Sandstone has cured her of that foolishness forever. She almost always meets at least one new man to have sex with on weekends. But in town she has never dated anybody she's met here. The fact is her social life is nil off the mountain. She breathes a rarified air at Sandstone and for sure doesn't find too many soulmates "down there."

Marilyn's shrink tells her Sandstone is good for her growth. How? I inquire. "Well, I never used to be able to scream in my apartment during my orgasm, which bottles me up. Here I feel free to shout, and he says that's important for me." Yes, who of us urban dwellers cannot sympathize with that one? "I'm also getting more and more relaxed about not having to run behind a closed door to express myself physically with a man. It wasn't easy for me at first, but I'm getting better every week." And from where I sit, Marilyn doesn't appear to have too many noticeable hangups left in the public inhibition department. By the time I leave that night, I have noticed her expressing herself with three separate fellows, in two different rooms, and in more positions than the Bolshoi Ballet.

I imagine that Marilyn is more popular and more at ease in this setting than in a conventional singles' scene, where games and pretense rule. And even more than the unattached females like Marilyn, married women appear to blossom erotically here. Here they have permission to be assertive, truly sexual and to claim what they need. Women at Sandstone do not appear to play the passive role, waiting to be chosen, ultimately feeling ripped off. I'm not sure if Sandstone has thoroughly succeeded in demolishing the American double standard for sexual license (good for guys, bad for girls) in its wee special realm, but on the surface it looks that way. And if so, that's virtue enough to justify its existence.

I watch the women a lot, off and on during the night, and I never see them being hustled; I do see several politely but firmly saying no to men who politely but firmly request. I also watch them being more sexually forthright—infinitely more—than I think women allow themselves to be in the real world.

Sandstone once looked to me like the proverbial candy store —just drop in and gorge yourself on the goodies—and that ethos was at least a chunk of my initial disgust and fear. Tonight it feels humane, which is certainly not to say that the kids aren't balling left and right. It's just nicer. "You can't come to Sandstone horny," Uncle Wally says when I confide this observation to him. We are currently side by side, sinking into the low, sexy couch, trying to balance our plates of Cornish hens, artichokes, wild rice and Caesar salad. "The vibrations will blow people away, they just won't want to be near you. Sometimes I feel like I just need to fuck, and I know I'm gonna be aggressive. So I just go to sleep instead. You've got to give here. If you come just to take, you're gonna get slapped down."

•   •   •

Herbie is a sharp-looking, twenty-eight-year-old Jewish knight from New York, in the "import-export business" (which in these parts sometimes signifies dope dealing). With a horrid Bronx nasal lilt, and a necklace of silver coins dangling down his hairy chest, he has been on the couch for several hours, being very clubby with Jessie. Pay attention now. Jessie is the stunning fortyish wife of Vic, a bearded psychologist who has been showing considerable interest in my friend Audrey. One fancies where all this will eventually end up, but at the moment it's difficult to predict. Although Herbie and Jessie aren't touching at all, they are conversationally engrossed and exclusive. As I squat on the floor to talk to them he is saying to her, quite solemnly, "When I talk to you I get real-person vibes." And his genitals are ever-so-slightly exposed from underneath his scarlet bathtowel, which he wears as the bottom half of his gauzy rajah shirt. My intuitions tell me Herbie has come to Sandstone horny, but that he is moving in stealthily, willing to "share" and "relate" to Jessie before getting down to business. I could be wrong. I don't trust rajah shirts. Jessie, I think, is not into sex, even though she is wearing a short Chinese silk robe which barely covers her crotch.

Herbie tells me his story. He is unmarried and, like Marilyn, spends his weekends here, every one of them, and he never sees the same girls in town. But he admits to definitely "looking for a primary relationship." Reflexively I want to matchmake Herbie and Marilyn, but each seems to be absorbed only in married folks. Hmm . . .

I ask, "What's in it for you to be here with so many married people?" I am praying I will not get one of those windy, tedious answers about fulfilling his potential, you know the kind I mean. Herbie does not disappoint me. "Sex," he says. "Fucking." "Do you get sexually involved every weekend?" say I, flinching at my automatic euphemism. "Christ, I hope so. Fuckin' waste if I don't." He sneaks a sidelong glance at Jessie.

I do too. She doesn't react. Maybe I'm wrong, maybe she *is* into sex.

Jessie and Vic have been married for eighteen years, have four children and are thoughtful, cheerful people. "We were looking for something exciting and scary to do," she says. "We've tried beach clubs and country clubs, but that wasn't giving us the stimulation we need. I like it up here, even though I'm sexually inhibited. Maybe one out of twenty times that we come up I make love with someone. That's all." (I peek sideways at Herbie. Is it my imagination or have his horny eyes suddenly begun to cruise the room?)

Vic usually indulges in the Sandstone feast, but in their agreement he cannot date anybody in town. "Have you ever watched him make love?" I ask. "Once," she says quietly, "and it was the most agonizing experience of my life. It felt like I was eight years old and walking through a blinding snowstorm and when I came to my house it was locked, so I pressed my nose against the window, and there was a strange woman opening my Christmas presents. I felt frightened to death, helpless and abandoned." I don't know what wellspring houses this story—memory, dream, fantasy or metaphor. But it moves me, and the source doesn't matter.

Vic, I am much relieved to note, does not have any liaison that night. I do not think I can bear identifying with Jessie, although she insists she's fine so long as she doesn't have to watch. That, and if she knows and likes the female—that arcane ethic again. "If I don't know her, she's Mata Hari," Jessie says.

Sexual jealousy. All roads lead back to that primordial, animal force. I know that it is possible to defeat sexual jealousy and that we would be richer without it. I know all the elements, I've examined them like paramecia under the microscope, and I can tell you precisely what to do to get rid of the Evil Fiend. And, sometimes, once every four years or so, I'm not jealous.

Yes, some mysterious human creatures are simply not victim

to it. Many others strive to conquer it and do. Most of us—almost all of us—are so invariably trapped in its oceanic currents that we cannot cope. We just cannot. We make monumental choices about our lives simply in order to elude its sheer madness. Choices like sexual fidelity.

Open relationships are a noble and engaging idea, an idea which—after my long pilgrimage—I can no longer fault. A form that, in theory, could cure many of the ills of American matrimony. And an idea, for the big majority of us, whose time has probably *not yet* come. There is only that one massive barrier, Sexual Jealousy, but for now it is an innate and/or cultural volcano too large to puff out. We got rid of smallpox finally; someday, perhaps in the next generation or the one after that, we'll get rid of jealousy.

I'm aware that the renegades I've met who have abolished sexual jealousy from their lives, or who manage to coexist with it, still seem to me like Martians. I admire them, wish I could join them for a jaunt on their miraculous flying saucers, pray they triumph as a model for us earthbounds. Me, I'm not like them. I know that now, finally. I need some gigantic freedoms for my days to feel full but I need, too, a snug and safe harbor. There has to be some niche, some small place that is peaceful, in our bloody and battered system. I am a product of these decades of American chaos and fast change, but enough, I think, is enough.

And I'm willing to forego the occasional stabs of lust for others, or the naggings of periodic Experience Greed. I don't have a lot of faith in monogamy, but I surely don't need the colossal beauty of watching my mate make wild love to my best friend, no thank you very much. Pass.

Tonight at Sandstone, at about nine-thirty, the troops begin filtering outside to the Jacuzzi. The night is cold, windless and clear, the tub hot and bubbling, and the combination of sensations on one's skin is electrifying. I don't know the origin of the Jacuzzi, but it must be a California invention, an emblem of our exaltation of hedonism. Dick and I are, much to our amazement, rather awakened by the good spirits, the wine, the water and air, the WICKEDNESS.

About twenty frolickers crowd the small tub—making random touching inevitable. We talk to an unlikely duo, in their fifties, who drive five hours from a little town up north to get here each weekend. The woman says, "We're members because we like the people and the ambiance, but we have no desire for free sex." I take her word, as she resembles a high-school Latin teacher and her husband an electrical supply salesman. But a few moments later I suddenly feel a hand inching lightly up my calf under the water, then up my thigh, and I whisper to Dick who is perched on my left, "Is that your hand on my leg?" He swears no, bringing his two arms out of the water to illustrate. By God, that bloody old lecher soaking on my right, that tame old electrical supply salesman who only comes here for the "ambiance," is talking heatedly to somebody and making Le Grand Tour of my inner thigh at the same time, hidden from his wife and even from me. I whisper to Dick, frantically, "What should I do?" He gets annoyed. "Tell him to get his fuckin' hands off you." "I can't," say I with uncharacteristic meekness. "I mean, he's not really *doing* anything, and it *is* Sandstone. I don't want to seem like a creep or humiliate him . . ."

There you have it. A lot of babies have been created in this world from just such guilt-stricken paralysis. How many consummations at Sandstone have occurred thus?

I speak with a dark-haired woman in her twenties named Louise, very chubby, her chubbier husband beside her in the water. Since they've had an open marriage, everything is superduper for them, she croons. She doesn't get a mite jealous even though he's currently in love with another chick. *What does she know that I don't?* Is it possible that I am more insecure than anybody on this outpost? Do I not care about Personal Growth?

A fat, curly-haired fellow approaches Louise, starts nibbling and stroking her. Right in front of her husband, who looks on, impassive. Is there something going on behind that stony face? Are his insides shredding, making like the motor of a Cuisinart? Curly and the lady leave together, next to be seen giving each other head in the playroom. Where would I be if that scenario had been my mate and another woman? What is the secret?

Dick has asked Wally the same question earlier: How come you can make an open relationship work? Dick, like me, would probably not be monogamous except for sexual jealousy. Like me, he would wish total sexual license for himself, while blind faithfulness from me. Wally has answered that nonmonogamy is a matter of reeducation, retraining the way we look at and interpret events. "That, and living in a supportive milieu, in the midst of a social process that everyone here is engaged in. I'm sure that it's a lot more difficult to carry off if you don't have a place, a system, like Sandstone, to reinforce you. If Ann and I lived in Beverly Hills we couldn't have done it."

Dick and I amble down to the playroom, where the bacchanale is just getting up steam. Our friend Audrey, whom we've not glimpsed for some time, is over in one dark corner, embroiled with an ethereal young boy wearing lace-up Indian sandals to the knee, but nothing else. We're all of us startled (But she left her diaphragm home!) and quite embarrassed, averting our eyes. It's one thing to view strangers doing it . . . When my eyes meet hers she leaps up, grabs the young buck's hand and pulls him off into the ballroom.

Finding an unoccupied waterbed, Dick and I settle down to observe the proceedings, I with notebook and pencil in hand. The bed undulates, is as warm as an electric blanket beneath our nakedness, and soon I find the Sandstone atmosphere getting to me. I feel as if I'm stoned and moving through some kind of filmy, unearthly erotic dream. Dick looks at me, and we know wordlessly that we're feeling the same moody arousal, and we begin slowly to make love. For a while I go with it, surprised at the unexpected truth that either of us would be free to do this in front of other people. Periodically, the sound of gasping or shrieking orgasm from another part of the black room sends us into uncontrolled giggles, and we sit up, becoming innocent bystanders once again. But after each interruption, in watching the rhythmic thrusting and rocking, the building heat of another couple near us, we again become excited and reach for each other.

That cycle repeats several times, for perhaps an hour. Ultimately, lust wins out over note-taking. During the act my head never quite stops its jabbering. What if Audrey or Larry see us doing this? What if we look ugly or klutzy? I handle those recurrent tunes, somewhat by 1) pulling off the orange scarf I've been wearing on my head—so nobody will recognize me, and 2) burying my face in Dick's chest and never lifting it until we have finished. I'm aware, afterward, that Dick was much more unrestrained; I evidently needed to withhold the final surrender that is so linked, in my mind, to private shelter. He admits to having been supremely turned on by the mirrors behind us in which he watched our entire deed, and by the extraordinary sinfulness of this whole adventure.

Four years ago I was gripped by hostile tension, visceral dislike for these outlaws and their shenanigans. I could barely manage a monosyllabic conversation. Tonight I have made love in Piccadilly Circus.

I know, at least, that my ancient iron-willed myths about monogamy, sexuality, relationships all have suffered pounding blows since I started this job. And Sandstone no longer seems dangerous or detestable. Tonight it has felt . . . well . . . right to join in. These women and men are partisans, not betrayers. The playroom is not Sodom but neutral territory.

Dick and I are like two naughty children, delighted with our mischief. We jump around chattering to people, peeking baldly at strangers screwing. I overhear Herbie, currently meshed with a lady who is not, by the way, Jessie, saying, "You know, if you're really into what you're doin', there's nobody else here." All the while, he is fucking surrounded by twenty-two others. In one unlit corner of the ballroom I spy my friend Fred, the potential *est* trainer. The silicone lady, still wearing her Tuesday panties, is going down on him. Somebody else is biting his neck and ears while he and I have a dialogue about the future of *est*. Later, as we're leaving, Dick and I return to say farewells to Fred, and blond Marilyn is gulping his cock. Dick whispers to me, "If she gets up to kiss me goodbye, I don't know what I'll do."

On the way down the mountain we four friends deliver our State of the Union reports. Unanimously, our sagas reverse those of panic that gripped us driving in the opposite direction. Audrey has met several men she likes, felt unruffled making love with one but couldn't quite handle a multitude in one sitting. She has been invited back for next Saturday night by the lace-up sandals; she will bring her diaphragm. Larry, as he prophesized and fulfilled, did not engage and is gloomy, sort of like he has failed an important exam. Dick feels evil, adolescent, and wonders when we can go again.

And I'm essentially bemused, rather in awe at discovering that unpredicted hidden corridor in myself. I am silent for a long time while everyone gabs merrily. I'm thinking about four years. As Larry drops us off at home, he calls out the car window, "You know, Sandstone is either incredibly healthy or terribly sick. And I'll be damned if I can tell which."

Four years ago I would have been fleet with an answer. Now I shrug and say nothing. I know I could blab on the subject for days without pause. A century has passed since I began.

When I began, I thought this expedition was going to be about sex. I believed that marriage doesn't work today because —among the army of explanations—fidelity doesn't work. But my eyesight has altered over these few years. I see that sex, as elemental a human function as it is, isn't the entire issue at all. Yeah, fidelity is difficult, and probably silly. And yes, we're voracious creatures with lusts for every lollipop beyond our grasp; satisfied with nothing for very long, what we don't have becomes itchingly more valuable than what we do. And sex is that mighty force which makes us itch above all else. But sex is not the most vital ingredient for most of us, either in life or in our relationships. Sexual license, nonmonogamy, erotic solutions, are mostly metaphors—overlays for matters much deeper and more meaningful. Among its other values, sex has forever stood as the symbol for possession, control and suppression of another human being, and humans have often assumed possession, control and suppression as parts of the definition of marriage. So that in breaking down the limitations of monogamy, my pilgrims are really addressing themselves to today's continuing struggle to destroy the decrepit roles and games and lies wedged in the heart of traditional marriage.

When I think about all the seekers I've encountered on this trip—the questionable unions as well as the unassailable triumphs—the same message echoes throughout: I'm not going to give up who I am because I'm married to you. *That* is the revolutionary credo, the thesis of the 1970's. And that is not about messing around, but is a demand and a freedom much more at the marrow of our lives than sexual liberty.

Most of us are fighting this good fight, but most of us will not choose the bedroom as our Omaha Beach. There is, you see, the matter of jealousy.

I've met and known enough journeymen to realize that open sexual relationships can prosper. I've come to see them not as weirdos but as pioneers of a long and slow cultural shake-up. They are single-minded, most of them, flamboyant, often blind and self-righteous, maybe misguided. But some of them succeed, and more and more will every day. And I'll be rooting and cheering for them. From the sidelines.

●　　　●　　　●

The chances for me as a possible recruit into the free-sexuality arm of this revolution became inescapably lucid several months after Sandstone. We took my mate's fifteen-year-old son to dinner one night. Drowning in his first full-fledged Love, he was consumed with the topic and all its branches and byways, and between enchilada mouthfuls he said to me, seemingly from nowhere: "What would you do if my dad made love to another woman?" I flinched from the imaginary fist that had just socked me in the stomach and said, without having to ponder even a second: "I would leave him." My own surefooted answer rattled me as much as it did the two males; we all think I'm a hipper creature than that. But at that moment I meant it, and we all knew that I meant it.

Bibliography

Books

Bach, George R. and Wyden, Peter. *The Intimate Enemy.* New York: Morrow, 1969.

Benson, Leonard. *The Family Bond.* New York: Random House, 1971.

Bernard, Jessie. *The Future of Marriage.* New York: Bantam, 1973.

Blankenship, Judy. *Scenes from Life.* Boston: Little Brown, 1976.

Casler, L. *Is Marriage Necessary?* New York: Human Science Press, 1974.

Comfort, Alex, ed. *More Joy.* New York: Crown, 1974.

Constantine, Larry L. and Constantine, Joan M. *Group Marriage.* New York: Macmillan, 1973.

Cuber, John and Haroff, Peggy B. *Sex and the Significant Americans.* New York: Appleton-Century-Crofts, 1965.

De Beauvoir, Simone. *The Second Sex.* Translated by H. M. Parshley. New York: Knopf, 1953.

Ellis, Albert. *The American Sexual Tragedy.* New York: Grove, 1962.

———. *The Civilized Couple's Guide to Extramarital Adventure.* New York: Pinnacle, 1973.

Farson, Richard E.; Hauser, Philip M.; Stroup, Herbert; Wiener, Anthony J. *The Future of the Family*. New York: Family Service Association of America, 1969.

Francoeur, Anna K. and Francoeur, Robert T. *Hot & Cool Sex*. New York: Harcourt Brace Jovanovich, 1974.

Francoeur, Robert T. *Eve's New Rib*. New York: Dell, 1973.

Gordon, Michael, ed. *The Nuclear Family in Crisis*. New York: Harper & Row, 1972.

Gordon, Suzanne. *Lonely in America*. New York: Simon & Schuster, 1976.

Gorney, Roderic, M.D. *The Human Agenda*. New York: Bantam, 1973.

Greer, Germaine. *The Female Eunuch*. New York: McGraw-Hill, 1971.

Howe, Louise Kapp, ed. *The Future of the Family*. New York: Simon & Schuster, 1973.

Hunt, Morton. *The Natural History of Love*. New York: Minerva Press, 1959.

———. *Sexual Behavior in the 1970's*. Chicago: Playboy Press, 1974.

Jourard, Sidney M. *The Transparent Self*. New York: Van Nostrand, 1971.

Kerkendall, Lester A. and Whitehurst, Robert N., eds. *The New Sexual Revolution*. New York: Donald W. Brown, 1971.

Lederer, William J. and Jackson, Don. *The Mirages of Marriage*. New York: Norton, 1968.

Lobell, John and Lobel, Mimi. *John and Mimi: A Free Marriage*. New York: Bantam, 1973.

Maslow, A. H. Introduction to *Religions, Values and Peak Experiences*. New York: Viking, 1970.

———. Preface to *Motivation and Personality*. New York: Harper & Row, 1970.

Masters, W. and Johnson, V. *The Pleasure Bond*. Boston: Little Brown, 1975.

May, Rollo. *Love and Will*. New York: Dell, 1974.

Mead, Margaret. *Male and Female*. New York: Morrow, 1967.

O'Neill, Nena and O'Neill, George. *Open Marriage*. New York: Avon, 1973.

Otto, Herbert A., ed. *The Family in Search of a Future*. New York: Appleton-Century-Crofts, 1970.

Packard, Vance. *The Sexual Wilderness.* New York: Pocket Books, 1970.

Peele, Stanton, with Brodsky, Archie. *Love and Addiction.* New York: Taplinger, 1975.

Rimmer, Robert H., ed. *Adventures in Loving.* New York: New American Library, 1973.

———. *Proposition 31.* New York: New American Library, 1969.

———. *Thursday, My Love.* New York: New American Library, 1972.

Rogers, Carl R. *Becoming Partners.* New York: Dell, 1972.

Smith, James R. and Smith, Lynn G., eds. *Beyond Monogamy.* Baltimore: Johns Hopkins University Press, 1974.

Taylor, G. Rattray. *Sex in History.* New York: Harper & Row, 1973.

Toffler, Alvin. *Future Shock.* New York: Bantam, 1971.

Werneck, Robert and the editors of Time-Life Books. *The Family.* New York: Time-Life Books, 1974.

Westermarck, Edward. *A Short History of Marriage.* New York: Humanities, 1968.

Wolfe, Linda. *Playing Around.* New York: Morrow, 1975.

Magazines, Lectures, Newspapers

Abeel, Erica. "Divorce Fever: Is It an Epidemic?" Lecture. New York, November 4, 1974.

Casler, Lawrence, "Permissive Matrimony: Proposals for the Future." *The Humanist,* March/April 1974.

Denfeld, Duane and Gordon, Michael. "The Sociology of Mate-Swapping." Journal of Sex Research 6:2, May, 1970.

Durbin, Karen. "On Sexual Jealousy." *The Village Voice,* October 18, 1973.

Farson, Dr. Richard E. "The Education of Jeremy Farson." State of California State Committee on Public Education, March 1967.

———. "Why Good Marriages Fail." *McCalls,* October 1971.

Levin, Robert J. and Levin, Amy. "The *Redbook* Report: A Study of Female Sexuality," September and October 1975.

Liddick, Betty. "Open Sexuality Reopens at Sandstone." Los Angeles *Times,* June 4, 1974.

Maslow, Abraham. "Critique of Self-Actualization." Reprinted from *Journal of Individual Psychology* 15:24–32, May 1959.

———. "A Philosophy of Psychology." Lecture. Cooper Union, New York City. March 7, 1956.

Rice, Richard H. "Sexuality, Pleasure and Growth at Sandstone Ranch." Master's thesis, UCLA, 1975.

Vesey, Laurence. "Communal Sex and Communal Survival." *Psychology Today,* December 1974.

"A Marriage with Room for One More," *Harper's Weekly,* May 16, 1975.

About the Author

The last time Marcia Seligson crisscrossed America to look at some of its stranger practices was for her book *The Eternal Bliss Machine: America's Way of Wedding*. In addition, she has written four humor books, one children's book and articles for most of the country's major magazines, including *New Times*, where she is a contributing editor. A native New Yorker, Ms. Seligson lives in Los Angeles.